PASSPORT

MW00963823

ETHNIC

TORONTO

*A Complete Guide
to the Many Faces
& Cultures of
Toronto*

ROBERT J. KASHER

Printed on recyclable paper

PASSPORT BOOKS
a division of *NTC Publishing Group*
Lincolnwood, Illinois USA

Contents

Maps

Introduction

Toronto has many attractions for visitors as a modern, clean, vibrant and attractive city, but its most interesting attraction lies in the diversity of its people. Toronto is the world's most multicultural city. Its close to four million inhabitants represent over seventy-five different cultures with at least 1,000 people each. Toronto has no majority culture or ethnicity. Its largest ethnic group represents only a little over 20 percent of its people. Over a dozen cultures have more than 100,000 people in the Metropolitan area. Known for many years as one of the most narrow-minded and uncosmopolitan of the British colonial cities, Toronto has become the most ethnically and culturally diverse city in the world in the last thirty years.

If you look at the history of settlement in this area, you will see that Toronto has long been a meeting place for different cultures. In fact its original Native name, *Temetegon,* identified this area at the confluence of the Humber and Don River portage routes as the meeting place of the five Huron tribes. It was here that Toronto's first European settlers came. These settlers were French, Irish, and Scottish fur traders who were part of Etienne Brule's expedition into Ontario in the 1600s. British settlement began in earnest only after the French and Indian wars gave Britain control of the territory, and loyalist refugees from the American Revolution gave them a population source to settle here.

With the expedition of John Graves Simcoe in 1793, the casual grouping of settlements that was Temetegon was formalized into the town of York, which was the precursor to Toronto. After York was burned down by the American invasion in the War of 1812 (an act that was avenged by the British bombardment of Fort McHenry and the burning of Washington, DC, made famous in *The Star-Spangled Banner*), Toronto came into its own as a scrappy, fast-growing city of immigrants from Europe and the United States. At that time one of the largest and most important immigrant groups in the city were thousands of escaped American slaves whose skills, hardworking ethic, and entrepreneurial drive helped bring about much of the city's early commercial success.

While many of these immigrants left Toronto to return to the United States after the Civil War, they helped provide the basis for the economic engine that would help Toronto grow into a major industrial and commercial center as well as an agricultural market for the surrounding areas. Agriculture was the main springboard for the next waves of migration, and while most of the German, Dutch, and Belgian immigrants moved beyond Toronto to settle in the growing farming communities of southwestern Ontario, enough stayed to bring further growth to the region. The town of Yorkville at the northern tip of what was then Toronto, was a particular center for Dutch settlement.

In the 1880s and 1890s the opening of the Trans-Canada railway system brought three sources of immigration to the area. First was the actual work on the rail system itself, which brought Toronto's first Asian immigrants to settle here as work ended and they moved into what was then the virgin commercial territory of laundry services. Second, the growth in the mining country of northern Ontario that was precipitated by the advent of the railroad brought a need for skilled miners from Poland, the Balkans, Silesia, and Hungary, many of whom settled in Toronto after their initial work contracts were over. Their skills also helped establish the city as one of the world's great mineral exchanges. Third, good access to resources, transportation, and a burgeoning population brought many people from the British Isles and Western and Eastern Europe to Toronto as well as many second-generation internal ethnic immigrants from the United States and the farming regions of Canada who came to Toronto looking for a better life.

In the post–World War II era, immigration was accelerated by Canada's tremendous industrial growth when it became, after the United States, the world's second leading industrial power for a brief period of time. Immigration at this time was heavy from Italy, Greece, and Central European countries, with many skilled laborers and craftsmen coming into the country. Refugees from iron-curtain, Eastern European countries accelerated throughout the 1950s and 1960s, with a large influx from Hungary after the abortive revolt of 1956, and from Czechoslovakia after the end of the Prague Spring in 1968. Chinese immigration from Taiwan and Hong Kong also grew steadily during this period, as did British Commonwealth immigration from the Caribbean and Indian subcontinent areas. Over 25,000 draft-dodging Americans also settled here, many of them having since found important positions in Canada's arts and cultural industries.

The growth in Asian and Caribbean immigration has been the largest driving force in immigrant growth over the past twenty years, though large numbers of Eastern, Central, and Western European families continue to settle here. A large Southeast Asian community established itself here after the takeover of South Vietnam and the collapse of the Cambodian government in 1972. As a result, Toronto has the world's largest expatriate communities of Chinese, Vietnamese, Indian, Pakistani, Hungarian, Italian, and Estonian peoples.

As one of the world's major entrepôts for immigrants, Toronto has continued to attract many people to its opportunities. Canada is proud of what it calls the multicultural "Vertical Mosaic," its cultural policy that has encouraged immigrants to keep and maintain their ethnic and cultural identities within the broader context of Canadian society. As a result, Toronto has become an international microcosm of different cultures in its neighborhoods. You can buy products from around the world in ethnic specialty shops, as well as find special foods, delight in unique and exotic entertainment, and just enjoy the ambience of being in a different world for a little while as you walk through neighborhoods like the Corso Italia or Little India.

Foreign-language books, magazines, newspapers, radio shows, and television programs are available as is foreign music. A wide range of community-based foreign-language educational programs also are available. A plethora of community and religious institutions deal with the unique needs of and provide interesting information and insights about Toronto's many cultural communities.

Ethnic Toronto is a guide to this incredible array of diversity. It gives you information on the history and background of these communities, as well as current listings of restaurants, shops, community and religious groups, special events, and media outlets. As such, it is a guide not just to Toronto but to the international element that is the cosmopolitan pulse of the city.

Getting Around

First-time visitors to Toronto will find it an easy city to get around. The Toronto Transit Commission (TTC) provides excellent service throughout the city via subway, streetcar, and bus, including a skeleton twenty-four–hour service throughout Metro Toronto. Connecting bus companies in Mississauga, Vaughan, Markham, and Pickering, as well as the GO Transit system, can also give you mass-transit connections to suburban communities.

Free TTC transit maps are available from the **Metropolitan Toronto Convention and Visitors Association,** 207 Queen's Quay West in the Queen's Quay Terminal, or the **Visitor Information Centre** in the Eaton Centre on Yonge Street near the Dundas Street entrance on "Level One Below."

For drivers, Toronto is laid out on a grid system of north-south, east-west streets. Highway 401 and the Gardiner Expressway are the main east-west freeways, while the Don Valley Parkway/Highway 404, Highway 427, and Highway 400 are the main north-south highways.

Accommodations

Toronto has many hotels, as well as lots of unique bed-and-breakfasts scattered throughout the city. Many of the latter are located in or near a number of the locales described in this book and can give you a multicultural, neighborly introduction to this vast and diverse city. For current listings check with the following organizations:

Toronto Bed and Breakfast, *253 College Street (416-588-8800).*

Metropolitan Bed and Breakfast Registry, *615 Mount Pleasant Road (416-964-2566).*

Downtown Toronto Association of Bed and Breakfast Guesthouses, *PO Box 190 Station B (416-368-1420).*

Bed and Breakfast Accommodators, *223 Strathmore Boulevard (416-461-7095).*

Bed and Breakfast Homes of Toronto, *PO Box 46093 (416-363-6362).*

For those interested in staying in hotels, the following are some of Toronto's better places to stay. All are in Toronto proper.

Best Western Chestnut Park, *108 Chestnut Street (phone: 416-977-5000, 800-528-1234; fax: 416-977-9513).*

Best Western has dramatically upgraded the quality of hotels in its chain. This hotel offers modern rooms in a recently built facility located in the heart of downtown near city hall and Chinatown, with an excellent recreation center, conference center, and good dining facilities, all at reasonable prices.

Bradgate Arms Hotel, *54 Foxbar Road (phone: 416-968-1331, 800-268-7171; fax: 416-968-3743).*

Once an exclusive apartment complex built in the early 1900s, the Bradgate Arms offers luxurious accommodation for the discriminating traveler a bit off the beaten path. Located in a lovely residential section of uptown Toronto near the Rosedale, Summerhill, and Forest Hills neighborhoods, the Bradgate boasts meticulously restored and redecorated rooms and suites. Many have balconies and fireplaces; all have wet bars. The dark rich woods that set the elegant tone for rooms and furnishings extend throughout the hotel, giving a rich, elegant yet comfortable feeling to the hotel. There is an excellent library and lovely garden for quiet contemplation, as well as good meeting room facilities. The Avenues dining room is one of the finest in Toronto. The Bradgate provides superb service and accommodation in an intimate setting. *An excellent and safe hotel for women travelers.*

Comfort Hotel, *15 Charles Street East (phone: 416-924-7381, 800-228-5150; fax: 416-924-7929).*

This charming European-style hotel, formerly the independently owned Brownstone, has been purchased by the Comfort Inn chain. Excellently located in the Yonge/Bloor Street area on the border of the Cabbagetown, Yorkville, and Rosedale neighborhoods, this hotel offers European charm and warmth in the small but pleasantly decorated rooms as well as good dining facilities. Conference and meeting rooms are also available.

Carlton Days Inn, *30 Carlton Street (phone: 416-977-6655, 800-325-2525; fax: 416-977-0507).*

This Days Inn offers updated and particularly well-maintained rooms with dining facilities. This facility offers very reasonable rates for downtown accommodation and is the closest hotel to Maple Leaf Gardens. Also close to Cabbagetown and downtown Chinatown.

Delta Chelsea Inn, *33 Gerrard Street West (phone: 416-595-1975, 800-268-1133 [Canada], 800-243-5732 [U.S.]; fax: 416-926-7809).*

Toronto's largest hotel complex is also one of its best. The Delta Chelsea has gone through a recent updating and expansion, now offering spacious, well-appointed, pleasantly decorated rooms. The Chelsea provides excellent conference and meeting facilities, as well as a comprehensive business center for the busy corporate traveler. Delta Privilege check-in, check-out services make getting in and out a pleasure. The hotel has a lot to offer family vacationers as well. Its second-floor children's activity center offers a full array of facilities including a pool, daycare center, and games room. It even offers a special weekend package for parents who wish to enjoy Toronto's nightlife by providing children with dinner, baby-sitting services, a movie, and other recreational activities. The Deck 27 recreation center offers adult recreational facilities, as well as a top-floor lounge. The Market Garden Emporium is a unique buffet-style café and market, open throughout the day for travelers who wish to pick up something to snack on or a whole meal. The Chelsea offers something for everyone at a price that is competitive with other hotels in the city. It's the closest to Chinatown.

Holiday Inn on King, *370 King Street West (phone: 416-599-4000, 800-465-4329; fax: 416-599-8889).*

Probably the best located hotel in Toronto, the Holiday Inn on King is in the heart of Toronto's theater district, only blocks away from the Queen Street Village, Skydome, and downtown. Its location on the King streetcar line gives you easy access to the ethnic communities in Parkdale, Bloor West Village, Dovercourt, and the Danforth as well. This recently built hotel has pleasantly decorated rooms, a good exercise center, access to numerous fine restaurants in and around the hotel, and a bright, well-lit parking lot. *An excellent hotel for women travelers.*

Hotel Inter-Continental, *200 Bloor Street West (phone: 416-960-5200, 800-327-0200; fax: 416-324-5920).*

A recently built, full-service hotel from one of the world's most renowned hotel chains, the Toronto Inter-Continental offers luxury accommodations in an interesting area bordering on the University of Toronto and the Annex and Harbord Street neighborhoods. Rooms have a very modern European flavor to them and come fully equipped with all the amenities. Fine dining, good conference facilities, and excellent recreational facilities are also available.

Quality Inn/Journey's End Hotel (Bloor), *280 Bloor Street West (phone: 416-968-0010, 800-668-4200; fax: 416-968-7765).*

Dependable and reliable for quality rooms at reasonable prices, Canada's Journey's End chain, now owned by Quality/Comfort Inn, remains one of the most consistent accommodation values in the country. This one is no different from the many other excellent facilities. A preferred traveler's program is available for speeding up check-in and check-out procedures. Well located near the Annex and Harbord Street areas and the University of Toronto campus.

Selby Hotel, *592 Shelborne Street (phone: 416-923-3177, 800-387-4788; fax: 416-923-3177).*

This charming, deceptive building has a long history of involvement in Toronto's various artistic and countercultural communities and has been recently renovated and restored to a comfortable, unique, and active hotel combining the Victorian graciousness of its interiors with the excitement and adventurousness of the surrounding Cabbagetown community. The Selby was home to Ernest Hemingway during his years in Toronto and is still a favorite haunt with scribes and artists.

chapter one

Afro-Caribbean Toronto

Toronto's growing black community has generally been identified with its large and active Caribbean community, but a very large amount of recent growth has occurred in its African-born neighborhoods. Both groups have distinct social and cultural backgrounds, making them vibrant additions to the city's ethnic blend.

Nationalities

African Americans

Immigrants and refugees from Somalia, Ethiopia, Nigeria, Ghana, Uganda, South Africa, and other African countries has grown dramatically in recent years. As a result, a variety of restaurants, shops, art galleries, music clubs, and cultural institutions have appeared representing the diversity of races, cultures, religions, and languages of this broad community. In addition to black Africans, many Arab and Indian peoples from Africa have established their own cultural and social groups in the city, such as the Asian Indians of East Africa.

Preceding both communities, however, are black Canadians whose heritage in Toronto goes back to the city's very earliest days. In the 1830s Toronto welcomed its first black American immigrants, many of whom were runaway slaves. In fact, in the years leading up to the American Civil War, Toronto became a major haven for such refugees, a terminus on the Underground Railroad from the United States. While immigration was slow at first (only fifty families had arrived by 1847), it picked up in the 1850s. Black immigrants became skilled craftspeople and highly trained service personnel, as well as carpenters, painters, and shoemakers.

While Toronto was just one stop for the many ex-slaves who headed for work in Ontario's burgeoning farming areas, it became a focal point for the province's broader black community. In the 1840s an Emancipation Day celebration was organized to help celebrate the work of both the white and black communities to assist in these efforts. From 1850 to the end of the Civil War, over 40,000 black Americans came to Ontario to escape slavery in the United States.

By the 1860s Toronto's own black population numbered over 1,500 and included a number of prominent citizens. One of the most successful, but by no means an exception, was William Peyton Hubbard, a founder of Toronto Hydro (Toronto's electric utility provider) and the city's first black politician, who served as acting mayor on a number of occasions. Many other black Canadians were successful businesspeople, professionals, and teachers.

Toronto also spawned media for the black community that have been present since 1853 with the establishment of the *Provincial Freeman,* whose Mary Ann Shadd has been acknowledged as the first black woman journalist in North America. The first black businessmen in the city go back to the founding of Toronto. Jack Mosee and William Willis opened a toll-road west from Yonge Street in 1799. James Mink, one of Toronto's wealthiest citizens in the 1840s, owned livery stables, an inn, and a stagecoach service.

After the Civil War Toronto's black population declined as many blacks moved back to the United States. By the 1890s only a few hundred families remained. During the first two decades of this century, that population increased as many American blacks migrated to Canada seeking jobs in industry, railroads, and construction.

Self-help leagues and antidiscrimination organizations sprang up to help support the burgeoning community, which numbered over 4,000 by 1950. Many black Canadians lived in the downtown East End area near Front Street East and Sherborne Street, as well as in the Dovercourt and Bloor Street West areas. Today there are over 25,000 black Canadians of non–West Indian, non-African origin living in Toronto who take great pride in their vital and important contributions to the development of this city.

Prominent black Canadians active in the Toronto community include the Honorable Lincoln Alexander, lieutenant governor of the province of Ontario; Salome Bey, a prominent singer and entertainer; and Daniel G. Hill, ombudsman for the province of Ontario.

While immigration to Toronto from Africa was sparse until the late 1960s, migration of Commonwealth-area citizens from Kenya and Uganda picked up in response to political upheavals there in the late 1960s and early 1970s. Many African immigrants originally arrived in Canada as students from Ghana, Nigeria, and other British Commonwealth countries. They came to Canada in increasing numbers during this time, many settling in Toronto.

Finally the political upheavals of the 1980s and 1990s have brought refugees from Ethiopia and Somalia, Angola and Mozambique, as well as immigrants from many other African countries. The Ethiopian community alone numbers over 3,500. Although Toronto's Somali community is second in size to the large Somali communities in Ottawa and Montreal, it still numbers over 10,000. Over 2,000 members of recently independent Eritrea's expatriate community reside in Toronto. There are over 4,000 Ugandans, most of whom are Asian-Indian refugees who fled Idi Amin's "Africanization" pogroms.

Metro's West African communities include peoples from Ghana, Sierra Leone, Gambia, Liberia, and Nigeria—the single largest source of immigrants from the West African area. Nigerians were among the earliest African arrivals in Toronto, some coming as students to the University of Toronto as early as the 1930s. Many Yoruba-speaking Nigerians live in the area, as do over 2,000 Ibo-speaking immigrants, some of whose families first arrived during the Nigerian civil war. The Nigerian community is by and large Christian, and religious activities revolve around **Saint Bartholomew's Church** at 509 Dundas Street East.

Other African immigrants include those from Zaire, Burundi, and Rwanda, as well as many from South Africa, Zimbabwe, Angola, and Mozambique. A fair amount of displacement has occurred in the South African community in recent years with the election of Nelson Mandela and the victory of the African National Congress (ANC), but over 16,000 white and 25,000 black South Africans remain in the area. The local Afrikaner clubs and ANC chapters remain active focal points for activities in these communities.

Caribbeans

For visitors the world over who have been to Toronto in early August, August is Caribana month, the single biggest Carnival parade in North America outside of the Caribbean. Over one million visitors annually watch the parade wend its way down University Avenue in a plethora of colorful costumes and gyrating dancers to the music of numerous soca, calypso, reggae, mambo, and steel drum bands. The festival itself lasts for over ten days and is a celebration of life in the world's third largest Caribbean city (after Kingston, Jamaica and Havana, Cuba), Toronto's Caribbean community numbering over 300,000.

Trinidadians, Jamaicans, Guyanese, Dominicans, Barbadjians, Bahamians, Antiguans, and Haitians are among the many peoples of the Caribbean who have found their way to Toronto. The community makes up more than half of Toronto's black population and comes from twenty-five different islands or nations in the Caribbean, including Antigua, Barbados, Bahamas, Dominica, Haiti, Grenada, Guyana, Jamaica, Montserrat, Saint Lucia, Saint Vincent, Saint Kitts, Trinidad and Tobago, Cuba, Belize, Aruba, Turks and Caicos, Anguilla, Guadeloupe, and Barbuda. Within this diverse range of countries and islands is an even more diverse mixture of cultures and peoples, including Portuguese, Spanish, English, French, African, Dutch, Lebanese, Indian, and aboriginal peoples from the various areas.

West Indians have been in Canada for generations. Trade between the Caribbean Isles and Canada first brought West Indian immigrants in search of work in Toronto's many industries. Another source of immigration was from Caribbean students who came to study in Canadian institutions. A great number of Trinidadian students came up in the 1950s, and many stayed to work as skilled professionals, engineers, and craftspeople. Many young women from islands like Jamaica and Barbados received sponsorships to enter Canada as domestic workers.

Major immigration began in the 1960s with large-scale influxes from many islands, Jamaica in particular. Many new immigrants went to work in factories and the construction industry, and many others came to work in the service and health sectors. An early community sprang up around the corner of Bloor Street West and Bathurst Street, but gradually moved north to the Eglinton Avenue West/Vaughan Road area between Oakwood and Dufferin Streets where the largest concentration of Caribbean shops, restaurants, and services are located today. The eastern suburb of Scarborough also has a large Caribbean community along Saint Clair Avenue, as does the suburb of North York in the Jane Street area north of Sheppard Avenue West.

The biggest cultural festival in Toronto is held by the Caribbean community. **Caribana** takes place every summer at the end of July through the first Monday in August, which is a civic holiday in Toronto. The festival includes a wide array of musical events and concerts, dance contests, costume parties, and beauty contests as well as the grand Caribana parade held on the Saturday before the civic holiday. Caribana attracts close to a million visitors to the Toronto area every year, and the parade is one of the biggest events of its kind in North America. It's great fun and a fabulous introduction to the many different Caribbean cultures that inhabit the Metropolitan area.

A number of Caribbean immigrants to Canada have become very prominent in Toronto-area affairs. Among them are Alvin Curling, a liberal MPP and former minister of housing; Wilson Head, a prominent human rights activist and professor of sociology; Charles Roach, a well-known political activist and human rights lawyer; Sherlene Shaw, a Scarborough city councilor; and Beverley Salmon, a Metro-area councilor.

Religion

There are three principal long-established black churches and congregations in Metro Toronto:

British Methodist Episcopal Church, *460 Shaw Street (416-534-3831).*
A United Church with a large African congregation.

Grant African Methodist Episcopal Church, *2029 Gerrard Street East (416-690-5169).*
Reaches a wide variety of Christian Africans belonging to the United Church. Of all the churches, Grant African takes one of the most active roles, though the Seventh Day Adventist congregation is probably the largest among the black Canadian community.

First Baptist Church, *101 Huron Street (416-977-3508).*
This is the oldest still-functioning black institution in the city, tracing its origins back to 1826 when it was started by a group of fugitive slaves.

The Ethiopian community focuses around the **Ethiopian Orthodox Church,** 425 Vaughan Road (416-651-8182), which celebrates many traditional Ethiopian holidays, including Ethiopian National Day on September 12 and the Julian calendar Christmas and Easter celebrations. The faithful fast all day before the evening Christmas mass and then at 2:00 AM enjoy a large meal that includes their native starch, injera. Similar late-evening Christmas dinners are popular with other African and Caribbean Christians who often have dinner celebrations at home at 1:00 or 2:00 Christmas morning.

The Evangelical Christian community is a rapidly growing one in Africa. The center for this community in Toronto is the **All Nations Full Gospel Church,** 4267 Steeles Avenue West (416-665-9964), which recently erected a new facility.

As part of the British Commonwealth, many African nations still have a strong Anglican Church influence, and many African Torontonians are associated with this faith. The two biggest African congregations are found at the main **Anglican Church of Canada,** 600 Jarvis Street (416-924-9192), which also serves as a focal point for local relief and aid efforts through CARE Canada. As noted earlier, **Saint Bartholomew Anglican Church,** 509 Dundas Street East (416-368-9180), has long been a center for neighborhood activities and has an active African congregation that provides a variety of community services.

The largest Islamic community among African Canadians is in the Somali community, although Islamic African Canadians come from other communities as well. The **Jami Mosque,** 56 Boustead Road (416-769-1192), is the place for most Islamic worship in the city. The **Somali Islamic Society Of Canada,** 1919 Weston Road (416-242-9464), also provides religious and community services for the Somali Islamic community.

The many peoples of the West Indies have varied religious backgrounds. Former British colonies like Jamaica have strong Anglican and United Church affiliations, whereas Spanish and French colonies like Trinidad and Haiti have strong links to the Catholic Church. Pentecostal, Baptist, and Evangelical movements have been very popular throughout the region as well.

The Anglican Church of Canada remains the central church for Anglican Caribbeans though the **Saint George the Martyr Anglican Church,** 205 John Street (416-598-4366), and **Saint Michael's and All Angels Anglican Church,** 611 Saint Clair Avenue West (416-653-3593), also have large Caribbean congregations. The latter church serves the growing communities in the Eglinton Avenue West and Vaughan Road areas.

Saint Matthew's United Church, 729 Saint Clair Avenue West (416-653-5711), serves the United Church members of this community and offers a variety of community service programs as well. The **British Methodist Episcopalian Church,** 460 Shaw Street (416-534-3831), which has a large African and black Canadian congregation, also serves the Caribbean community. **Oakwood Wesleyan Church,** 22 Brandon Avenue (416-536-3357), has a large Caribbean community, serving the burgeoning community near Oakwood Street and Eglinton Avenue West. **Saint David's Presbyterian Church,** 1300 Danforth Road (416-267-7897), serves the Caribbean neighborhood on the east side of the city.

The **Caribbean Canadian Catholic Church and Centre,** 867 College Street (416-534-1145), and **Catholic Caribbean Centre** at the same address is the main congregation for West Indian Catholics, in particular members of the Trinidadian community. A variety of social and educational programs undertaken by the Catholic Caribbean Centre are open to the West Indian community as a whole.

Agincourt Adventist Church, 2 Norbert Avenue (416-636-2471); **Christian Centre Church,** 4545 Jane Street (416-661-6770); **Church of God of Prophecy,** 114 Pape Avenue (416-465-6321); **First Baptist Church,** 101 Huron Street (416-977-3508); and **Perth Avenue Seventh Day Adventist Church,** 243 Perth Avenue (416-535-1909), all serve various Evangelical and Christian reformist movements. The First Baptist Church is one of Toronto's oldest Protestant churches and has a large black Canadian congregation that goes back to the very beginnings of Toronto's settlement.

Organizations

A number of umbrella organizations help support awareness of African-American heritage and provide community services to the black community in Toronto:

The **Harriet Tubman Centre,** *2029 Gerrard Street East (416-693-2378).*

Located on the Grant African Methodist Episcopal Church grounds, the center includes the Sapodilla Gallery, which features local black Canadian artists; a youth center; and facilities for programs in music, dance, and crafts, as well as lectures on black history.

The **Ontario Black History Society,** *Ontario Heritage Centre, 10 Adelaide Street East (416-867-9420).*

An organization established in 1978 to study and foster awareness of black history in Ontario. It sponsors a traveling historical exhibit on the role black Canadians have played in Toronto's and the province's history. The society also provides tours of the city emphasizing sites of importance to black Canadians and conducts slide shows, educational programs, and discussions.

The Black Secretariat, *394A Euclid Avenue*
(416-924-1104).

An organization that provides information on services in the black community and publishes a directory of black services, organizations, community groups, and businesses.

The **Black Action Defense Committee,** *393 Vaughan Road (416-656-2232).*

One of the most prominent of a number of political organizations that have sprung up in recent years to combat racism and discrimination against the black community in general and that of Metro Toronto in particular.

Black Business and Professional Association, *675 King Street West (416-504-4097).*

Works on issues of concern to the black business community and hands out the annual Harry Jerome awards for black achievement.

Black Community Committee and **Black Development Committee,** *156 Front Street West (416-979-2001).*

Perform fundraising and educational work in the black community.

Black Artists Service Organization, *56 The Esplanade (416-214-2276).*

Does work with Toronto's black performing arts community.

A large number of African cultural organizations also exist to help perpetuate local languages, arts, crafts, and music, and act as meeting places for community members:

African Community Development Centre of Ontario, *14 College Street (416-925-8598).*

A major cultural center for the African community, it holds lectures, community forums, educational programs, and theater and dance performances, while providing job placement and counseling services. It publishes a monthly magazine about the African-Canadian community as well.

African Resource Centre, *366 Adelaide Street East (416-863-6240).*

An information and community resources clearinghouse covering all African groups. Primarily an educational resource center.

Ashanti-Canadian Multicultural Organization, *Box 181, Station A.*

An organization representing one of Ghana's larger cultural groups.

Association of Ghanaians in Toronto, *264 Dupont Street (416-972-6290).*

Puts on a variety of community and cultural events and publishes a bi-monthly newsletter on events of interest to the Ghanaian community.

Eritrean Canadian Community Centre, *347 Oakwood Avenue (416-658-8580).*

Provides information, community services, and cultural events for the Eritrean community in Toronto. Also supports dance and choral singing groups.

Ethiopian Association In Toronto, *851 Bloor Street West (416-535-2766).*

Provides assistance to newcomers, as well as practical job training in skills like computer work and other community-oriented services and heritage programs in the Amharic language.

Friends of the Springboks, *1491 Yonge Street (416-920-5466).*

An Afrikaner social group that provides local get-togethers for the community as well as charter travel packages for members.

Nigerian Canadian Association, *4544 Sheppard Avenue East (416-298-0502).*

The main center for Nigerian social, cultural, and community activities in Toronto.

South African Support and Information Centre, *276 Augusta Avenue (416-966-4059).*

A social club and community services center for South African immigrants to the Toronto area.

Ugandan Community, *585 Dovercourt Road (416-531-0885).*

Provides cultural and social gatherings for the Ugandan community in Toronto.

Umunna Cultural Organization, *205 Hilda (416-223-7613).*

A cultural awareness and community services organization for the city's Ibo-speaking population. It brings in speakers and sponsors forums and language classes.

Yoruba Cultural & Heritage Association, *572 King Street West (416-504-0922).*

Provides heritage-language classes and sponsors cultural events, dance programs, and concerts among the Yoruba people of Toronto.

The Somali community in Toronto has a large number of organizations aimed at helping Somali refugees and immigrants integrate into Canadian society and find support from other Somali-speaking peoples in the city. The Somalis in Toronto have also been particularly effective organizers of relief services and aid to fellow Somalis through the crises of the last few years. The following are the most prominent groups:

Somali Badar Organization of Toronto, *100 Mclevin (416-754-9411).*

Somali Canadian Community Association in Ontario, *2379 Dundas Street West (416-537-1417).*

Somali Canadian Integration Society of North York, *1315 Finch Avenue West (416-635-6415).*

Somali Community Centre of Etobicoke, *2428 Islington Avenue (416-745-2548).*

Somali Immigrant Aid Organization, *698 Weston Road (416-766-7326).*

A major center for immigrant integration, cultural heritage programs, and community support services. Provides language classes and sponsors a dance troupe.

Somali Islamic Society of Canada, *1919 Weston Road (416-242-9464).*

Somali National Community Service Ontario, *8 Appleton (416-658-6643).*

Somali-Canadian Association of Etobicoke, *925 Albion Road (416-742-4601).*

The heyday of political action in the overall African-Canadian community reached its apogee with the recent victory of Nelson Mandela in the South African elections. The **African National Congress,** 292-A Danforth Avenue (416-461-4255), remains a potent political organizing force in the broader African-Canadian community though its focus now revolves particularly around South Africa itself rather than Pan-African concerns.

Other groups like the **African and Caribbean Student Association,** 44 Saint George Street (416-978-6636), have become preeminent in voicing broader community issues and concerns. Likewise the Canadianization of the African community has brought new political and social concerns to the forefront as represented by the **African Women's Support Group,** 366 Adelaide Street East (416-363-8780), and the **African-Canadian Entrepreneurs Association,** 2347 Kennedy Road (416-754-0700), each providing services to its own distinct community interests.

A variety of cultural organizations serve the Caribbean community:

Antigua Barbuda Association, *PO Box 6 Station F.*

Undertakes a variety of cultural and community programs aimed at helping to integrate citizens from Antigua and Barbuda into the community.

Association Hatienne de Toronto, *1262 Don Mills Road (416-444-1582).*

An umbrella organization that helps Haitian immigrants to the Toronto area and organizes social and cultural events.

Barbados Canadian Association, *PO Box 111, Station B (416-392-7178).*

Helps newcomers from Barbados settle in Toronto.

Bermuda Social Club, *61 Palmdale Drive (416-493-3512).*

A social club for Bermudan immigrants to Toronto.

Black Perspectives, *58 Sumach Street (416-863-0498).*

Offers cultural programs for West Indian people, including music and creative-writing workshops.

Calypso Association of Canada, *PO Box 85, Station B (416-284-1252).*

A cultural group devoted to the playing and promotion of calypso music in Canada, conducts workshops and music schools.

Canadian Caribbean Excelsior Fraternal Association, *334B Silverthorn Avenue (416-656-7313).*

A fraternal organization engaged in charitable work in the Caribbean community.

Caribbean Cultural Committee, *474 Bathurst Street (416-925-5435).*

Organizes the Caribana parade and annual Caribana events.

Caribbean Youth Program, *2885 Jane Street (416-636-8367).*

Undertakes a variety of cultural and recreational activities for Caribbean youth.

Commonwealth Sports Club, *146 Bobolink Avenue (905-738-8077).*

A sports club sponsoring Caribbean sports teams in cricket, soccer, rugby, and other sports.

Federation of Trinidad and Tobago Organizations of Canada, *24 Mountjoy Avenue (416-393-0741).*

An umbrella group for a variety of community and social organizations serving the Trinidadian community in Toronto and throughout Canada.

Guiness Domino League, *10 Glenholme Avenue (416-656-4317).*

Sponsors competitive events. Dominoes are a very popular recreational activity in the Caribbean.

Guyana Canadian Association, *5109 Steeles West (416-749-7162).*

An association devoted to helping the Guyanese-Canadian community.

Jamaican Canadian Association, *1621 Dupont Street (416-535-4476).*

A social organization that also runs a community center. It organizes Independence Day festivities; helps new immigrants find housing and work; and provides educational, cultural, and arts programs. It also produces a newsletter and a variety of social and cultural events throughout the year.

National Council of Barbadian Associations in Canada, *211 Consumers Road (416-497-0079).*

Acts as an umbrella group for community and self-help groups dealing with Barbadian immigrants to Canada.

National Council of Jamaicans, *PO Box 7237, Station A (416-924-8188).*

A social and cultural group working within the Jamaican-Canadian community.

NEVCAN, *1529 Islington Avenue (416-239-2648).*

A social organization devoted to helping immigrants from the Island of Nevis.

Ontario Society for Studies in Indo-Caribbean Culture, *York University, 4700 Keele Street (416-736-2036).*

A social and cultural organization that sponsors academic lectures, discussions, and conferences as well as an annual boat cruise.

Rastafarian Cultural Workshop, *PO Box 221, Station Q (416-658-0576).*

Conducts cultural and educational programs on Rastafarian religion and culture.

Tringo Sports Club, *719 Military Trail (416-286-0026).*

A sports club sponsoring Caribbean sports teams in cricket, soccer, rugby, and other sports.

Ujamaa Young Peoples Association, *PO Box 3233, Markham Industrial Park (905-490-0628).*

An organization doing community work with African and Caribbean youth.

In addition to its cultural organizations, the Caribbean community supports a number of political and social groups aimed at promoting causes both within the community and with surrounding groups and communities.

Caribbean Immigrant Services, *1621 Dupont Street (416-535-4476).*

Provides services and acts as an advocate group for Caribbean immigrants.

Congress of Black Women, *PO Box 781, Station P (416-534-3114).*

Feminist organization working with the specific concerns of black women.

Organization for Caribbean Initiatives, *563 Cummer Avenue (416-222-5955).*

Works to articulate the political and social needs of the Caribbean community as a whole.

West Indian Social and Cultural Society, *PO Box 298, Station E (416-493-1292).*

A project to work with and provide counseling for Caribbean youth.

The **Cross Cultural Communications Centre,** *2909 Dundas Street West (416-760-7855).*

Provides a wealth of information on cultural and political issues of concern to the Caribbean community.

═══ Holidays and Celebrations ═══

February	*Black History Month.*
February 23	*Guyana Republic Day,* celebrating the day in 1970 when Guyana became the Cooperative Republic of Guyana.
March 6	*Ghana National Day.*
March/April	*Carnival* (before Lent).
April 19	*Republic Day,* celebrated in the Sierra Leone community.

May 21	*Grenadian Cultural Day.*
May 31	*South African Republic Day.*
June 25	*Mozambique Independence Day.*
June 26	*Somali Independence Day,* celebrating the independence of Northern Somaliland from Great Britain in 1960.
July 5	*Cape Verde Independence Day.*
July/August	*Caribana Festival,* running from the last week in July to the first Monday in August.
August 6	*Jamaican Independence Day.*
August 31	*Trinidad and Tobago Independence Day.*
September 11	*Ethiopian New Year.*
September 12	*Ethiopian National Day.*
October 1	*Nigerian Independence Day.*
October 9	*Ugandan National Day.*
November 30	*Barbados Independence Day.*

Ethiopian Orthodox Church members celebrate Christmas and New Year's according to the Julian calendar. Ethiopia's Falasha Jews celebrate a variety of Old Testament religious days, and the African-Islamic community celebrates the high holy days of the Islamic religion.

Restaurants, Cafés, and Nightclubs

A number of African and Afro-Caribbean restaurants serving African specialties are available in the Metro Toronto area. Most are in offbeat parts of town but are generally close to mass-transit stops and other restaurants and shops. The greatest concentration seems to be in the Bloor Street West area between the Dufferin Street and Dundas Street West subway stations.

Most African restaurants in Toronto tend toward East African cuisine, which is an amalgam of Arab, Indian, and African influences, mixing mild curries with saffron and cloves. It comprises many stews and hot pots of beans, lentils, and meat, often goat or lamb. The halaal Islamic food purity code, very similar to the Jewish religion's kosher food purity code, has a strong influence on cooking methods and ingredients even though most Africans in Toronto are not Islamic.

With some exceptions, most of the restaurants listed are inexpensive and transient. It's best to call before going to make sure they are still in business and still at the same location, since some restaurants have moved in recent years and will probably move again in years to come depending on rents, neighborhood demographics, and relative prosperity.

North American black cuisines such as creole and soul food are limited in their availability.

Caribbean cuisine is a mixture of a variety of interesting, often spicy dishes from its many islands. While Toronto does not have a restaurant specializing in the more refined creole cooking from Martinique and Guadeloupe, it does provide a number of restaurants, take-out houses, and fast-food places whose cuisine generally reflects the cooking specialties of Jamaica and Trinidad. Jamaican cooking tends toward *jerk spices*—a peppery combination used in grilling or stewing meat—or the ever-present *roti,* a large unleavened bread dumpling filled with anything from goat meat to potatoes and vegetables. A variation on the roti is the *patty,* which has become a staple fast-food item with many Torontonians and is available in many stores.

Trinidadian cuisine is a combination of South Asian and Chinese cooking in which stir-fries and stews are made with a decidedly curry-like flavor that is generally much milder than its South Asian or African counterparts. Trinidadians spice up their foods with a variety of hot sauces, some of which verge on the dangerous.

The following listings include some of Toronto's better Caribbean restaurants. Don't expect haute cuisine settings; these are all down-home cookeries that serve good West Indian food at very reasonable prices. Most are licensed, and many serve English or West Indian beers like Red Stripe or Dragon Stout on tap.

African bands and musical groups, dance troupes, and theater companies often come to Toronto's major halls. King Sunny Ade, Manu Dibango, Hugh Masakela, Youssou N'Dour, and Mory Kante are among the many African performers who have played in Toronto.

As far as North American black entertainment goes, Toronto has long been a prominent stopping point for many black blues musicians, as well as producing more than a few of its own fine blues and jazz performers. In ages past prominent blues performers like Hound Dog Taylor and Muddy Waters often played in Toronto at the El Mocambo, Colonial Tavern, or Coq D'or on their way to a fishing vacation in Northern Ontario.

Reggae, soca, and calypso are the staple musical forms for Toronto's West Indian entertainment scene. Besides the clubs mentioned here, many other music clubs in the city feature local reggae artists and West Indian bands, like the Sattalites, as well as major performers like Ziggy Marley and Reel 2 Reel.

Addis Ababa, *1184 Queen Street West (416-536-0059).*

The African decor matches the wide array of African cuisine, including traditional Ethiopian stews and vegetarian purées such as shiro wat (roast ground peas in a spicy red pepper sauce), yatakilat wat (braised cabbage, carrots, and potatoes with garlic and ginger), and tibs (cubes of lamb on the bone braised with onions, garlic, rosemary, and some very hot peppers). This restaurant shows the full range of flavors that make up this underrated cuisine.

Afro-Caribbean Village Restaurant, *736 Saint Clair Avenue West (416-653-8477).*

A large modern restaurant serving a variety of Caribbean East and West African dishes, including excellent rotis, meat patties, stews, and mild curries.

Albert's Real Jamaican, *542 Saint Clair Avenue West (416-658-9445).*

This unprepossessing little take-out restaurant is considered by many to have some of Toronto's best Jamaican cuisine, including excellent rotis, cod fritters, and beautifully braised oxtail stews.

Ali's West Indian Roti Shop, *1446 Queen Street West (416-532-7701).*

Provides good, hearty rotis, patties, and stews; take out or eat in.

Babes Restaurant and Dining Lounge, *805 Brimley Road (416-269-6779).*

A nightclub and dining lounge serving a variety of West Indian specialties, including akee and cod (*akee* looks like scrambled eggs but is actually a very delicious and hearty Caribbean vegetable) and the ubiquitous roti. The nightclub features live local bands and a disco with West Indian music.

Bahamian Kitchen, *14 Baldwin Street*
(416-595-0994).

A small restaurant in the Baldwin Street village, serving West Indian staples as well as Bahamian seafood specialties like conch chowder and curried chicken stewed in coconut milk with lemon grass.

Bamboo Club, *312 Queen Street West*
(416-593-5771).

A Queen Street West music club specializing in African, West Indian, and Third World musical styles. Brings in both top-notch local and out-of-town talent on a regular basis. Also has an excellent tropical cuisine restaurant with some good Caribbean food as well as Thai, Malayan, and South Asian dishes. Cover charge for music.

Blue Bay Café, *2243 Dundas Street West*
(416-533-8838).

French-African cuisine reminiscent of seafood dishes from the Ivory Coast, Martinique, and Senegal. The food is spicy and hot but reasonably priced, and the dining room is very pleasantly decorated.

Bukom Restaurant and Catering, *322 Wilson*
Avenue (416-633-2028).

Toronto's main restaurant for West African cuisine, specializing in dishes like plaintain with bean stew, *waatse* (rice and beans, often served in West Indian cooking), *banku* (made from cornmeal), and okra stew and kenkey.

Calypso Hut, *2011 Lawrence Avenue West*
(416-244-1160).

Caribbean cuisine served to a calypso beat. The Hut serves Trinidadian specialties like tripe stew and various run-downs, such as seafood sautéed in coconut cream with a variety of exotic herbs and spices. Another popular specialty is mackerel with green bananas.

Calypso Palace, *120 Norfinch Drive (416-667-8986).*

Another Trinidadian restaurant, this one serves all the major West Indian dishes in a roomy, comfortable atmosphere.

Caribbean Kitchen, *727 Bloor Street West (416-535-1977).*

A small unprepossessing spot serving excellent down-home cooking. Especially noteworthy are the rotis and stews.

Caribbean Queen Roti Hut, *2990 Lakeshore Boulevard West (416-503-3419).*

A small but tidy take-out restaurant in the Long Branch area serving excellent Caribbean food.

Caribbean Spring Garden, *2300 Finch Avenue West (416-744-1620).*

A combination of Caribbean cuisines with a Chinese flavor. The Chinese immigrated to Trinidad on a large scale in the early 1900s and had a strong influence on the local cuisine, as demonstrated by the pilau rices served here.

Club Ecstasie, *1263 Saint Clair Avenue West (416-652-0746).*

A discotheque specializing in West Indian music with occasional live bands on the weekends.

Cutty's Hideaway, *538 Danforth Avenue (416-463-5380).*

A large room sometimes a bit difficult to find on Danforth, serving good, hearty West Indian staples like rotis and patties. Excellent live music on the weekends. The main club for Trinidadian (soca and calypso) music in the city with occasional reggae bands as well.

Cutty's West Side Lounge, *105 Kennedy Road South (905-455-9181).*

More subdued than the Danforth location, this Cutty's serves lovers of West Indian food in the Brampton and Mississauga areas.

Dirre Restaurant, *1415 Bloor Street West* *(416-588-6889).*

West and East African specialties, including a variety of curried stews and meats, as well as *kinche* (cracked wheat with spicy butter), an Ethiopian breakfast specialty.

Ethiopian House, *4 Irwin Street (416-923-5438).*

Kenyan and Ethiopian specialties include excellent curried rice dishes with spicy stew mixtures of meats and East African vegetables, as well as hot purées. Local African beers are also available.

Ethiopia Palace, *699 Bloor Street West* *(416-536-8386).*

An Ethiopian restaurant serving Ethiopian specialties such as injera and *wats,* which is meat—chicken, lamb, beef, or sometimes goat—that has been seasoned with *berbere,* a very hot red sauce. Traditional stews and vegetarian dishes are also available.

Finfinay Restaurant, *1710 Eglinton Avenue West* *(416-789-2277).*

Ethiopian and Italian cuisine, specializing in spiced meats and vegetables on wheat and rice pancakes. Also serves an Ethiopian breakfast on weekends that includes *fouli* (lemon-spiced fava beans), spiced tea, and strong coffee, as well African-tinged Italian pastas and sauces.

Icy Hot, *760 Saint Clair Avenue West (416-654-3363).*

Specializes in spicy curries and rotis as well as excellent codfish fritters.

La Sunset Restaurant Dining Lounge, *1286 Bloor Street West (416-533-3115).*

A reggae club with top-notch local and occasional imported talent playing on weekends and serving good Jamaican home cooking for lunch and dinner.

Mesob Restaurant, *1051 Bloor Street West* *(416-516-2332).*

An Ethiopian restaurant that also serves some Northern African and Eritrean dishes.

Michidean's Take-out, *758 Dovercourt Road (416-531-1474).*

A small but very good Caribbean take-out place making foods for the Caribbean palate (meaning well spiced).

Modern Mogadishu Restaurant, *1480 Saint Clair Avenue West (416-658-3941).*

A popular spot with Toronto's Somali community. Traditional dishes served include *sambusa* (spiced ground meat rolled into a patty) and *sukhar* (rice with spicy beef), as well as spicy teas.

Mr. Jerk, *1552 Eglinton Avenue West (416-783-1367); 3050 Don Mills East (416-491-3593); 1166 Morningside Drive (416-724-9239).*

A group of fast-food outlets specializing in West Indian foods like rotis, patties, stews, and jerk-food plates served with the ever-present rice and bean dishes that are the Caribbean starch staples.

Pepperpot Café, *1170 Sheppard Avenue West (416-638-2842).*

Spicy and exotic Caribbean cuisine from a variety of different islands, including French, Spanish, Jamaican, and Trinidadian dishes all spiced up in a comfortable north Toronto setting.

Queen of Sheba, *1198 Bloor Street West (416-536-4162).*

One of Toronto's best spots for Ethiopian food. Popular dishes include the *kitfo* (a spicy steak tartare) and the *injera* (also *enjera*), the ubiquitous pancakelike leavened bread used in Ethiopian cooking. The spicy lamb or goat wat is good, as is the *tej,* a local Ethiopian intoxicant appearing as a fermented honey drink.

Randy's Takeout, *1569 Eglinton Avenue West (416-781-5313).*

A good take-out restaurant in the heart of Little Jamaica.

Real Jerk, *709 Queen Street East (416-463-6906).*

The best-known and probably overall best-quality Caribbean restaurant in the city, the Real Jerk also has great pizzazz. It inhabits a wonderfully redecorated concrete-block building on the corner of Queen Street East and

Broadview that shows what a little innovation and creativity can do. The food is scrumptious, especially the oxtail stew which is not only the best of its kind in the city, but possibly the best in the country. Also excellent are the jerk chicken and pork dishes on which the restaurant built its original reputation. A noisy, active, lively place with great reggae music playing all the time. Very welcoming to families with children.

Roti-King West Indian Restaurant and Dining Lounge, *1688 Eglinton Avenue West (416-781-8432).*

A more upscale licensed take-out house serving a variety of West Indian dishes to a primarily West Indian clientele.

Round P Restaurant, *813 Saint Clair Avenue West (416-654-9922).*

Home cooking Caribbean style, with milder flavors than some of its counterparts.

Selam, *875 Bloor Street West (416-588-5496).*

A wide array of Ethiopian and Eritrean dishes are available, including spicy grilled meats, vegetarian stews, and various braised-meat dishes served on the spongy unleavened breads for which this regional cuisine is noted.

Silver Dollar Saloon, *484 Spadina Avenue (416-964-2245).*

The primary spot for authentic blues in Toronto, presenting prominent North American blues performers from Monday through Saturday nights.

Somalian Safari Restaurant, *2215 Dundas Street West (416-538-4385).*

Another popular Somali restaurant in Toronto's West End.

Southern Accent, *595 Markham Street (416-536-3211).*

Serving creole, cajun, Southern American, and soul food dishes, this is a comfortable, reasonably priced restaurant in the Markham Village area near Bathurst and Bloor Streets.

Tina's No. 1 French African Restaurant from Paris, *2007 Lawrence Avenue West (416-245-5760).*

A restaurant specializing in African creole cooking with a distinctly French accent. Tina's is eccentric, eclectic, and interesting, if a little off the beaten path.

Vijay's International Restaurant, *154A Cumberland Street (416-967-4135).*

An eclectic African and Caribbean restaurant serving a wide array of foods and using a variety of cooking styles. Excellent oxtail and beef stews as well as foo foo and salt cod.

Visions Restaurant and Nite Club, *2915-A Dufferin Street (416-783-5685).*

Primarily a West Indian disco with occasional live music acts.

Zaidy's, *225 Queen Street West (416-977-7222).*

More cajun than creole, Zaidy's includes a number of dishes from Southern black cuisine and has long been a popular restaurant in the Queen Street Village.

================ **Food Sources** ================

Several Toronto stores carry African specialties, as well as East and West Indian foods:

Somali Halaal Food Centre, *2371 Weston Road (416-244-8248).*

Carries a wide variety of Halaal African meat specialties as well as many other spices and imported Somali foods.

Caribbean Foods, *3322 Keele Street (416-633-9268);*
India Africa Grocers, *2121 Jane Street (416-241-5435)* and *40 Rexdale Boulevard (416-748-5720);*
Mercy Tropical Foods *1129 Saint Clair Avenue West*

(416-658-8727); and **Ray's Tropical Foods,** *1640 Jane Street (416-248-9690).*

All have a variety of African and Caribbean specialties including fresh produce items like kokonte, cassava, mango, yams and cocoyams, and coconut, as well as other specialty foods like *gari* (fermented cassava), *abe* (palm nut soup), and hot kenkey.

Abyssinia Food Market, *191-A Baldwin Avenue (416-979-9746).*

Specializes in Ethiopian delicacies and spices, as does the **Ethiopian Spice Shop,** 60 Kensington Avenue (416-598-3014).

Africana Grocers, *65 Kensington Avenue (416-599-8928).*

Carries a wide array of African groceries and produce.

Florence Meat Supply, *81 Florence Drive (905-842-2066).*

Offers South African delicacies such as wors sausage, sosaties, kingklip, and beef biltong (a beef jerky–like product).

A West Indian roti shop is sort of a combination bakery–fast-food restaurant that produces both filled rotis and roti bread, the thin unleavened bread used for rotis. Roti shops also sell meat patties (deep-fried turnovers filled with spiced meat) and a variety of doughy breads and pastries for the West Indian palate.

Ali's West Indian Roti Shop, *1446 Queen Street West (416-532-7701).*

Sells rotis and a variety of West Indian foods.

Bacchus Roti Shop, *1394 Queen Street West (416-532-8191).*

A bakery that provides rotis to many of the West Indian restaurants in town.

Pati-Mahn, *848 Bathurst Street (416-532-9204).*

Specializes in Jamaican patties and sponge breads and cakes. Pati-Mahn sells patties throughout the city at other locations as well.

Patty King, *187 Baldwin Street (416-977-3191).*
Offers fresh-baked patties, rotis, breads, and cakes.

Spence's Bakery, *1539 Eglinton Avenue West (416-782-7850).*
A full-line West Indian bakery.

Sunlight Bakery, *2512 Eglinton Avenue West (416-658-2846).*
One of the bigger and better West Indian bakeries in the city.

West Indian fruits and vegetables like mangos, plantains, and papayas can be purchased at an increasing number of grocery stores along with more specialized products and spices. The following are some of the better places to shop.

Caribbean and Oriental Specialty Mart, *1170 Morningside Road (416-284-9457).*

Caribbean Foods, *3322 Keele Street (416-633-9268).*

Gus' Tropical Foods and Delicatessen, *1582 Eglinton Avenue West (416-789-2387).*

Joyce's West Indies Food Store, *854 Bathurst Street (416-533-4872).*

West Indian and African Home Food, *547 Rogers Road (416-658-5383).*

West Indian Fine Foods and Fruit Market, *3601 Lawrence Avenue East (416-431-9353).*

West Indian Food Store, *1804 Eglinton Avenue West (416-787-8069).*

Shops

A number of excellent African art galleries, craft shops, and clothing stores are in the Toronto area, as are several specialty record and book stores. The following is a list of some of the better stores.

Akwaa-Harrison Gallery, *183 Queen Street East (416-947-1379).*

An excellent gallery showing a variety of contemporary and historical arts and crafts from countries throughout the African continent. Showings of contemporary African artists are held throughout the year. The gallery is open Tuesday through Saturday.

Africa and More Art and Books, *1921 Eglinton Avenue East (416-750-0418).*

African arts and books about Africa and in African languages are available here, as are African magazines and newspapers.

African Fashion Centre Arts and Crafts, *827-A Bloor Street West (416-537-8520).*

Owned by Nigerian-born designer Esther Akinbode, this store sells traditional and modern African clothing including dashikis, caftans, and robes. Some crafts and jewelry are also available.

African Heritage Clothing, *2072 Lawrence Avenue West (416-244-9998).*

African clothing and jewelry. Clothing styles represent traditional African designs and styles.

African Tribal Art, *121 Scollard Street (416-929-3103).*

An upscale gallery showing heritage art and crafts from throughout Africa. Located in the Yorkville area of town. The pieces are interesting, but this is a relatively pricey gallery.

Charles Mus Gallery, *182 Davenport Road (416-921-5870).*

A gallery of contemporary and heritage African art, as well as rare books, prints, and portfolios of African history, sketches, drawings, and travelers' tales.

Kenya Crafts Canada, *108 Lansbury Drive (416-291-5349).*

Crafts and clothing from Kenya and East Africa.

Third World Books and Crafts, *942 Bathurst Street (416-537-8039).*

Excellent English-language bookstore carrying a wide variety of books on Afro-Caribbean history and current events, Afro-Caribbean newspapers and magazines, and fiction by Afro-Caribbean writers.

World Art and Decor, *803 Queen Street West (416-363-6340).*

The best selection of African music in Toronto, as well as traditional carvings, masks, snakeskin belts, and other artifacts and crafts from Africa.

A number of shops listed in the "Food Sources" section carry West Indian products other than food. Many carry clothing, jewelry, and other paraphernalia in addition to their main lines, very much like the general variety stores one finds throughout the West Indies.

A store specializing in Caribbean fashion is **Jamaica Jamaican Fashions,** 544-A Saint Clair Avenue West (416-656-2274), which has clothing with the bright tropical patterns and cloths so familiar in the Caribbean.

Hair weaves, braids, and other Caribbean beauty and haircare supplies can be purchased at **West Indian Golden Beauty Supply,** 862 Bathurst Street (416-533-6033).

A number of record stores specializing in Caribbean music can be found throughout the city. One nice thing about these small specialized shops is that like old record stores of the past they will play music for you at the shop so you can hear what it sounds like before you buy it. Some of the shops providing these services along with excellent selections of reggae, soca, and calypso music are:

Bobby's Records, *1007 Bloor Street West (416-535-1049).*

Distinctive Sound of Music, *68 Kyla Crescent (416-410-5110).*

George's Records, *1553 Eglinton Avenue West (416-789-5722).*

Gospel Records and Health Products, *872 Bathurst Street (416-537-4852).*

Play de Record, *357A Yonge Street (416-586-0380).*

Record Factory, *1489 Eglinton Avenue West (416-782-8116).*

Top Ranking Records, *1547 Eglinton Avenue West (416-784-5560).*

========== **Media** ==========

Publications

African Letter, 230 Brown's Line, Suite 205 (416-252-4667).

Newspaper published every two weeks covering events in Africa and Toronto.

African Canadian Report, 20 College Street, Suite 7 (416-924-3450).

A monthly publication highlighting local news of interest to African Canadians as well as initiatives being taken by Canadian-based development groups and non-governmental organizations (NGOs) in Africa.

Contacts International, PO Box 375, Willowdale Station A (416-731-6911).

A yearly directory aimed at Toronto's South African community.

Share, 1554A Eglinton Avenue West (416-789-0691).

Well known in Toronto's Caribbean community, *Share* had to pick up some of the slack in covering black Canadian issues that occurred when the long-established *Contrast* magazine folded.

Spear, PO Box 3243, Station D (416-535-9727).

A monthly magazine covering issues of interest to black Torontonians.

Echo, *120 Norfinch Drive (416-665-6969).*
A monthly publication for the Caribbean community.

Indian Frontiers (416-283-7671).
An annual magazine on the Caribbean-East Indian community.

Indo-Caribbean World, *312 Brownridge Drive (416-738-5005).*
A bimonthly publication on the Caribbean community as a whole, with special emphasis on the East Indian Caribbean community.

Inter Caribbean News, *4800 Sheppard Avenue East (416-498-8866).*
A monthly publication covering island news.

Our Lives (Black Women's Collective) (416-532-2672).
A monthly publication covering issues of concern to African and Caribbean women.

Viewpoint, *1680 Jane Street (416-249-7554).*
A biweekly newspaper of news and opinions on the Caribbean community.

Radio and Television

Toronto has a very active African-Canadian community radio production group that helps produce a number of weekly African music radio shows. Check with the radio stations for current time slots:

"Sounds of Africa," CKLN-FM 88.1, *380 Victoria Street (416-595-1477).*

"Akasanoma," CHRY-FM 105.7, *4700 Keele Street (416-736-5293).*

"African Program," CHIN-FM 100.7, *637 College Street (416-531-9991).*

"African International Radio," CIVT-FM 98.5, *91 Saint George Street (416-595-0909).*

"Night Cruise" and **"Night Moves,"** CHIN-AM
1540, *622 College Street (416-531-9991)*.
Cover issues of interest and concern to Toronto's black community.

"Soul in the City," MUCHMUSIC, *299 Queen Street West (416-591-5757)*.
A music show covering the world of black music as well as prominent features on local black musicians.

A number of good Caribbean music and community news shows are offered locally, including:

"Caribbean Connection," CHIN-AM 1540, *622 College Street (416-531-9991)*.

"Caribbean Program," CIAO 790 AM, *50 Kennedy Road South (905-453-7111)*.

CIUT-FM, 89.5 FM, *91 Saint George Street (416-595-0909)*.

The University of Toronto station has a number of Caribbean music and news shows throughout the week, as does **CKLN-FM,** 88.1 FM, 380 Victoria Street (416-595-1477), Ryerson Polytechnical Institute's radio station. **Energy 108,** 107.9 FM, 4144 South Service Road (905-681-1079), Toronto's main dance-music station, also carries West Indian musical shows on the weekends.

"Music Connection," CKQT 94.9 FM, *360 King Street West, Oshawa (905-686-1350)*.

"Nightcruise," CHIN-AM 1540, *622 College Street (416-531-9991)*.

"Nightmoves," CHIN-AM 1540, *622 College Street (416-531-9991)*.

"Clip Trip," MUCHMUSIC, *299 Queen Street West (416-591-5757).*

Carries videos from around the world, including many West Indian groups.

There is also a television station carrying programming for the African and island communities:

"Upfront," CFMT Channel 47, *545 Lakeshore Boulevard West (416-593-4747).*

A news and current events program on the West Indian and black community in Toronto.

—The Caribbean Shopping Center: Little Jamaica—

A center of Caribbean shopping, eating, and even some nightlife of sorts has grown up in the Eglinton Avenue West area between Oakwood Avenue and Vaughan Road. Myriad record shops, roti houses, variety stores, and bakeries catering to the needs of the Caribbean have sprung up here, close to one of the city's centers of Caribbean population.

While not as sophisticated as the Corso Italia or as noticeable as the Greek Danforth neighborhoods, this area nonetheless has slowly evolved from a working-class Italian area to a mixed neighborhood with a strong West Indian flavor. American visitors shouldn't prejudge Little Jamaica by their experience with black ghettoes in the United States. This is a safe, lively area full of bargains, exotic products, and interesting people. A bit off the beaten path, it can be a rewarding visit for the traveler looking for a bit of the tropics in Toronto.

How to Get There: *Take the Spadina branch of the Yonge Spadina subway and get off at the Eglinton Avenue West station. Catch the Eglinton Avenue West bus or the Oakwood Trolley and go west on Eglinton Avenue West to Oakwood Avenue. You can also walk; it's only about five blocks from the subway station.*

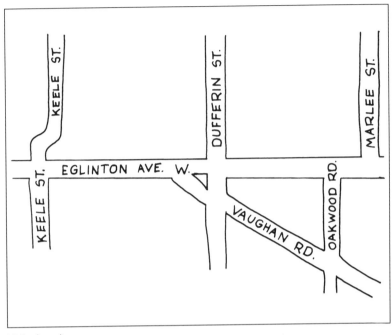

Little Jamaica

Arab and Middle Eastern Toronto

History

Toronto's Arab and Middle Eastern population is a diverse and complex group of peoples who have come here from over twenty different countries. Adjusting to a cold climate, living in a country with different religious and social structures, and trying to preserve a language and alphabet quite distinct from Canada's has been challenging enough to the members of this community. In addition, the diverse range of Arabic cultures from Egyptian to Syrian to Iraqi has balkanized the broader population of Arabs in the city.

Immigration to Canada from the Levant began in 1882 with the arrival of Salim Shaykh, a Syrian-Lebanese immigrant and Toronto's first Arab-speaking settler. Early on, a Syrian enclave formed around Saint Patrick's Church near McCaul and Dundas Street West, but that has long since been superseded by other developments in the area. Later the neighborhood around Shuter Street near Saint Vincent de Paul Hall became known as Little Syria and abounded with Arab confectionery shops and merchants. A few merchants and pawn shops along Church Street are the only remnants of this neighborhood today.

Almost all early Arab immigrants to Canada were Christian. The Melkites (Eastern Rite Catholics) worshipped at Our Lady of Assumption parish on Jarvis Street, while the Maronite Christians worshipped at Our

Lady of Mount Carmel Church. This East Side downtown area was the focus for the small Arab community which remained primarily Syrian and Christian throughout the 1930s and 1940s.

After the Second World War a broader religious and cultural mix of Arabs began arriving in Toronto. Immigrants and refugees from Egypt, Iraq, Jordan, Algeria, Libya, the Sudan, Bahrain, Mauritania, Yemen, and Palestine all came, including many Islamic and Coptic Christian believers. Today half of all Toronto's Arab peoples are of Syrian-Lebanese origin, one quarter are of Egyptian descent, and the rest are from other Arab countries.

In the 1970s the Lebanese population grew larger as many Lebanese moved to Canada to escape the chaos in their own country. These immigrants became active merchants, traders, and professional people in the community. Although some have returned to their homeland as peace has come to Beirut, many others have remained in Toronto, commuting between Canada and the Levant and acting as brokers for Arab-Canadian business interests. In spite of its tremendous diversity in terms of ethnicity and religious belief, Toronto's Arab community has been able to speak as a coherent group through a variety of its social and cultural organizations, in particular the **Canadian Arab Federation** and the **Canadian Arab Friendship Society.** There is no particular area in the city where this population currently congregates, although pockets of Arab peoples exist in west Toronto and central Etobicoke.

Both Iran and Turkey have also sent many people to Toronto. After the rise of the Ayatollah Khomeini and the success of the Iranian revolution in the late 1970s, Toronto's Iranian population swelled with thousands of professionals and businesspeople fleeing the consequences of the upheaval in their native land. Canada as a whole received almost 100,000 refugees; over 20,000 of these settled in the Toronto area, where they joined a small Iranian/Persian community. The first immigrants of this latter group began to arrive in the post–World War II era around 1946. Most of them were students who remained in Canada after receiving a college education, and the community slowly grew throughout the 1950s and 1960s. A further influx of Montreal-based Iranian immigrants, who moved to Toronto in the wake of the rise of the Separatist movement in Quebec, occurred in the early 1970s. Finally, a number of Iranian refugees of the Baha'i faith, which was severely persecuted in Iran in the early 1980s, were sponsored as immigrants by Toronto's existing Baha'i community.

The tremendous growth of the Iranian community in the early 1980s led to the development of a number of institutions aimed at helping preserve the Persian language and heritage. The **Persian Traditional Art and Cultural Foundation of Ontario** organizes a number of cultural events, and plans are afoot to open a library and community center as well. Even though the community hasn't been in Toronto long, it has produced a number of prominent citizens, including Lofti Mansouri, the owner of Hakim Optical, a large chain of eyeglass stores; Dian Babayan, former director of the Canadian Opera Company; and artist and concert violinist Payman Vesal. The Iranian community is spread throughout the Metropolitan Toronto area, but the largest concentration is in the North York area.

Like their Balkan neighbors, the Bulgarians and Macedonians, Turkish immigrants began coming to Canada in the 1880s, though at the time they were far fewer than those from other cultures. Large numbers of Turks didn't start arriving in Toronto until after World War II. Today there are over 9,000 Turkish speakers in the Metropolitan area.

Immigrants came not only from Turkey, but from Cyprus, Greece, and Germany, where many Turkish immigrants had originally gone as guest workers. One of the first community groups formed in the Turkish community was the Turkish-Canadian Friendship Association, which was established by former Turkish-German guest workers. In the 1970s the Turkish community established its own mosque on Pape Street and has been active in relief efforts to its home country.

The community itself is spread throughout Toronto, with a high concentration of Turkish Cypriots in the Mississauga area and of native immigrants from Turkey in the South Riverdale area. Turkish settlers include professional businesspeople, designers, engineers, financiers, and professors. Prominent Turkish Torontonians include computer designer B. Dartok and professor M. Uzumeri.

Religion

Toronto's Arab community is served by a variety of churches that relate to the eclectic nature of its prevalent beliefs.

The **Saint Mar Barsaumo Syrian Orthodox Church,** *72 Birchmount Avenue (416-694-4500)* and **Saint George's Antiochian Orthodox Church,** *9116 Bayview Avenue (905-731-7210).*

Both serve the Syrian Orthodox and Lebanese Marianite community, one of Toronto's largest Arab groups.

Our Lady of Lebanon Catholic Church, *1515 Queen Street West (416-534-7070).*

Serves the Lebanese Catholic community.

The **Apostolic Assyrian Church of the East,** *1155 Indian Road (905-278-2025).*
An Eastern Rite Catholic Church.

The **Marianists of Toronto,** *655 Spadina Avenue (416-593-1710).*
Acts as an umbrella group for the Marianite community.

Saint Mark's Coptic Orthodox Church,
4 Glendinning Avenue (416-494-4449).
The main church for Toronto's Egyptian Coptic Christian community, Saint Mark's holds a variety of special festivals, community events, and cultural activities.

Toronto's Arab Islamic community is served by the **Jami Mosque,** 56 Boustead Avenue (416-769-1192), as well as by the newly built **Zainabia Muhammadi Mosque,** 7340 Bayview Avenue (905-881-1763).
The **Turkish Canadian Islamic Heritage Association/Turkish Mosque,** 336 Pape Avenue (416-469-2610), is the main religious center for the Turkish community.
Among those faiths widely persecuted in Iran was the Baha'i; many practitioners of this faith worship at the **Baha'i Faith National Administrative Centre,** 7200 Leslie Street (905-889-8168). The center has been active in promoting the peaceful values of the Baha'i faith, as well as in trying to work to end the persecution of its members in Iran.

Organizations

There are many well-funded community organizations helping to preserve the Arab language and the many cultural variations present in Toronto's Arab community:

Arab Canadian Club of Toronto, *51 Fieldcroft Court (416-832-3158).*
Primarily a social and fraternal organization sponsoring various social get-togethers.

Arab Community Centre, *5298 Dundas Street West (416-231-7746).*

The main center for Toronto's Arab community. Established in 1972, it provides social, cultural, and educational programs, as well as heritage-language courses. The active center also publishes a newsletter.

Arab Palestine Association, *5298 Dundas Street West (416-275-7818).*

A subgroup of the Arab Community Centre that specializes in activities for Toronto's Palestinian community.

Arabian Sahara Dancers, *247 Dundas Street West (416-368-1797).*

A group specializing in teaching and performing Arab dancing, including belly dancing.

Assyrian Community of Canada Welfare Committee, *964 Albion Road, Suite 102 (416-742-5676).*

A social welfare group aimed at helping members of the broader Syrian-Canadian community.

Canadian Arab Youth Club, *44 Gerrard Street West, #1406 (416-599-7823).*

A social and fraternal club for Canadian Arab youth.

Canadian Druze Community, *PO Box 338, Station R (416-490-1756).*

A social organization for the Druze Christian Lebanese community in Toronto.

Canadian Egyptian Club, *PO Box 368, Station R (416-239-5282).*

A social and cultural organization for Toronto's Egyptian community sponsoring a variety of discussions and social events. **Cercle des Canadiens d'Egypte** is a group that aims to provide support to French-speaking Egyptians.

Federation of Canadian Turkish Associations, *253 College Street (416-597-2026).*

An umbrella organization for a dozen different Turkish community groups including the **Turkish Canadian Islamic Association,** the **Anatolian Folk Dancers,** the **Turkish Culture and Folklore Society, Turks from Bulgaria** (416-429-4180), and the **Association of Canadian Turkish Cypriots.**

Jordanian Club of Ontario, *PO Box 519, Station T (416-890-9483).*

A social and cultural organization for Jordanian immigrants.

Nile Association of Ontario, *1041-A North Service Road (905-410-8580).*

A social and community service organization covering Toronto's Egyptian and Sudanese communities.

Syrian Canadian Cultural Association, *265 Dixon Road, #1712 (416-247-9527).*

A community services organization for Toronto's Syrian community.

World Lebanese Cultural Union of Toronto, *221 Victoria Street, Suite 10 (416-366-7025).*

A Lebanese cultural organization sponsoring a variety of events and discussions.

In recent years the Toronto Arab community has felt the need to take a more public position within the city. Much of this was due to the widespread hysteria stirred up by the Gulf War that was directed at the broader North American Arab community. The irony here was that many Arab Canadians supported the United Nations' intervention but, because of a lack of understanding about the cultural and political differences with their homeland, the community was seen by the Canadian public as holding the opposite view. The **Canadian Arab Federation,** 5298 Dundas Street West (416-231-7524), has long been the preeminent group speaking on behalf of the Arab-Canadian community. It has supported a wide variety of educational, cultural, and political initiatives designed not only to provide services to the community but to provide a more complex and accurate portrayal of its members to the Canadian public at large.

Other political and social organizations of importance include the **Canadian Arab Friendship Society,** Box 352; **Assyrian Society of Canada Social Club,** 1150 Crestlawn Drive (416-624-5194); and the **United Holy**

Land Fund, 1586 Onondaga Place (905-891-1233), a political advocacy group centered on the Middle East conflict. While many Arab Canadians hold strong opinions on a personal level regarding the Middle East conflict, the community organizations have generally taken a low profile in this area.

The **Persian Traditional Art and Cultural Foundation of Ontario,** PO Box 1137, Adelaide Street Station, is an umbrella organization that helps promote Iranian art and culture through lectures, conferences, seminars, and publications. It also works as a community agency to help new immigrants to Canada.

Persian-language courses are available from **Forest Manor Elementary School,** 25 Forest Manor Road (416-491-5331), and **Glenview Public School,** 401 Rosewell Avenue (416-393-9390).

Other community groups and organizations include:

Iranian Community Association of Ontario, *1110 Finch Avenue West (416-736-4090).*

Iranian Women's Organization, *2975 Don Mills Road (416-496-9566).*

Iran's Ethnic Foundation, *39 Kimbercroft Court, Suite 507 (416-297-7680).*

In spite of their political differences on the question of Israel, there is actually a surprising amount of interaction between Toronto's Arab and Jewish communities, with many of the most popular Arab restaurants located in Toronto's Jewish north end.

══════ Holidays and Celebrations ══════

February 9	*Feast of Saint Maron,* patron saint of the Maronite Christians.
March	*Anatolia Ball.*
March 21	*Iranian New Year,* with celebrations and dinners.

March 30	*Day of the Land,* a Palestinian celebration marking their commitment to hold onto their lands in occupied Palestine.
April	*New Year's* according to the Antiochian-Syrian calendar, occurring early in the month.
May 8	*Saint Mark's Day,* honoring the patron saint of the Coptic Church.
June 29	*Feast of Saint Peter and Saint Paul,* founders of the Church of Antioch.
July	*Kurban Bayrami/Great Festival,* a religious celebration.
September 11	*New Year's* celebration in the Coptic Church calendar.
November 15	*Declaration of the Palestinian State.*
November 21	*Arab Heritage Day.*
December 22	*Celebration of the Winter Solstice.*

Restaurants

There are a number of different styles of Middle Eastern cooking, including Lebanese, Turkish, Persian, and Syrian. Lebanese specialties include the ubiquitous *falafel* (a chickpea-based salad) and *shawarma* (sliced chicken or lamb with tahini sauce and vegetables), as well as the lesser-known *kebbi* (deep-fried ground beef with buckwheat meatballs). Persian cuisine is similar to those of many Mediterranean, Middle Eastern, and North African countries, with a heavy emphasis on grilled, delicately marinated meats and spicy yogurt sauces in addition to unique specialties such as *gheimeh* (spicy veal stew), *gormeh sabzi* (vegetable stew), *bademjan* (eggplant casserole), and *dolmeh* (Persian-stuffed green peppers).

Moroccan cuisine is also available at a number of restaurants that provide an interesting array of saffron-based sauces and marinades with grilled-meat specialties, as well as excellent and underrated Moroccan wines. Turkish food is very similar to the Greek and Levantine cuisines that abound in the Mediterranean. Specialties include grilled pork, lamb, and chicken, and stuffed green peppers. Baklava and kadaiff are popular desserts served with thick, strong Turkish coffee.

Aida's Falafel, *553 Bloor Street West (416-537-3700).*

The full-service restaurant branch of this large chain of take-out cafés, this location serves full meals, including excellent lamb and chicken dishes and a variety of dips.

Armenian Kitchen, *1646 Victoria Park Avenue (416-752-8122).*

Primarily an Armenian restaurant, the Armenian Kitchen also carries a variety of Arab dishes, including various grilled, seasoned meats, dips like hummus, and baba ganoosh. (See also the listing on page 305.)

Boujadi, *220 Eglinton Avenue East (416-440-0258).*

An excellent addition to the Toronto restaurant scene serving superb Moroccan and Levantine specialties with intensely spicy tejas, beautiful grilled and braised lamb and other meats, and saucy slow-cooked couscous dishes.

Cedars Lebanese Cuisine, *394 Bloor Street West (416-923-3277).*

A full-service restaurant in Toronto's annex area serving Lebanese specialties, such as shish kebab and *tabbouleh* (a salad of mint, parsley, bulgur wheat, tomatoes, onions, and lemon juice), at reasonable prices in a comfortable atmosphere.

Cleopatra Restaurant and Nightclub, *977 Bloor Street West (416-539-0259).*

An Egyptian-Lebanese restaurant and nightclub that looks a bit dowdy on the outside but has a pleasant and entertaining atmosphere once you get inside. The food is well prepared and moderately priced.

Darvish Persian Restaurant, *1549 Bloor Street West (416-535-5530).*

A traditional down-home–style restaurant well known for its chelow kebab served with yogurt herbs and mint, Cornish hen marinated in saffron, and spiced ground beef kebabs served with rice. Persian tea and desserts are also available.

Efes Restaurant, *605 Bloor Street West (416-588-2708).*

A pleasant, popular Turkish restaurant serving a variety of dishes.

El-Basha Restaurant, *415 Bloor Street West (416-921-9094).*

A small restaurant serving primarily take-out foods such as shawarmas. Well known for its kebbi and *shish taouk* (spit-roasted chicken).

Haifa Restaurant, *3022 Bathurst Street (416-783-6406).*

A long-established Middle Eastern restaurant serving many specialties from the Levant, including a variety of grilled meats, salads, and appetizers.

Jerusalem Restaurant, *955 Eglinton Avenue West (416-783-6494).*

Another well-established favorite with a small but comfortable dining area. Among its specialties are lamb shish kebab, *foule* (flavored fava beans), and *labaneh* (yogurt cream cheese).

Kensington Kitchen, *124 Harbord Street (416-961-3404).*

A superb restaurant presenting a variety of reasonably priced continental and Middle Eastern dishes in pleasant surroundings. Excellent wine list values are complemented by superb grilled lamb chops, a creamy richly flavored hummus, and tabbouleh, as well as vegetarian specialties such as *lubya* (green beans stewed in tomato sauce) and *baba ghanouj* (puréed eggplant and tahini). In the summer they open up a lovely outdoor patio on the back deck of the restaurant's second floor.

Mandaloon, *113 Yorkville Avenue (416-324-9814).*

A new Middle Eastern restaurant in the heart of Yorkville serving an eclectic array of Levantine and North African dishes with an emphasis on Lebanese specialties. A comfortable dining room warmed by a fireplace.

Marrakesh Restaurant, *8362 Kennedy Road (416-479-4241).*

Owned by the same people who own the Sultan's Tent, the Marrakech is a smaller, more intimate restaurant serving superb saffron-tinged Moroccan cuisine.

Pars Restaurant, *455 Queen Street West (416-862-0527).*

Decorated in the floral patterns found in Persian palaces, the Pars is Toronto's premier Persian restaurant, serving such specialties as *barg* (char-grilled racks of lamb), badjeman, and appetizers like *torshee* (spiced and aged vegetables in vinegar). There are various kinds of baklava and Persian honey pastries for dessert. Another specialty is *shole-e-zard*—a ride pudding dessert combining saffron, cinnamon, almond, and rose water.

Sammy's Bay Street Exchange, *330 Bay Street (416-361-3133).*

Persian dancing and music are available here on Saturday nights, as are some Persian menu specialties throughout the week.

Star of Omar Khayam, *934 College Street (416-533-4333).*

A very pleasant neighborhood restaurant serving Middle Eastern and Persian specialties, including a variety of grilled meats and yogurt-based dips and sauces.

Stone Cottage Inn, *3750 Kingston Road (416-266-6200).*

Located in an old Coach Stop Inn originally built in 1867, the Stone Cottage Inn is Toronto's oldest Egyptian restaurant. Specialties include *zagazig dip* (yogurt, cucumbers, garlic, and spices), *moza bel forne dani* (marinated lamb on a bed of rice), and *Sultan effendi* (curried lamb stew), as well as a variety of Arab desserts such as the honeyed pistachio nut baklava pastries.

Sultan's Tent Restaurant, *1280 Bay Street (416-961-0601).*

A superb restaurant presenting Moroccan cuisine and Arab entertainment in a large tent-like environment. The saffron-tinged flavors of Moroccan cooking permeate the air, and specialties include *b'stila* (Cornish hen in a sweetened saffron sauce served with eggs and almond) and *khizzu* (puréed carrots cooked with lemon, hot pepper, and cumin).

Turkish Delights Istanbul, *444 Yonge Street (416-340-1946).*

A restaurant and nightclub with belly dancing and a variety of Turkish foods.

====== **Cafés and Nightclubs** ======

Arab fast foods, in particular falafel, shawarmas, and kebabs, have become staple items in the diets of many Torontonians. Falafel is a kind of chickpea and vegetable filling in a soft taco-like pita bread covered with tahini and red-pepper hot sauce. Very healthy and very popular with vegetarians. Shawarmas are made of lamb, pork, or chicken that has been slow-roasted on a spit and is then sliced off and added to salad vegetables and again covered in tahini and hot sauce. Kebabs are individually roasted chunks of meat served in a similar fashion. Kebbi is a kind of Middle Eastern meatball made with ground lamb and bulgur wheat. Likewise, Arab coffee, thick and rich, or its spiced teas and honey-drenched desserts are often available at cafés. A number of falafel/shawarma cafés can be found throughout the city, but among the best are:

Aida's Falafel, *1921 Queen Street East (416-699-3377); Eaton Centre Food Court (416-971-9050); 553 Bloor Street West (416-537-3700); 2439 Yonge Street (416-488-2426); 3410 Sheppard Avenue East (416-299-4888).*

Falafel-Falafel, *1280 Bay Street (416-962-0639).*

Falafel Hut Village, *105 McCaul Street (416-598-4252).*

Falafel Plus, *388 Bloor Street West (416-921-1674).*

Falafel Queen, *576 Queen Street West (416-594-9736); 181 Dundas Street West (416-596-0449).*

Falafel Villa, *1700 Wilson Avenue (416-245-2723).*

Falafel World, *2396 Bloor Street West (416-769-9336); 3128 Dundas Street West (416-762-9658).*

Jerusalem Restaurant, *955 Eglinton Avenue West (416-783-6494).*

Lebanese Falafel House, *977 Bloor Street West (416-537-7823).*

Arab entertainment, with its ecstatic music, belly dancing, and other lively attributes, can be found in a variety of clubs in Toronto:

Cleopatra Restaurant and Nightclub, *977 Bloor Street West (416-539-0259).*
Full-scale Arabian entertainment with belly dancing, musical groups, even floor shows, nightly throughout the week and on weekends.

Haifa Restaurant, *3022 Bathurst Street (416-783-6406).*
Arab performers entertain on weeknights and weekends.

Sahara Palace, *300 Dundas Street East (905-897-0977).*
This nightclub/restaurant attempts to conjure up as much of the exotic atmosphere of North Africa as possible, with belly dancers and Arab musicians performing in a decor reminiscent of an Arab tent. Performances are nightly throughout the week and on weekends.

Star of Omar Khayam, *934 College Street (416-533-4333).*
On Fridays and Saturdays, music only.

Stone Cottage Inn, *3750 Kingston Road (416-266-6200).*
Belly dancers and Arab musicians on weekends in Toronto's oldest Arab restaurant/nightclub located in this historic coach stop building on the old road to Montreal.

Sultan's Tent Restaurant, *1280 Bay Street (416-961-0601).*
A well-known restaurant and nightclub on Bay Street near the Yorkville neighborhood, the Sultan's Tent has belly dancing and Arab music nightly.

Tehran's Night Restaurant, *4949 Bathurst Street (416-229-4444).*
A newly opened Persian and Arab restaurant with some Middle Eastern entertainment in the evening.

Turkish Delights Istanbul, *444 Yonge Street (416-340-1946).*

Restaurant and nightclub with belly dancing and a variety of Turkish foods.

Food Sources

Bakeries

Beautifully baked unleavened Arab pita breads, almond pastries, phyllo pastries, and other specialties such as *kul wa-shkur* (almond-and-cashew–filled pastries) and marquq can be bought along with a variety of other Levantine foods and baked goods at the following bakeries:

Ararat Bakery, *1800 Avenue Road (416-782-5722).*

Armenian Bakery, *1646 Victoria Park Avenue (416-757-1559).*

Haddad Bakery, *4610 Dufferin Street (416-661-8046).*

Mediterranean Bakery, *190 Norelco Drive (416-743-6634).*

Zakarian Family Variety, *2190 Warden Avenue (416-493-5649).*

Carries a variety of Turkish foods and baked goods.

Foods and baked goods popular with Persians include saffron, basmati rice, dried fruits, baklava, Persian tea and coffee, and various kinds of produce unique to the area. Some stores and bakeries specializing in these products include:

Country Harvester, *2339 Dundas Street West (416-530-1530).*

Garni Bakery, *508 McNicoll Avenue (416-492-7200).*

Millwood Variety, *1495 Bayview Avenue (416-421-9911).*

Nasr Mini Mart, *1996 Lawrence Avenue East (416-757-1611).*

Butchers

Most Mediterranean meats can be bought fresh at a variety of butchers. Check the listings in the Italian and Greek chapters. Also, halaal meat specialties can be bought at the following butchers:

Alaqsa Halal Meat, *2233 Dundas Street West (416-516-3319).*

Araina Halal Meat, *927 Danforth Avenue (416-461-7205).*

House of Halaal Meats, *803 Danforth Avenue (416-461-2839).*

Khartoum for Halaal Meat, *1018 Bloor Street West (416-534-4775).*

Delis/Grocers

Saffron, Arab spices, figs, assorted dried fruits, bulgur wheat, and scented Arab coffees and teas are available at a number of local stores, including the following:

Al-Amin Grocery, *2768 Danforth Avenue (416-699-2849).*

Byblos Mini Mart, *2667 Islington Avenue (416-749-8959).*

NASR Foods, *1996 Lawrence Avenue East (416-757-1611).*

A large store with a wide array of foods and produce.

Zakarian Variety, *2190 Warden Avenue (416-493-5649).*

Shops

Persian carpets are noted the world over for their quality, craftsmanship, and beauty. A number of Persian carpet stores exist in Toronto. Among the better ones are:

Aban Persian Rugs, *922 Yonge Street (416-960-1139).*

Asian Persian Rug Co., *2025 Dundas Street East (905-624-3081).*

Indo-Iranian Carpet Co., *241 Queen Street West (416-593-5870).*

Isfahan Oriental Rugs, *474 McNicoll (416-494-3123).*

Pak Persian Oriental Rugs, *1280 Bay Street (416-924-5688).*

Persian Carpet Centre, *348 Davenport Road (416-925-2278).*

Scollard Carpet Ltd., *54 Scollard Street (416-967-4776).*

Turco-Persian Rug Co., *452 Richmond Avenue East (416-366-0707).*

Stores selling Arab-language music, books, newspapers, and videos include the following:

Azir Video, *520 Carlaw Avenue (416-778-0693).*

NASR Video, *2004 Lawrence Avenue East (416-750-0900).*

Other Middle Eastern art and craft specialties are available from many of the grocers noted earlier and at:

Egyptian Art, *517 Yonge Street (416-944-9688).*

This store carries a variety of Egyptian crafts and art as well as some knock-offs, so be careful.

Stone Cottage Inn, *3750 Kingston Road (416-266-6200).*

Carries a variety of Middle Eastern crafts and gifts, including wood carvings, jewelry, brass, and copper pots.

Media

Publications

Al-Petra, *PO Box 519, Station T (416-479-6939).*

A monthly newspaper published by the Jordanian Club of Ontario.

Arab Dawn, *5298 Dundas Street West (416-231-7524).*

Arab Guide, *511 Queen Street East (416-362-0307).*

Arab News of Toronto, *370 Queen Street East (416-362-0304).*

Haber Bulteni, *336 Pape Avenue (416-469-2610).*

News magazine published six times a year by the Turkish Canadian Islamic Heritage Association.

Iranian Women, *238 Davenport Avenue (416-920-5228).*

Quarterly magazine on the concerns of Iranian women.

Lisan Al-Arab, *5298 Dundas Street West (416-231-7524).*

Rouydad, *7 Hayden Avenue (416-260-0218).*

A publication citing items of interest to the Iranian community.

Sesimiz/Our Voice, *7305 Woodbine Avenue.*

A quarterly publication by the Turkish Culture and Folklore Society.

Radio and Television

"Arabic Program," CHIN 1540-AM, *637 College Street (416-531-9991).*

A weekly radio and television show produced in the Arab language covering cultural events and political issues of concerns to Toronto's Arab community.

"The Good News of Liberty," MTV Channel 47, *545 Lakeshore Boulevard West (416-593-4747).*

News and current-event television show of interest to the Iranian community.

"Iranian Program," Rogers Cable Channel 10, *855 Yorkville Avenue (416-446-6500).*

"Light for All Nations," MTV-CHANNEL 47, *545 Lakeshore Boulevard West (416-593-4747).*

"Namy Iran," CITY TV Channel 5, *299 Queen Street West (416-591-5757).*

Balkan Toronto

A number of Toronto's ethnic communities come from the volatile regions of Eastern Europe's Balkan Mountains. There are similarities in culture and cuisine as well as overlapping religions among these diverse peoples, but tremendous differences in language and politics.

Nationalities

Albanians

Although not one of Toronto's larger ethnic communities, Albanians make up one of its older ones. The first Albanian immigrant to Toronto, a Mr. Shamata, arrived in 1902 and owned and operated a shoe store on Bloor Street for over fifty years. Subsequent immigrants started arriving after 1904. Most of these went to work on building Canada's then-burgeoning railway and in many local factories and restaurants.

Albanians descend from the ancient Illyrians associated with Greek and Mycenaean civilizations. King Pyhrrus of the infamous Pyhrric victory was an Albanian. Like the Bosnians, the Albanians are by and large Orthodox Muslims, though many Albanians also belong to the Albanian Orthodox and Eastern Rite Catholic Churches.

Early cultural and social activities in the Albanian community centered around *konaks,* or boarding houses, since most Albanian immigrants to Canada were single working-class men. Religious organizations, especially the Islamic Church, were also important because Albanians were among the first Muslims to live in Toronto.

Following the Second World War and the rise of the Hoxha regime in Albania, many families came to join their Canadian-based relatives. There also were a number of immigrants who were Hoxha supporters and supported some neo-Maoist political groups in Toronto in the 1960s and 1970s.

Other Albanians also came from Italy, Greece, Yugoslavia, Egypt, and Turkey. As a result, one of the largest Albanian social organizations is the **Alleanza Albanese Italo Di Toronto,** a group of Italo-Albanians.

There are over 15,000 Torontonians of Albanian descent currently living in the city. Most live in the west Toronto district bordered to the north and east by Dundas Street West and Jane Street and to the south by Annette Street. A number of Albanian businesses and restaurants are located in these areas as well.

Bulgarians

Toronto's first wave of Bulgarian immigrants arrived with the outbreak of the first series of Balkan wars in 1908. More arrived as the conflicts deepened, and in 1910 the community's first church, **Saints Cyril & Methodius Macedono-Bulgarian Orthodox Cathedral,** which remains the focal point for the community to this day, was established.

The earliest Bulgarian immigrants were from small rural towns and were recruited to come to Canada and build the railroads and canals that were springing up in the early 1910s and 1920s. Others went to work in the many mines that were opening up in the Canadian shield during this time. The community slowly grew through the 1930s but received a very large influx following the Communist takeover of Bulgaria in 1946.

The early community was focused around Church, Parliament, Queen, and Dundas Streets. With the coming of new immigrants and the arrival of many Macedonian refugees from Bulgaria, a number of joint Macedonian-Bulgarian organizations were formed. Churches and benevolent societies were created, the Macedonian community in particular becoming a very large and active presence in Toronto.

Bulgarian choral music, folk dancing, and language classes have been greatly encouraged by this small (3,000 people) but active community. Many Bulgarian Torontonians have been active in the Toronto arts and classical music scene. Some prominent members of the community include film director Ted Kotcheff and one of Toronto's biggest real estate developers, Ignat Kaneff.

Croatians

The Croatian community in Toronto goes back to the earliest days of Canadian exploration. Sailors from the Dalmatian port of Ragusa served on both Jacques Cartier's and later Samuel de Champlain's explorations of Canada and were mercenaries in the French armies brought to defend New France in the 1750s. Settling in the farming areas opened up after the French and Indian wars, some Croatian settlers began to move to the growing urban area of Toronto in the early 1800s.

This small community was joined by a continuous wave of Croatian immigrants driven out of their homeland by the Balkan Wars accompanying the decline of the Ottoman Empire. The community greatly increased in size following World War II, with two waves of Croatians fleeing both the repressive Nazi puppet state of the Kingdom of Croatia set up in the forties and the successive communist regime of Tito.

A darker side to one portion of this community was its involvement (similar to members of the Slovakian community) in an assortment of marginal political activities throughout the sixties and seventies, but generally the citizenry has been a productive and proudly Canadian community, producing some of the great sports heroes of this city, including boxer George Chuvalo and hockey stars Frank and Peter Mahovlich.

With the increase in population in the 1950s and 1960s, the Croatian community began to take a more active cultural role and established its first parish and school, as well as a number of social and cultural organizations. Its proudest moment came when Toronto's first soccer team (at the time called the Metro-Croatians because of the Croatian community's strong involvement) won the 1976 North American Soccer League Championship.

Over 25,000 Torontonians of Croatian descent currently live in the city, many of them in the Parkdale area surrounding what is now called Croatia Street, where **Our Lady Queen of Croatia Roman Catholic Church** remains as the religious, cultural, and social center of the neighborhood.

Unfortunately the current conflicts in the former Yugoslavia have strained relations between Toronto's Croatian and Serbian communities, which live close to each other in Parkdale and have seen their numbers increase with the wave of refugees from their homeland.

Macedonians

Macedonia is a Balkan region best known as the home of Alexander the Great. It has gone through various periods of self-rule over the years, last achieving independence from Ottoman rule in 1903. Macedonians live in an area that now spans northwestern provinces of Bulgaria and Greece and the Republic of Macedonia in the former Yugoslavia. Toronto boasts one of the largest Macedonian communities in the world.

Macedonians didn't start coming to Toronto until the turn of the century. With the failure of the Ilinden Uprising and the devastating impact of the subsequent Balkan wars which focused around the Macedonian territories, many Macedonians fled their homeland. Early immigrants to Canada came to work in the tannery and fur-processing plants located in the Cabbagetown area of Toronto. Others went to work in the iron industry and machine and tool factories, as well as the meatpacking industry. When the meatpacking and tanning industries moved west in the city, a Macedonian community formed around their center in the Niagara Avenue area of Toronto and in the west Toronto district known as "the Junction."

Unlike other ethnic groups, Macedonian immigrants were primarily laborers who were looking for factory work. As such, they played a disproportionately large role in early Toronto industrial development as well as in unionization. Labor exchanges, a steamship line, and a banking company were all started by Macedonian immigrants. As factory workers grew in experience to become shop stewards and supervisors, the Macedonian community began to produce many small auto repair, metal work, and butcher shops. Many Macedonians own restaurants in the city, although generally they sell either Canadian or Greek food. Much Macedonian cuisine is similar to Greek cooking.

A third wave of immigrants came to Toronto after the Second World War, when many Macedonians were expelled from their homeland by various regimes. Today there are over 50,000 Macedonians in the city. Prominent community members include former National Hockey League coach Tommy Ivan, businessman John Bitove, and physicist Dr. Boris Stoicheff.

Romanians

Probably the most famous Torontonian of Romanian descent is that denizen of late-night music commercials, Zamfir, whose haunting Romanian folk music played on the pan pipes has become familiar to insomniacs everywhere. Toronto's Romanian settlers came here in the 1880s around the same time as those from many other Balkan countries. This was a time of tremendous upheaval in that area, as new countries were forming out of the remnants of the Ottoman Empire.

The earliest Romanian immigrants, many of whom were priests, came from the provinces of Transylvania and Bukovina, which at the time had been newly acquired by the Austrian-Hungarian Empire. More Romanians came from the capital city of Bucharest throughout the late 1800s. They came as farm laborers, many initially moving to Quebec, since for many of them French was their second language. Former army officers and soldiers also joined the ranks of immigrants in an attempt to find work.

Romanians from Europe and the United States slowly collected in Toronto, with the opportunities afforded by a growing industrial and commercial economy. Growth in immigration to the city continued throughout the post-World War I era, with many Romanians finding jobs as gardeners, butchers, and tailors. The **Romanian Cultural Society** was set up at this time, and two congregations of the Romanian Orthodox Church arose which later united as the **Saint George Romanian Orthodox Episcopate Church of America and Canada.**

The community now numbers almost 20,000 people, most of whom are dispersed throughout the city, though pockets of Romanians live in the Junction and Bloor West areas frequented by many other Balkan peoples. The nearby communities of Hamilton and the Kitchener/Waterloo area also have large Romanian populations. The Romanian community has produced its share of well-known Torontonians besides the aforementioned Zamfir, including opera singer Cathy Dumitrascu, industrialist Dan Chirtu, and architects Constantine and Iona Maruntescu.

Serbs

With over 30,000 members, Toronto's Serbian community is the city's largest ethnic group from the former Yugoslavia. Members are actively involved in the community through their church. Serbian settlement in Toronto goes back to 1850 when a group of Serbs arrived to work in railroad construction and other industries. The first substantial group came just at the turn of the century, with many working in the Ontario mining and lumber industries. By 1916 the first fraternal organization was established, along with a number of Serbian-owned businesses and a coffeehouse.

A second wave of Serb immigration occurred in the 1920s when more families came to work primarily in the meatpacking and iron industries. The community then began work on organizing a local parish of the Serbian Orthodox Church. As immigration continued in the 1930s, other cultural and educational institutions were created, primarily focused around the Parkdale and Junction areas where the greatest amount of settlement occurred.

The period following the Second World War saw the largest increase in the community. Serbs left a Yugoslavia devastated by World War II where per capita deaths were higher than for any other country. The majority of the arrivals settled in the Riverdale area, around which a new parish church was organized.

Immigration continued into the 1960s and 1970s, with many skilled academics, musicians, and artists coming to Toronto. Dr. Luigi Von Kunits, a Serb immigrant from an earlier phase, was one of the founders of the Toronto Symphony and also started the *Canadian Music Journal*. Other recent immigrants, such as composer Marinko Michael Pepa, continue this tradition with the promotion of chamber music concerts.

Unfortunately the current troubles in the former Yugoslavia undermined what were close and cordial relations between Toronto's Bosnian, Serbian, Croatian, and Slovenian communities. Tensions have calmed since the early years of the war, but the communities' previous level of interaction has not been reestablished.

A unique Serbian custom is that of "Patron Saint Day" *(Krsna Slava)*. This day is passed down from father to son and commemorates when the family originally became part of the church. Each Serbian home has an icon of its patron saint, and on the patron saint day the family holds a church service and feast.

Slovenians

Slovenia is a small mountainous country that was a region in the former Yugoslavia and has been a prosperous and relatively peaceful independent country since the larger nation's breakup. In many ways Slovenia has more in common with nearby Austria and Switzerland than with the rest of the Balkans. Its main symbol is the linden tree, a fragrant tree renowned for its medicinal properties and a symbol of prosperity and fertility.

Slovenian settlement in Toronto goes back to the 1830s, when Frederick Baraga, a missionary and later a bishop, came to preach among the Native

Canadians of Upper Canada (as Ontario was known at the time). He was well known and respected for his work in codifying Native Canadian languages. He also corresponded with his fellow countrymen in Slovenia.

Intrigued by reports of his adventures in Canada, a large group of Slovenians began arriving in the 1800s, most of them between 1875 and 1900. These were mainly miners and construction laborers who became involved in the many road-building projects going on in Ontario at the time. Slovenians settled in Toronto as well as the northern communities of Timmins and Kirkland Lake, from which some internal migration to Toronto occurred.

This nascent community was greatly enlarged by almost 25,000 Slovenians who arrived in Canada as a result of the communist takeover in Yugoslavia after World War II. The community began organizing churches, community groups, and fraternal charitable organizations and came to settle in the area that is still their central focus, west Toronto. Over the years, Slovenian parishioners purchased a plot of land in the Assumption Catholic Cemetery in Mississauga with a memorial stating, "Here Slovenians wait for Resurrection." As far as their homeland goes, that miracle occurred five years ago. Well-known Slovenes include geologist Ludmilla Dolar-Mantuani, artist Ted Kramolc, and internationally known accordion player Joe Petric.

Religion

Most Albanians are of the Sunni Muslim religious persuasion and, as pointed out earlier, were among the first immigrants of this faith to arrive in Toronto. While they worship at the major mosques—including the **Medinah Mosque,** Danforth Avenue (416-465-7833), and the **Jami Mosque,** 56 Boustead Avenue (416-769-1192)—they also have their own community mosque—the **Albanian Mosque,** 564 Annette Street (416-763-0612), which is also a major focal point for most community and cultural activities through the **Albanian Muslim Society.**

There are three main churches in the Bulgarian community, but the oldest and most prominent is **Saints Cyril & Methodius Macedono-Bulgarian Orthodox Cathedral,** 237 Sackville Street (416-368-9410), which also maintains an active language school and music choir. Two other Eastern Orthodox churches having large Bulgarian congregations are **Saint George's Macedono-Bulgarian Eastern Orthodox Church,** 17 Regent Street (416-

366-1810), which was established in 1941 and also has a choir and school, and **Holy Trinity Macedono-Bulgarian Eastern Orthodox Church,** 201 Monarch Park Avenue (416-461-2214), which maintains a choir.

The Croatian community is predominantly Catholic, although some members are Islamic, and there are three principal places of worship:

Our Lady Queen of Croatia Roman Catholic Church, *7 Croatia Street (416-536-3669).*

The religious and cultural heart of the community, the church features a statue of Aloysius Cardinal Stepinac, the former archbishop of Croatia. Besides the impressive cathedral, it also houses **Our Lady Queen of Croatia Community Centre** (see listing in next section).

Roman Catholic Church of Croatian Martyrs, *4605 Mississauga Road (416-826-8844).*

Serves the growing suburban Croatian community.

The **Croatian Islamic Center,** *75 Birmingham (416-255-8338).*

A mosque serving both the Croatian and Bosnian Islamic community and holding a variety of Arabic-language classes as well as maintaining a large library of Croatian-Islamic books, newspapers, and magazines.

Macedonians in Toronto belong to the Byzantine Orthodox tradition. The two main churches are:

Saint Clement of Ohrid Macedonian Orthodox Church, *76 Overlea Boulevard (416-421-7451).*

Built in 1964, it also houses a twenty-voice male choir and holds language classes.

Saint Ilija Macedonian Orthodox Church, *Derry Road (905-564-0570).*

The main church for the Romanian community in Toronto is Saint George Romanian Orthodox Church, 247 Rosethearn Avenue (416-651-

1321). It operates a library and an art gallery and is beautifully decorated with icons and statuary imported from Romania.

Serbs by and large attend the Serbian Orthodox Church. The main one in Toronto is **Saint Sava Serbian Orthodox Church,** 203 River Street (416-967-9885). It includes a school on Serbian language, history, and culture, and is home to the **Saint Sava Church Choir,** the **Serbian National Federation,** and **Queen Alexandra Circle of Serbian Sisters.**

The other church in the area is the **Serbian Orthodox Free Church of Saint Archangel Michael,** 212 Delaware Avenue (416-531-0275), which also houses a church choir, a folk dance group, a library, and language classes.

The predominant religion among Slovenians is Roman Catholicism. The two major churches are also centers for community, cultural, and social activities, including language classes:

Our Lady Help of Christians Church, *611 Manning Avenue (416-531-2316).*

The first Slovenian church built in Canada with religious art from Ted Kramolc and the stations of the cross sculpted by Franc Gorse. It also publishes the monthly magazine *Bozda Beseda.*

Our Lady of the Miraculous Medal Parish, *739 Brown's Line Road (416-255-2721).*

The largest Slovenian parish in Canada. The church's statues and stations of the cross were sculpted by Franc Gorse.

Organizations

A number of Albanian social, cultural, and sports clubs exist in the city, including:

Albanian House, *223 Mavety Street (416-766-7272).*

A center for Albanian cultural activities sponsoring a folk dance troupe, music nights, lectures, and discussion groups.

Albanian Muslim Society, *564 Annette Street (416-763-0612).*

A major religious and charitable society providing community support for many members of the Albanian community.

Albanian Socer Tiem *(416-251-2996).*

The local Albanian community soccer team.

Alleanza Albanese Italo Di Toronto, *190 Rosemount Avenue (416-652-1143).*

An active organization of Italo-Albanians hosting a variety of social and charitable events.

Klubi Kulturoro-Patriotik, *395A Keele Street (416-624-6200).*

A patriotic and nationalist organization supportive of the Albanian homeland.

The Bulgarian community supports a variety of cultural, social, and political organizations of its own:

The **Bulgarian Canadian Society of Toronto,** *1092 Islington Avenue (416-239-3051).*

Organizes a number of social and cultural activities for the community, including the National Liberation Day celebrations.

The **Bulgarian National Front,** *55 Wynford Heights Crescent (416-449-8649).*

Established in 1951, it has helped provide assistance for new immigrants, as well as charitable and social work in the Bulgarian community and relief efforts overseas. This organization has taken a strong anticommunist political stance over the years and has sponsored a number of political forums and activities. It also supports cultural activities like a woman's choir.

All three religious centers in the Croatian community maintain Croatian-language schools and a variety of cultural and community services. **Our Lady Queen of Croatia Community Centre** has displays of arts and crafts by local Croatian artists, as well as historical portraiture, many made particularly poignant by the destruction to the picturesque cities of Dubrovnik and Mostar that has been wrought by the wars in the former Yugoslavia. The center also houses the **Association of Croatian Women,** a **Croatian Catholic Youth Group,** two church choirs, a variety of benevolent and charitable institutions, and the **Tamburitza Orchestra,** a musical performing group using traditional Croatian instruments.

The **Roman Catholic Church of Croatian Martyrs** houses a choir, the **Zupna Kolo Grupa Sljeme** folk dancing group, and another folk music ensemble, the **Croatian Tamburitza.**

Other cultural and artistic groups in the community include:

Croatian Community Services, *240 Brunel Road (905-712-0992).*

Croatian Information Center, *918 Dundas Street East (905-270-2532).*

Croatian Canadian Business and Professional Association, *1745 Thornybrae Place (905-858-4442).*

Croatian Club, *1989 A Dundas Street East (905-624-4111).*

A local soccer club holding a variety of meals and social events, with excellent Croatian food and local Croatian musical entertainment every Sunday.

Croatian Folklore Ensemble and the **Folklore Ensemble Croatia Mississauga,** *41 Pindar Crescent (905-895-1662).*

Both help preserve Croatian musical and folk dance traditions.

Croatian Social and Cultural Center, *9118 Winston Churchill Drive (905-456-3203).*

The **Father Kamber Parish Recreational Park** in the Toronto suburb of Mississauga has been an important recreational and social center for the community, and now includes a large indoor recreational center to accompany the beautiful outdoor picnic areas along the banks of the Credit River. There is also an extensive social and recreational complex at the **Croatian**

Social and Cultural Center, PO Box 97 (905-456-3202), in nearby Norval, Ontario.

Croatian political groups have been focused around the concept of the return of an independent Croatia, as well as relief work and support of the Croatian community during the war following the breakup of Yugoslavia. These groups include the **Hrvatski Narodni Otpor/Croatian National Resistance** and **Hrvatsko Narodno Vijece/Canadian Croatian National Congress,** 48 Douglas Crescent (416-921-9301), the **Croatian Democratic Union,** 4040 Creditview Road (905-602-5430), and the **United Croats of Canada General Committee,** PO Box 236, Station E (416-746-5409). The **Croatian Family Relief Fund,** 5359 Timberlea (905-625-4454), is the major relief and charitable agency providing aid overseas.

Other Croatian political groups tie into the working-class heritage of many Croatian families and their involvement in the construction and craft unions. These include the **Croatian Workers Association of Canada,** PO Box 357, Station D; the **Croatian Fraternal Union;** and the **Croatian Catholic Union.**

Organizations and clubs in the Macedonian community include:

Canadian Macedonian Place, *76 Overlea Boulevard (416-421-7451).*

The major community center houses a number of organizations, including **Makedonka,** an award-winning folk dancing ensemble with over 200 dancers; the **Macedonia Drama Group;** the **Miladonov Brothers,** a Macedonian literary association; a Macedonian-language school; three large halls; a ballroom; and a library.

Canadian Macedonian Hockey League, *71 Gooderham Drive (416-759-5309).*

Canadian Macedonian Recreational Soccer League, *76 Overlea Boulevard (416-421-7451).*

Macedonian-Canadian Human Rights Committee, *97 Agincourt Drive (416-291-6424).*

"Selyani" Macedonian Folklore Group, *4 Osborn Avenue (416-698-1747).*

Association of Refugee Children from Aegean Macedonia, *982 Midland Avenue (416-266-8108).*

Macedonian Canadian Media Network, *2020 Bathurst Street (416-789-2905).*

United Macedonians of Canada Organization, *PO Box 334, Station O (416-940-8596).*

A number of organizations operate out of Saint George Romanian Orthodox Church at 247 Rosethearn Avenue (416-651-1321), including the **Romanian Cultural Association,** the **DACIA Dance Ensemble/Romanian Cultural Association, Saint George's Church Choir,** and the **Romanian Cultural Association.**

The **Romanian National Council of Canada,** 170 Garden Avenue (416-889-8228), acts as the major political lobbying organization for the community in Canada.

Organizations supported by the Serbian community address social, cultural, and political concerns.

Canadian Serbian Club of Toronto, *1900 Sheppard Avenue East (416-498-6853).*

The main umbrella group coordinating activities of the Serbian community in Canada.

Serbian Heritage Academy, *2381 Dundas Street West (416-588-8550).*

Serbian Information Directory, *75 Havenbrook (416-497-1949).*

Keeps citizens up to date on community activities.

The **Canadian Serbian National Committee,** *1 Secroft Crescent (416-663-3409),* and **Serbian National Shield Society,** *1900 Sheppard Avenue East (416-498-6853).*

The two main political organizations supporting Serbian interests in Canada and overseas.

There are also a number of societies and associations in the Slovenian neighborhood:

Slovenian Linden Foundation, *52 Neilson Drive (416-621-3820).*

Slovenian-Canadian Center (Slo-Can Center), *618 Manning Avenue (416-531-8475).*

Provides a cultural information service and publishes a variety of materials in Slovenian.

Slovenian Home Association, *864 Pape Avenue (416-463-2616).*

This group is developing a property that will be the cultural home of many Slovenian cultural associations, including the **Slovenian Playhouse** which currently performs Slovenian-language theater and drama in a variety of community centers across Canada.

Slovenian Hunters and Anglers Club, *43 Cowley Avenue (416-622-6655).*

Slovenian Information Center, *770 Brown's Line Road (416-255-4626).*

Provides information on events taking place in the Slovenian community.

Slovenska Narodna Zveza, *79 Watson Road (416-766-4848).*

════ Holidays and Celebrations ════

January 6/7	Serbian *Christmas* and *Christmas Eve.*
January 18	*John the Baptist Day.*
January 24	*Celebration of the Union of Principalities of 1859,* when Muntenia and Moldova were united to form the single state of Romania with Bucharest as the capital.

January 27	*Saint Sava Day,* celebrating the Serbian prince who became the first Serbian archbishop and helped establish the autonomous Serbian Church.
February 4	Commemorates the birthday of Gotse Delchev, who led the 1903 Ilinden Uprising.
February 10	Commemoration of the death of Aloisius Cardinal Stepinac, a Croatian spiritual leader who died while imprisoned by Yugoslav authorities in 1960.
March 3	*National Liberation Day,* honoring the day in 1878 that Bulgaria became an autonomous principality after 500 years of Ottoman rule.
March 27	*Bessarabia and Bucovina Day,* commemorating the day in 1918 when these two provinces were united with the rest of Romania.
April 10	*Croatian Independence Day.*
April 30	Honors Peter Zrinski and Frane Krsto Frankopan, national heroes who fought against the Austrian-Hungarian empire.
May	*Victoria Day,* commemorating the 1945 Bleiburg Massacre, as well as the celebration of the Croatian Folklore festival.
May 6	*Saint George's Day,* honoring a patron saint of Bulgaria, who was a high-ranking Roman soldier and was executed by the Emperor Diocletian for his Christian faith.
May 10	*Independence Day,* marking the day in 1877 when Romania gained its independence from the Ottoman Empire.
May 24	*Saints Cyril and Methody Day,* honoring the patron saints of Macedonia and creators of the Cyrillic alphabet.
May/June	*Feast of Corpus Christi.*

June	Memorial service for Slovenians killed in World War II, on the first Sunday of the month.
June 28	*Feast of Saint Lazarus.* Also *Memorial Day* for Serb resistance to Turkish conquest in 1389.
July	*Slovenian Day,* on the last Sunday of the month.
July 17	Memorial services for General Draza Mihailovich, a leader of Serb resistance to the Nazis.
August	*Bishop Baraga Day,* on the last Sunday of the month.
August 2	*Commemoration Day of the Ilinden Uprising.* Ceremonies are generally held on the first Sunday in August.
August 8	Commemoration of the death of Radic Stjepan, leader of the Croatian Peasant Movement, who promoted national unity through nonviolence and was killed in 1928.
September	*The Banat Festival,* held the first weekend of the month, which draws Romanians from across North America to celebrations in the nearby Kitchener area.
September 6	*Birthday of King Peter II.*
September 9	*Mourning Day,* a day of mourning observed by anticommunist Bulgarians marking the day Bulgaria became a communist regime.
October 9	*Croatian Music Festival.* Also, Serbian memorial of the assassination of King Alexander I, who was to have proposed a mutual defense treaty against Hitler.
October 11	Formation of the Republic of Macedonia in 1944.
October 22	Observance of the founding of the first Croatian parish in Toronto.

October 29	*Slovenian National Day*
November 2	*Feast of All Souls.*
November 28	*Albanian Independence Day,* celebrating the independence of Albania from the Ottoman Empire in 1912. Speeches, discussions, and cultural performances are all scheduled to help celebrate this event.
December	*Serbian Mother's Day,* on the second to the last Sunday of the month.
	Serbian Father's Day, on the last Sunday of the month.
December 1	Celebration of the Union of Transylvania with Romania.
December 8	*Saint Clement's Day,* honoring Saint Clement, a disciple of Saints Cyril and Methody.

Restaurants, Cafés, and Nightclubs

Albanian cuisine is a mixture of hearty Italian and Greek dishes that tend toward the baked casseroles of the border areas. Conversely, Croatian food can be divided into two different categories, sea and mountain. The coastal Croatian cuisine was heavily influenced by the Italians who controlled much of the Dalmatian coast throughout history, particularly the Venetians, as well as by the general transfer of flavors that marks much of the cuisine of the northern Mediterranean. The mountain cuisine is more Germanic and Balkan, with lamb, pork, and veal the main meats; hearty dishes and thick stews with potatoes, rather than the risottos and noodles of the coast, are the main source of starch. Specialties include *cevapcici* (spicy ground veal or beef fingers that are grilled), *raznjici* (barbecued veal or pork on a skewer), seafood risottos, and *rolati* (sponge cake rolls).

In addition to the listings in this chapter, you should consult those for Greek restaurants (page 156), whose cuisine is very similar to that of Macedonia.

Romanian cuisine consists of a number of uniquely spiced dishes mixed with other specialties commonly found in the Balkans, such as smoked sausages. *Mamliga,* a spicy cornmeal cooked until firm, is similar to a panchetta. Other specialties include baked carp, *foi de vita* (ground meat served in grape leaves with yogurt or sour cream), and *ghiveci calugaresc* (vegetables stewed in oil). *Masticka* (grape brandy) is a popular after-dinner liqueur.

Serbian cuisine is very similar to other Balkan cuisines, such as Romanian, Bulgarian, and Macedonian. Specialties include roast lamb or pork, as well as *gibanica* (phyllo pastry filled with cheese and eggs), raznjici, and placzinki. *Slivovitz* (plum brandy) is a favorite after-dinner liqueur.

Slovenian food is influenced by nearby Hungary, the Czech Republic, and Austria and includes specialties such as *golaz* (the Slovenian version of goulash), *vampe* (potato and tripe soup), *krvavice pecenice* (sausages made with pork and rice), Slovenian *polenta* (made of cornmeal and sauerkraut), and *buta repa* (turnip and pork hock soup).

Andy's Place, *2290 Dundas Street West (416-588-0113).*

Serbian cuisine.

Café Sofia, *272 Parliament Street (416-362-0846).*

A small, unpretentious neighborhood restaurant that serves some Bulgarian specialties, such as *kebabches* (broiled meat rolls on skewers), thick vegetarian stews, and bulgur and kasha grains with vegetable side dishes.

Captain John's Restaurant, *1 Queen's Quay West (416-363-6062).*

A seafood restaurant located on board a former Slovenian ship, the *Jadran* (Adriatic), docked at Harbourfront. It serves mainly seafood but includes a few Slovenian fish and dessert recipes on its menu.

Ilie's, *300 Eglinton Avenue West (416-483-2654).*

One of Toronto's two Romanian restaurants, decorated with folk crafts and artifacts throughout. Specialties include *miti-tei* (Romanian smoked sausage), eggplant pâté, and, on special occasions, mamliga prepared with chicken, sour cream, dill, and bay leaf.

Istria, *303 King Street West (416-598-5656).*

A lovely new restaurant that was opened on the King Street West strip just west of the Royal Alexandra Theatre, Istria serves Croatian delicacies like *shevepnece,* a grilled lamb and spiced ground-beef sausage, as well Northern Adriatic specialties such as seafood risotto and thin-crust pizzas.

Jeric's Dining Lounge, *1340 The Queensway (416-259-8372).*

Serves Serbian dishes.

L'Europe Dining Room, *469 Bloor Street West (416-921-6269).*

A Germanic/Hungarian restaurant serving a variety of Croatian delicacies. Located on Bloor Street West's "schnitzel strip" (see listings for Hungarian restaurants on page 338), L'Europe offers a variety of Croatian stews and hearty mountain fare.

Linden Restaurant, *1574 The Queensway (416-255-1496).*

The Linden serves a variety of Eastern European foods, including Slovenian specialties.

Majestik Restaurant, *751 Queen Street West (416-362-0813).*

A popular Queen Street hangout particularly well known for its hunter's platters.

Mary's Restaurant, *1608 Queen Street West (416-532-6394).*

Serbian cooking.

Penguin Restaurant, *824 Sheppard Avenue West (416-633-9628).*

Serves a wide array of Romanian specialties, including miti-tei and Romanian shish kebabs. There is also musical entertainment on weekends.

Queen's Pasta Café, *2263 Bloor Street West (416-766-0993).*

An Albanian-owned restaurant that serves Italian and Albanian specialties.

Steve's Restaurant and Tavern, *876 Brown's Line Road (416-259-1329).*

A local down-home diner featuring Croatian specialties from the coast and mountains in a casual environment. Inexpensive and hearty.

Food Sources

Croatian bakeries make a variety of sweet delicacies, including the ever-present baklava, lemon *krempite* (custard squares), and different kinds of flavored rolatis. Those specializing in these pastries include:

Pastry Villa, *2179 Bloor Street West (416-766-0609).*

Tilly's Bakery and Delicatessen, *3380 Lakeshore Boulevard West (416-259-7008).*

Mississauga Meat and Delicatessen, *3058 Hurontario Street (905-276-2710).*

Shops where you can obtain Slovenian specialty meats and imported foods include:

Alderwood Meat Market, *880 Browns Line Road (416-251-0209).*

Family Meat and Delicatessen, *278 Browns Line Road (416-255-1098).*

Slovenija Meat Delicatessen, *2409 Dundas Street West (416-535-8946).*

Willy's European Meat and Delicatessen, *2500 Hurontario Street (905-270-4206).*

Other Balkan food specialties can be found at:

Cheese Boutique and Delicatessen, *2286 Bloor Street West (416-762-6292).*

Besides providing an excellent array of Albanian meats, sausages, and cheeses, this Bloor Street West institution has a superb array of foods from throughout Eastern Europe and is a definite must for the traveling gourmand.

Sweet Gallery Pastry Shop, *2312 Bloor Street West (416-766-0289); Toronto Eaton Center (416-979-3118); 694 Mount Pleasant Road (416-484-9622).*

Serves some of the best pastries in the city including many Eastern European baked goods and some Serbian specialties. Most locations include a very pleasant café.

Shops

Caravan Imports, *840 Browns Line Road (416-252-5856).*

Brings in books, records, gifts, and crafts from Slovenia.

Serbica Books, *47 Keegan Crescent (416-630-1675).*

A bookstore with Serbo-Croatian–language books.

=========================== **Media** ===========================

Publications

Bozja Beseda/Word of God, *739 Browns Line Road (416-255-2721).*

A Slovenian publication.

Bratstvo/Fraternity, *1 Secroft Crescent (416-663-3409).*

A Serbian publication.

The **Croatian News Agency,** *1001 Cedarglen Gate (905-279-0379).*

Provides information on activities and news from Croatia and other overseas Croatian communities.

Cuvautul Romanesc/Romanian Voice, *PO Box 4217, Station D (905-387-1852).*

The largest Romanian newspaper in the world outside of Romania.

Glas Kanadskib Srba/Voice of the Canadian Serbs, *1900 Sheppard Avenue East (416-498-6853).*

Ilinden, *PO Box 334, Station O (416-221-8190).*

A Macedonian publication.

Istocnik, *80 Parklawn Avenue (416-255-5631).*

A Serbian publication.

Kanadski Srbobran/Canadian Srbobran, *335 Britannia Avenue (905-549-4079).*

Serbian.

Makedonija, *76 Overlea Avenue (416-421-7451).*

Macedonian.

Slovenska Drzava/For a Free Independent Slovenia,
79 Watson Avenue (416-766-4848).

Slovenski Lovski Vestnik, 43 Cowley Avenue (416-
622-6655).

Svoboda, 55 Wynford Heights Crescent (416-449-
8649).

A monthly periodical published in Bulgarian, covering events of interest to and about the Bulgarian community in Canada.

Zdravets, 76 Overlea Avenue (416-755-9231).

Macedonian.

Radio and Television

"Bulgarian Program," CHIN-FM 100.7, *622 College*
Street (416-531-9991).

A weekly show playing Bulgarian music and covering events of interest to the Bulgarian community in Toronto.

"Sounds of Croatia," CHIN-FM 100.7, *622 College*
Street (416-531-9991).

Music from Croatia played Monday through Friday, 12:30 to 1:30 PM.

"Croatian Program," CHIN-FM 100.7, *622 College*
Street (416-531-9991).

A weekly current events show on Sunday from noon to 1:00 PM.

"Glas Nade," CHIN-FM 100.7, *622 College Street*
(416-531-9991).

A religious program on Sunday from 8:30 to 9:00 AM.

"Macedonian Mosaic," CITY-TV Channel 57, *299 Queen Street West (416-591-5757),* and **"Macedonian Nation,"** Graham Cable TV, *31 Scarlett Road (416-762-3633).*

Two television shows covering current events in the Macedonian community, as well as music, dance, and variety acts.

"Macedonia World Radio," CJMR-AM 1190, *27 Hallen Road (905-456-3819).*

A weekly radio show covering current events and music in the Macedonian community.

CHIN-AM 1540/FM 100.7, *622 College Street (416-531-9991)*

Produces a number of radio programs of interest to the Serbian community:

• **"Canadian Yugoslav Program"**

• **"Serbian Chetnick Program"**

• **"Sumadija"**

• **"Vojvodina Cabaret"**

"Slovene Caravan," CHIN-AM 1540/FM 100.7, *622 College Street (416-531-9991).*

chapter four

British and Irish Toronto

History

Before it became the world's most multicultural city, Toronto was known derisively as the most English town in the British Commonwealth. Travel writers such as Jan Morris berated Torontonians as "small E" Englanders overly dominated by an obeisance to the patina of the English way of life. The English of course dominated Toronto's early days, though they were not the first European settlers here; that distinction belongs to the French.

Large-scale English immigration to the area, then known as Upper Canada, began at the end of the American Revolution. The town of York, founded by Governor John Graves Simcoe, quickly became the largest settlement of English loyalists in Upper Canada, and York became the capital of the territory, changing its name to Toronto in 1834. As a result of its important status York was invaded and burned by the American armies in the War of 1812 (the subsequent bombardment of Baltimore Harbor by the British immortalized in the *Star Spangled Banner* was in retaliation for this act).

As an English colony, Canada in general and Toronto in particular was dominated by English law, culture, and customs, but in Quebec the large French-language population resisted these forces. Because of the large influx of Loyalist immigrants and its relatively small French population,

Toronto quickly became the cultural and political center of English Canada, although it was many years before it would supersede Montreal as the most important city in Canada as a whole.

English immigration to Toronto accelerated dramatically in the years following 1816. The post-Napoleanic War depression that hit the British Isles forced many small farmers, ex-soldiers, artisans, and factory workers to emigrate. Almost one million British immigrants came to Canada during this time, many settling in the growing city of Toronto as well as the surrounding farming areas.

After World War I, another economic downturn encouraged the British government to pass the Empire Settlement Act to provide financial and educational assistance to new settlers, encouraging over 100,000 immigrants to pervade the Toronto area in a short period of time. The end of the Second World War sparked another series of arrivals, this time including many skilled workers looking for jobs in Toronto's burgeoning industries as England attempted to rebuild.

The last major wave of immigrants from England came in the years immediately following the Suez Crisis though emigration from England, particularly of skilled tradesmen, is still encouraged by the Canadian government on a regular basis. People of English background continue to make up almost 30 percent of Toronto's population though they have long ceased to be the majority.

Many reminders of Toronto's English beginnings remain, especially some of the older Anglican churches, many of which can be found in the Cabbagetown area. This elite neighborhood contains a number of fine homes and buildings from its early English heritage.

The Toronto Cricket Club is another vestige of the English past, being North America's oldest cricket club, founded by British soldiers in the nineteenth century. This bastion of British culture has gone multicultural in recent years with cricket superiority passing from the British Isles to the Caribbean.

The number of prominent Torontonians of English descent would be too numerous to list here, but a few of the better-known celebrities include actress Rita Tushingham, businessman Conrad Black, sculptor Henry Moore, scholar Northrop Frye, and jazz vibraphonist Peter Appleyard.

While many examples of English architecture abound in the city, one of its best-known buildings, **Casa Loma** at 1 Austin Terrace (416-923-1171), built by Sir Henry Pelatt, is as much a monument to English eccentricity as to the various Gothic and Medieval decorations that abound amidst its castle-like walls. This ninety-eight–room mansion comes complete with secret panels and castle towers, as well as stone walls from Scotland.

A far lovelier example of the grand English house can be found next door at the **Austin House,** 3 Austin Terrace (416-923-1171). This beautifully restored home shows off the subtle country taste of one of Toronto's more prominent business families in a beautiful setting overlooking a wooded ravine, with a lovely English garden in the back. The **Grange House,** 317 Dundas Street West (416-977-0414), is a good example of what better-off settlers lived in. Built in 1817, the house has been restored by the attached Art Gallery of Ontario and is open to the public.

Besides the English, other peoples from the British Isles have major communities in the Toronto area. For example, the city's Scottish legacy has been a strong one. Toronto's oldest church, **Little Trinity Church** on King Street East, was built under the patronage of Scotsman John Strachan, the first Anglican bishop of Toronto and founder of King's College, whose name crops up on a number of buildings and streets throughout the city. Toronto's first mayor and the founder of *The Globe* newspaper (the precursor to *The Globe and Mail,* Canada's national newspaper) were both of Scottish descent as well.

Scots were among the earliest settlers in Canada. In fact, according to one theory that is gaining credibility, the Scottish Prince Henry Sinclair may well have set sail for and landed on Nova Scotia in 1398, his crew settling there for a year before going back to Scotland. This would have preceded Columbus by almost 100 years. In any event, the first officially recorded Scottish immigrants arrived in 1621, when they settled in what would become the province of Nova Scotia (New Scotland).

Following the fur trade into Quebec and what was then Upper Canada (now Ontario), Scotsmen arrived at the time Toronto was first established and also helped to found a number of surrounding cities, including Guelph and Galt (now Cambridge). Almost 80,000 Scots came through Toronto in the late 1870s, and over 500,000 have migrated here over the years.

The community now numbers over 250,000, and cultural activities center around the **Saint Andrews Society** and the **Caledonia Society,** which act as gathering places for historical and cultural exchange and research. Highland Games are also held each summer throughout Ontario and in nearby cities (see "Nearby Excursions: Fergus and the Scottish Highland Games" on page 98). Curling, a Scottish game involving rocks and brooms, has also become a popular sport at which Canadians have come to excel. Numerous Curling rinks are found throughout the city, generally operating during the winter months. Finally, the annual blessing of the tartans is held every June with a procession from Queen's Park to Saint Andrew's Presbyterian Church, the oldest Scottish church in the city, on Simcoe Street.

A number of historical sites relating to the Scots influence can be seen in the city. **Lucy Maud Montgomery Park** on Riverside Drive was named for the world-famous author of Scottish descent who wrote *Anne of Green Gables* and lived in Toronto for much of the latter part of her life. **Mackenzie House,** 82 Bond Street (416-392-6915), honors the family that so strongly affected Toronto's and Canada's early days. Originally built in 1850, the restored home of William Lyon Mackenzie includes a replica of his early print shop as well as a wealth of information on the history of early Toronto and the role the Mackenzie family played in Canadian history.

Another historic home is **Campbell House,** 160 Queen Street West (416-597-0227) which was built in 1822 for Scottish-born Chief Justice William Campbell. This lovely restored mansion contains a model of the early city of York, as well as many other furnishings and artifacts from Toronto's early days.

One of the smaller communities of British immigrants, the Welsh presence in Canada goes back to the very earliest expeditions of the explorer John Cabot, who is still officially credited as the first European to voyage to the coast off of Newfoundland. Among the earliest pioneers in Toronto, Welsh settlers included Elizabeth Gwillum, the wife of Toronto's founder Lieutenant Governor John Graves Simcoe. A diarist and artist, her chronicles of the early years of York's settlement are among the primary historical documents describing Toronto's early history.

Other Welsh settlers were among the area's first planners, judges, and political leaders. The largest group of Welsh settlers came in the 1880s and 1890s. Many were also among the Loyalist regiments that fled to Canada after the American Revolution. The community formed its first Welsh Association in 1887 with the founding of the **Saint David's Society** and 20 years later erected the first and only Welsh church in Canada—**Dewi Sant Welsh Church.** The Welsh community now numbers around 50,000, many Welsh immigrants having arrived in the years following the two world wars.

Probably the best-known Canadian of Welsh descent is the author Robertson Davies, whose books *Fifth Business* and *The Manticore* have achieved world-wide popularity. Other famous Welsh Torontonians include hockey player Dave (Tiger) Williams and opera singer Gaynor Jones Lowed, who is also Master of Massey College at the University of Toronto. Welsh rugby, song, dance, and poetry festivals are held in the city throughout the year.

The Irish presence in Toronto and Ontario goes back to the earliest days of European settlement in the province, when it was still a French colony. Irish and Scottish settlers were recruited by the French to help populate the vast wilderness of New France, and, by the time the British inherited this French possession in the eighteenth century, the Irish made up over 5 percent of its population.

Emigration to Canada continued under British rule, and a large number of Irish settlers arrived in the Toronto area. There were Irish working-class areas along the early Toronto waterfront. The best known of these areas is the neighborhood known today as Cabbagetown—made infamous by a Hugh Garner novel of the Irish working class set in this area—which is reputed to have received this name due to the cabbages planted in its Irish residents' front yards.

One of the best-known and most famous Toronto family names, the Eatons, goes back to this period when Irish merchant Timothy Eaton set up shop here in the 1860s. By 1907 his department chain employed over 9,000 people in Canada and Eaton's remains one of the best-known businesses in the country.

Irish immigration to the Toronto area hit its peak in the 1800s with the massive influx of settlers following Ireland's potato famines in the 1840s. It was at this time that the first Irish churches in the city were established, including **Saint Michael's Cathedral, Saint Basil's Church,** and the original **Saint Patrick's Church.** The charitable Saint Vincent De Paul Society was set up at the same time, and its members later went on to form the Catholic Children's Aid Society.

In the 1850s, **Saint Michael's College,** now part of the University of Toronto, was founded as a seminary school under the Basillian Fathers to provide higher education for Irish Catholics. Special private high schools and elementary schools were also established, including De La Salle, the Sisters of Loretto, and Saint Joseph. **Saint Michael's,** and later **Saint Joseph's** and **Our Lady of Mercy** hospitals, all of which have become major institutions in Toronto and originate from charitable Irish organizations, were also established at the time.

In the second half of the nineteenth century the large number of southern Irish residents were joined by a number of immigrants from the northern counties of Ulster. Lodges of the Orange Order, a predominantly Protestant society founded in Northern Ireland in 1795, were established in the late 1800s and came to play a prominent role in Toronto and Ontario politics of the day. In fact, in the 1800s twenty of twenty-three Toronto mayors were from the Orange Lodge Brotherhood.

Other well-known figures from the Irish community included banker William MacMaster, who went on to found both the Imperial Bank of Commerce as well as MacMaster University; Canadian boxing champion Sean O'Sullivan; labor leader Bob White; and former Toronto Maple Leaf owner King Clancy. Nowadays the community as a whole numbers over 500,000 and is the fourth largest Irish community on the continent after New York, Boston, and Chicago.

Irish-born architects John Lyle and Edmund Burke were responsible for the design of many of Toronto's best-known commercial buildings, including the **Royal Alexandra Theatre,** the **CHUM/CITY Television Building, Customs House on Front Street, Union Station, Simpson's** department store, and the **Royal Conservatory of Music** building, as well as the **Gooderham Building (Flatiron Building)** at the corner of Wellington/Front Streets and Church Street and the **York Club** at Saint George Street and Bloor Street West.

A number of historic buildings available for tours in the city have Irish-Canadian backgrounds, including **Montgomery's Inn,** 4709 Dundas Street West (416-394-8113), which was operated by Irishman Thomas Montgomery in the 1840s and today houses a museum commemorating early British and Irish settlement in the Toronto area. The **Enoch Turner Schoolhouse,** 106 Trinity Street (416-863-0010), was originally established by Irish brewer Enoch Turner as Toronto's first free school and was restored in the 1970s as a small museum dedicated to education in the city. Finally, **Spadina House,** 285 Spadina Road (416-392-6910), is the beautifully restored and tastefully decorated counterpoint to nearby Casa Loma. This house was once the home of financier James Austin and was built in 1866.

Irish-born explorer-artist Paul Kane, who traveled the Great Lakes extensively, painted his views on over 100 canvases which are housed in the **Royal Ontario Museum.** There is a commemorative plaque to him at 56 Wellesley Street East, the site of **Paul Kane House** and **Paul Kane Park.**

Two of Canada's brewing giants were also founded by Irish Torontonians. Labatt's Beer was founded by John Labatt, who was born in Laois, Ireland; and Eugene O'Keefe founded O'Keefe Breweries. Both companies are now owned by other companies, but their beers still bear the original brewers' names.

══════════════ Religion ══════════════

Most Canadians of English descent (over 50 percent) belong to the Anglican Church, which has remained the church of the English establishment in Toronto. Other churches with large English congregations include the United Church, an amalgam of many Protestant groups, including Methodists, Presbyterians, and Congregationalists. The United Church is particularly strong in the Scottish community, and the main Welsh congregation is part of this church as well.

There are over 100 Anglican churches throughout the city. The head office of the **Anglican Church of Canada,** 600 Jarvis Street (416-924-9192), includes a bookstore and houses a number of community charities and social groups. The main cathedral in Toronto is **Saint James Cathedral,** 65 Church Street (416-364-7865), which was designed in Gothic style by Frederick Cumberland and finished in 1874. The land here was originally on Toronto Harbour (the area where Church and Jarvis Streets slope down below Front Street marks the original harbor) and the spire, the tallest in Canada, was used to guide ships to the harbor. Other well-known names in

Toronto's history can be found among the stones and stained-glass windows of the church, marking much of the history of the early political and business establishment in the city. The church is also home to a variety of classical and chamber music events, including annual public performances of Handel's "Messiah."

The best-known United Church in the city is **Bloor Street United Church,** 300 Bloor Street West (416-924-7439). It mirrors Saint James Cathedral almost perfectly as the antiestablishment church of Toronto, housing a variety of social activist concerns and playing as strong a role in the development of the provincial socialist political movements as Saint James has in the development of the Toronto establishment.

Other Anglican and United churches of historic importance include:

Christ Church, *Deer Park (416-920-5211).*

One of the most beautifully located churches in the city, as well as a beautifully designed and appointed one. Set amid the wealthy tree-lined neighborhood of Rosedale, it is a quiet, tasteful statement of the power and wealth that surround it.

Emmanuel Howard Park Church, *214 Wright Avenue (416-536-1755).*

Built at the turn of the century, Emmanuel Howard has beautiful acoustics and one of the best church organs in the country. The likes of Glenn Gould and the Oxford String Quartet have played there, and a number of classical recordings have been made there.

Holy Trinity Church, *19 Trinity Square (416-598-4521).*

A lovely University chapel built in 1847 and reminiscent of the chapels at Oxford and Cambridge.

Little Trinity Church, *417 King Street East (416-367-0272).*

A small, intimate church built in the 1840s with Tudor Gothic features.

Saint James-the-Less Chapel, *635 Parliament Street (416-964-9194).*

Built in 1858 in the style of a thirteenth-century parish church.

Saint John's Norway Anglican Church, *470 Woodbine Avenue (416-691-4560).*

Has some of the most beautiful stained-glass windows in the city and over-looks one of the larger cemeteries, which houses the graves of many of Toronto's earliest settlers from the British Isles.

Saint Paul's Anglican Church, *227 Bloor Street East (416-961-8116).*

The city's largest Anglican church, built in 1861 in the style of an English medieval church.

Prominent churches in the Scottish community include:

Knox Presbyterian Church, *630 Spadina Avenue (416-921-8993).*

Saint Andrew's United Church, *117 Bloor Street East (416-929-0811).*

Saint John's Presbyterian Church, *415 Broadview Avenue (416-466-7476).*

Saint Andrew's Presbyterian Church, *75 Simcoe Street (416-593-5600).*

Built in 1872 in the Norman Romanesque style.

The Welsh have their own church—**Dewi Sant Welsh United Church,** 33 Melrose Avenue (416-485-7583)—which holds services in Welsh and English. It also serves as a community center and sponsors a variety of song and dance festivals celebrating Welsh culture. Every Good Friday the church holds a *Gymantfa Ganu* (Festival of Sacred Songs) to promote hymn singing and Welsh unity.

The **Toronto Necropolis,** near Castle Frank subway station at the north-eastern edge of Cabbagetown, houses the graves of Toronto's earliest set-tlers, including many of its most prominent English and Scottish families.

The Irish in Toronto belong to two distinct religious persuasions, Catholic Irish and Protestant Irish. Churches with major Catholic Irish con-gregations include:

Saint Basil's Church, *50 Saint Joseph Street (416-656-3772).*

Saint Cecilia's Church, *161 Annette Street (416-769-8163).*

Saint Michael's Cathedral, *200 Church Street (416-364-0234).*

Protestant Irish churches are:

Timothy Eaton Memorial Church, *230 Saint Clair Avenue West (416-925-5977).*

Toronto Free Presbyterian Church, *1335 Warden Avenue (416-752-2454).*

Organizations

Three "Saints" organizations handle most of the cultural and social events for the British community in Toronto.

Saint George's Society of Toronto, *Saint George's Hall, 14 Elm Street (416-597-0220).*
Founded in 1834, this society has endeavored to further and preserve English culture and heritage. In addition to these cultural activities, it maintains a strong tradition of doing charitable work. Social events include Christmas and Saint George's Day dinners, as well as other social and cultural events throughout the year.

Saint Andrew's Scottish Societies of Toronto, *75 Simcoe Street (416-593-5600).*
Coordinates the activities of a number of Scottish social, cultural, and charitable organizations in the city. Sponsors the annual Kirkin' o' the Tartan festival, as well as other events and celebrations throughout the year.

Saint David's Society, *33 Melrose Avenue (416-485-7583).*
Originally one of the loyalist societies, Saint David's became a Welsh cultural club in 1887. The society sponsors song fests, dances, and other cultural activities and acts as a focal point for the Welsh community in Toronto.

Other groups with activities of interest for the English community include:

British Pensioners Association of Canada, *605 Royal York Road (416-253-6402).*

Queen's Own Rifles of Canada, *100 Adelaide Street West (416-362-3946).*

Toronto Cricket, Skating and Curling Club, *141 Wilson Avenue (416-487-4581).*

The **Kew Beach Lawn Bowling Club,** *Lee Avenue (416-694-4371).*
One of the oldest recreational organizations in Canada. Patrons can be seen in their dress whites throughout the summer.

A number of clubs in the Scottish community are also active. Most are a part of the **Clans and Scottish Societies of Canada,** 75 Simcoe Street (416-593-0518), which represents over forty different groups and provides information on upcoming events and activities, including concerts, ceilidhs, dances, and lectures. It also holds an annual heritage ball every fall.

The **Dewi Singer Welsh Choir,** the **Welsh Rugby Club,** and the **Dawnswyr Y Ddraig Goch** dance group are all based at the **Dewi Sant Welsh United Church.**

The **Irish Canadian Centre,** 1650 Dupont Street (416-762-2858), is the main community center for the Irish community in Toronto. It has two lounges and a restaurant and sponsors a variety of social and cultural events. It also houses the **Irish Canadian Immigrant Aid and Cultural Society of Toronto,** which sponsors drama, music, lectures, and sports groups, as well as county social associations such as **The Dub Club, The Cork Association,** and **The Mearth Association.**

The **Saint Patrick's Day Parade Society,** 10 Craigmuir Court (416-755-5001), has been more and more active in recent years. These parades are well-known hallmarks of the Irish community in many American cities, but in Canada it has become a big event only in recent years. It is now growing in popularity.

A number of sports clubs are supported by the community, including the **Toronto Emerald Soccer Club** (416-489-9688), **Gaelic Athletic Association** (416-762-6127), and **Irish Rugby Club** (416-482-4164).

A variety of arts groups have become popular in recent years with a revival of interest in Celtic culture and music.

Canadian Celtic Arts Association, *1650 Dupont Street (416-868-8441).*

Comhaltas Ceoltari Eireann, *21 Ironshield Crescent (416-764-0154).*

Irish Dance Teachers Association, *1650 Dupont Street (416-792-9026).*

Toronto Irish Players, *1650 Dupont Street (416-762-2858).*

Toronto's Protestant Irish have been represented by the **Canadian Orange Headquarters,** 94 Sheppard Avenue West (416-223-1690), which carries on a wide array of social and cultural activities, including organizing a number of parades and festivals.

The **Ireland Fund of Canada,** 100 Simcoe Street (416-594-7833), is a major fund-raising group for development projects in both northern and southern Ireland.

═════ Holidays and Celebrations ═════

January 25   *Robbie Burns Day,* honoring Scotland's best-known poet. It has become a bigger and bigger annual event each year; for the Scottish community it is like Saint Patrick's Day. Commemorative dinners are held throughout the city with piping and the serving of haggis. Poetry readings, dances, and song festivals are also held.

March 1   *Saint David's Day,* honoring the patron saint of Wales, celebrated on the closest weekend to March 1. The Welsh wear leeks in their hats to celebrate either a victory over the Saxons (wearing leeks prevented the Welsh from killing their own men) or the blooming of daffodils (maybe in Wales, not usually in Canada). Dinners and dances are held.

March 17	*Saint Patrick's Day,* commemorating the patron saint of Ireland with parades and parties.
April 23	*Saint George's Day,* honoring the patron saint of England with dinners and a dance as well as church services.
April 25	*Anzac Day,* in memory of those who fought and died at the Battle of Gallipoli.
March/April	*Gymanfa Ganu,* the Welsh festival of sacred songs held on Good Friday.
June	*Kirkin' o' the Tartaini,* when Scots take their tartans to Saint Andrew's Church to be blessed.
June 16	*Bloomsday celebration,* honoring the day detailed in James Joyce's novel *Ulysses.*
July	*Highland Games* in Fergus.
July 12	Celebration of the Battle of the Boyne in the Orange community with parades and bands.
November 30	*Saint Andrew's Day,* religious and secular services held to honor Scotland's patron saint.
December 31	*Hogmanay,* a day of feasting at the end of the year (sort of like New Year's Eve).

Restaurants and Pubs

Although English cuisine is now ranked ahead of Italian cuisine by the Michelin guides in their comparison of world cuisines, it is still not seen as haute cuisine by the general population. Roasts, pies, and pasties are among the staples of English cooking, and perhaps North Americans simply take these foods too much for granted to really appreciate their culinary significance. Toronto has a number of restaurants serving both refined and pedestrian versions of British foods, as well as enjoyable pubs with classic fare.

Feathers, *962 Kingston Road (416-694-0443).*

A genial British pub in the Upper Beaches area with traditional pub fare as well as good roasts.

Fitzgerald's, *2298 Queen Street East (416-691-1393).*

Another pleasant English eatery in an elegant setting in the East Beaches area.

Griffith's Coffee House, *2086 Queen Street East (416-690-4022).*

A coffeehouse, deli, pub, and gift shop serving Scottish food specialties, including haggis, steak pie, and roast beef. There is also a roof garden café open during the summer months.

Pimblett's, *263 Gerrard Street East (416-929-9525).*

A wonderfully eccentric British pub and restaurant specializing in roasts. Every day sees a different roast as a specialty of the house, and the decor is early Victorian–Toronto garage sale, with a beautifully restored setting that isn't too precious for words but has lots of bohemian charm and class. Also has good English ale on tap.

Pawnbroker's Daughter, *1115 Bay Street (416-921-4679).*

A large English pub with a variety of pub and restaurant fare, as well as good ale on tap.

Sherlock's on Sheppard, *12 Sheppard Avenue (416-366-8661).*

Fine dining English style in an elegant Victorian setting. Portions are generous.

Traditional afternoon tea with scones and Devon cream, cucumber sandwiches, English jams, and a variety of teas all served on Royal Doulton china is provided at some of Toronto's finer hotels, including the **King Edward Hotel,** 37 King Street East (416-863-9700), and the **Four Seasons Hotel,** 21 Avenue Road (416-863-9700), as well as at **Wilson's Fine Foods,** 3249 Yonge Street (416-488-2030).

Traditional English fish and chips can be obtained from a number of fast-food outlets around the city, but the best is **Duckworth's Fish and Chips,** 2638 Danforth Avenue (416-699-5865) and 2292 Kingston Road (416-266-0033). This long-established "chippie" has been making authentic fish and chips for many years, and its crowded restaurants are a testimony to the quality of its food.

The pub has long been a way of life in England, a place for socializing and conviviality. It has only recently become a part of the Toronto scene, primarily due to the relaxing of what used to be a very onerous liquor code that prevented pub patrons from walking around with their drinks in hand. Since pubs have become legal, they have grown in popularity throughout the city and a number of excellent and enjoyable ones are available, some of which include entertainment.

Rose and Crown, *2355 Yonge Street (416-488-5557).*
A very popular establishment with entertainment on weekends.

Victoria and Albert, *4854 Yonge Street (416-223-6146).*
A busy and active pub in North York with a large menu of British specialties.

Artful Dodger, *12 Isabella Street (416-964-9511).*
An active pub on weekdays and in the summer with a large outdoor patio.

Pints, *518 Church Street (416-921-8142).*
A large active pub with an outdoor patio and an extensive array of English beers.

Jack Russell, *27 Wellesley Street East (416-967-9442).*
A popular pub and restaurant with some entertainment on weekends.

The popular "Dukes" chain of English pubs was the first to bring English draft beer to Toronto and still provides a number of pleasant and enjoyable pubs with traditional atmosphere, food, and prices.

Duke of York, *39 Prince Arthur Street (416-964-2441).*

Duke of Gloucester, *649 Yonge Street (416-961-9704).*

Duke of Kent, *2315 Yonge Street (416-485-9507).*

Duke of Westminster, *First Canadian Place (416-368-1555).*

Irish pubs and restaurants serve hearty foods, such as stews and assorted Celtic pub food, as well as the obligatory Guinness and harp lager on tap. Most have musical entertainment in the evening. The following is a list of some of the better and more active establishments.

Harp and Shamrock Restaurant, *848 The Queensway (416-251-0096).*

Irish Rose Pub, *1095 Weston Road (416-763-2478).*

Mick East Fynn's, *3 Gerrard Street East (416-598-0537).*

New Windsor House, *124 Church Street (416-364-9698).*

Paddy's, *2409 Yonge Street (416-484-1455).*

Unicorn An Irish Rovers Free House, *175 Eglinton Avenue East (416-482-0115).*

Food Sources

Bakeries

The **Little Pie Shop,** *2568 Yonge Street (416-485-6393).*

Produces an excellent array of English-style pies, tarts, and biscuits (cookies), all at a very reasonable price.

The Cake Shop, *832 Sheppard Avenue West (416-638-2253).*

McCall's Cake Shop, *3864 Bloor Street West (416-231-4459).*

A number of Scottish bakeries produce excellent shortbreads, scones, and other Scottish delicacies.

Burke's Scottish Bakery, *1156 Danforth Avenue (416-461-1585).*

John Baird Scottish Bakers, *2141 Weston Road (416-244-2307); 4 Racine Road (416-745-9879); Eglinton Square (416-755-1522).*

Mary MacLeod's Shortbread, *2579 Yonge Street (416-482-0683).*

Butchers, Delis, and Grocers

For English delicacies, the **Marks and Spencer** department store chain offers a variety of English culinary specialties and baked goods at their various Toronto locations, including:

- Fairview Mall (416-494-9764)
- Manulife Centre, 55 Bloor Street West (416-967-7772)
- Toronto Eaton Centre (416-979-1907)
- Yorkdale Shopping Centre (416-781-4639)

Other grocers and butchers with specialty English, Scottish, and Welsh products include:

But' n' Ben Butchers, *1601 Ellesmere Avenue (416-438-4214).*

Crawford Scottish Butchers, *55 Selby Road (905-455-9180).*

Hamish's Kitchen, *641 Pharmacy Avenue (416-759-1251).*

Shops

Besides the **Marks and Spencer** chain mentioned previously, a number of other shops specialize in English clothing, linens, and china. For Scottish tartans and woolen goods, try:

Ada MacKenzie Ltd., *94 Cumberland Street (416-922-2222).*

MacNeil Scottish Supplies, *1825 Avenue Road (416-782-5227).*

Richardson Tartan Shop, *546 Yonge Street (416-922-3141).*

China, glassware, and silverware may be found at:

Ashley China, *50 Bloor Street West (416-964-2900).*
Wedgewood.

Shane Jewellers, *55 York Street (416-368-5866).*
Royal Doulton.

The Royal Doulton Store, *Fairview Mall (416-496-8243).*

The British Toby, *121 Main Street (905-472-8629).*
The largest selection of Royal Doulton figurines in the area.

Britania Silversmiths, *6 Magnolia (416-266-4251).*

There are also several shops that carry Irish linens, crafts, glassware, and china:

Emerald Charms, *2390 Eglinton Avenue East (416-752-7177).*
Celtic knitwear, rugby shirts, Celtic music, videos, and books.

Irish Linen Shop, *527 Danforth Avenue (416-463-9518).*
An extensive array of Irish linen and textiles.

Irish Shop and Irish Shop for Men, *110 Bloor Street West (416-922-9400).*
Irish clothing and knitwear.

Irish Traditions, *444 Yonge Street (416-977-7917).*

Irish linen, glassware, books, and records, as well as gifts and crafts.

Keltic Touch, *2998 Bloor Street West (416-236-1441).*

Wools, cottons, and linens; Victorian-style Irish blouses; Celtic jewelry; and Waterford crystal.

Media

Publications

Britannia Magazine, RR1 (613-399-3634).

A monthly color magazine which also holds an annual Britannia show celebrating English culture and crafts, with exhibits from travel boards, artists, and entertainers ranging from folk singers to Scottish marching bands.

The British Post, 4 Racine (416-745-8242).

A weekly tabloid covering events of interest to Anglophiles in Canada.

Scottish Banner, 1598 Queen Street East (416-469-3939).

The largest Scottish newspaper in the world outside Scotland, the *Banner* is in its eighteenth year of monthly publication.

The Sentinel, 94 Sheppard Avenue West (416-223-1690).

An Irish publication.

Toronto Irish News, 1650 Dupont Street (416-762-2858).

Radio and Television

"Calling All Britons," CFRB-AM 1010, *2 Saint Clair Avenue West (416-924-5711).*

Provides news, old-time music, messages from home. and soccer and cricket scores. Daily, from 6:00 to 9:00 PM.

"BBC World News," CBC-NEWSWORLD, *250 Front Street West (416-975-5603).*

Weekday evenings at 11:00 PM.

"Frankie Benson Show," CJMR-AM 1190, *Box 1190, Port Credit Postal Station (905-279-1190).*

A variety of British news and music shows can also be found on CFNY-FM 102.1 and MUCHMUSIC. Many Canadian broadcasters and cable stations broadcast a broader range of British television than do American stations, with British soap operas such as *Coronation Street, East Enders,* and *Neighbors* being very popular. Likewise many British mysteries and comedy shows can be found on TVOntario, WTN, CBC, Showcase, and Bravo networks.

Celtic-based music is going through a considerable revival worldwide and in Canada as well. Some shows focusing on Irish music include:

"Songs from Home," CHIN-AM 1540, *622 College Street (416-531-9991).*

"The Long Note," CKLN-FM 88.1, *380 Victoria Street (416-595-1477).*

"Radio Erin Show," CJMR-AM 1320, *46 Sparklett Crescent (416-846-3746).*

"Highway 10," Rogers Cable TV Channel 10, *855 York Mills Road (416-446-6500).*

A community cable television show dealing with Irish community concerns.

—Rosedale: The English Neighborhood—

Rosedale is the epitome of English living in Toronto. One of the area's wealthiest neighborhoods, its stone and brick houses in forested neighborhoods punctuated with little parks, charming churches, and ivy-covered Tudor mansions makes it a beautiful drive. Of note is Rosedale United Church on Glen Road and the Toronto Necropolis at the southern end of Rosedale near Cabbagetown.

Prime ministers, leaders of business and industry, and famous artists and actors all have lived in the area, and it remains a gracious and serene sanctuary for the rich. Rosedale isn't quite the WASP enclave it once was, but it is still a testament to the taste of the British upper classes in Canada.

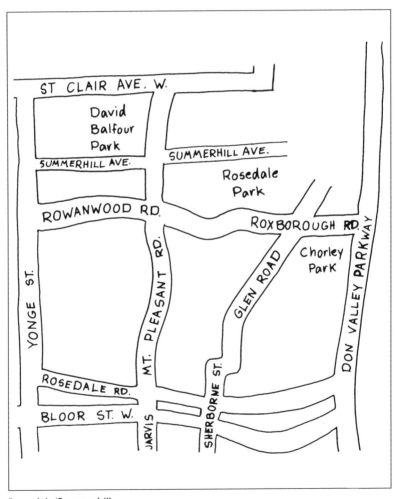

Rosedale/Summerhill

How to Get There: *Rosedale is located just north of Bloor Street West at Sherborne. A good drive that takes you past a nice array of the area's houses starts at the corner of Bloor Street West and Sherborne. Proceed north on Sherborne to Elm. Turn right on Elm to Glen Road, then turn left and take Glen Road north to Summerhill Avenue. Go left again and take Summerhill Avenue west to Mount Pleasant. You can also take the Yonge Street subway to Rosedale station and take the Rosedale bus to the Sherborne subway station.*

—The Beaches: English Gardens and Tudor Mansions—

The Beaches has become quite a trendy neighborhood in recent years, with its popular Boardwalk along Lake Ontario, a series of parks, and the activity along Queen Street East. This shopping area contains a number of fine English restaurants and pubs, as well as some interesting book and craft shops. It is also home to Kew Gardens, a lovely turn-of-the-century park with a bandstand, lawn bowling club, and Tudor-styled library.

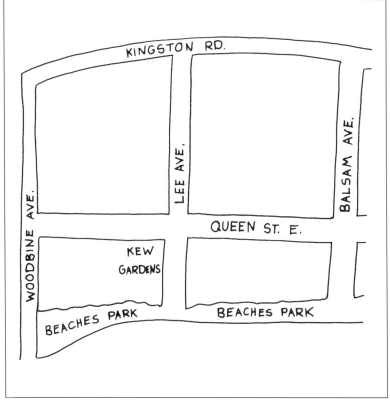

The Beaches

Another park along Glen Manor Road borders a number of beautiful old English mansions built along the Glen. This is another lovely, quiet neighborhood that reaches north up to Danforth into the heart of an old English working-class district, and it still retains many of its old Scottish bakeries and fish-and-chip restaurants to this day. This excursion makes a lovely drive or walk in the summer, with numerous outdoor cafés, pubs, and shops mixed in with stately homes and tree-shaded parkland.

How to Get There: *The Beaches area is at the end of the Queen Street streetcar line going east. You can get off anywhere after Woodbine Avenue, perhaps starting your journey at Kew Gardens and walking down to the lake and along the Boardwalk east to Neville Park Crescent, then up to Queen Street East along which you head back west to Glen Manor Road.*

—Cabbagetown: A Modern Neighborhood—
with an Irish Background

In Canadian literature, "Cabbagetown" refers to the area south of Bloor Street West along Parliament Street that is the home to Hugh Garner's immigrant Irish working-class community. It grew with the rest of the city in the late 1800s thanks to the factory complexes at the south end of the Don River (where it meets Toronto Harbour) that provided employment from the 1890s on. Irish settlers were attracted to this area and became the predominant group there for over fifty years.

Though the area has gentrified and changed its ethnic composition in recent years, the solid brick homes and tree-lined streets of Hugh Garner's world are still visible as are the remnants of the old industries that used to support the area. The central parts of Cabbagetown were transformed by massive housing projects built in the 1950s and 1960s, but the northern and southern parts still have the architectural flavor of that era and are an interesting walk through Toronto's architectural past as well as its Irish history. One obvious indicator of the community is the number of Anglican and Catholic churches that dot the area.

How to Get There: *Take the Parliament Street bus south from the Castle Frank station and get off at the corner of Wellesley Street East and Parliament Street. The old neighborhood is east and south of this area.*

—Nearby Excursions: Niagara-on-the-Lake and Stratford—

These two summer-theater resort towns are urban museums of fine English houses and architecture from the late nineteenth and early twentieth centuries. Niagara-on-the-Lake is an hour's drive southwest of Toronto in the

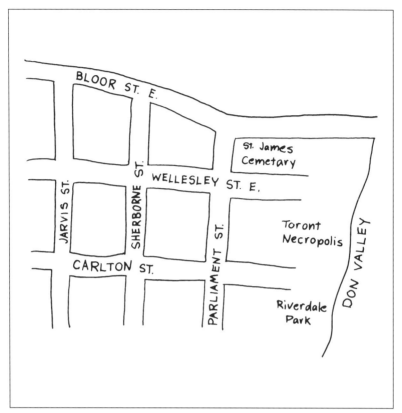

Cabbagetown

heart of Ontario's wine country. It is home to the Shaw Summer Theatre Festival, honoring the works of the late British playwright George Bernard Shaw, as well as to one of the prettiest and best-preserved British-colonial downtowns in North America. Numerous mansions and quaint bed-and-breakfasts abound in the area, which also features the remains of Fort George. English high tea is served in a number of atmospheric cafés throughout the town, and there are a number of fine restaurants and pubs.

Stratford, home of Canada's other major summer theater, is a larger city of over 25,000 residents that has an industrial and agricultural history as well. In the 1950s, the Stratford Shakespearean Festival was started and has been a hallmark of the Canadian theater scene ever since. Three main theaters show a variety of Shakespearean plays as well as an annual musical revival, Gilbert and Sullivan, and other classics from Moliére to Christopher Marlowe.

The downtown area has some beautiful turn-of-the-century shops and buildings, and numerous examples of lovely Victorian- and Edwardian-era architecture abound throughout the city. The park that borders the main theater district is reminiscent of the quiet river and lake parks that dot the countryside in Oxfordshire, England. This is a lovely destination for an excursion even if you're not a theatergoer.

How to Get There: *Take the Gardiner Expressway west to the QEW and remain on the QEW for approximately one hour. Take the Highway 55 exit (just south of the Welland Canal and St. Catherines, Ontario) and go south and east to the end of the highway, which will take you right to the heart of Niagara-on-the-Lake.*

How to Get There: *Take Highway 401 west to the Highway 8 exit (approximately 60 miles). Take Highway 8 north and then west to Stratford (approximately 30 miles).*

—Nearby Excursions: Fergus— and the Scottish Highland Games

North and west of Toronto, about an hour away, is Fergus. This small town, carved in stone amid the dramatic setting of the Elora Gorges Park areas along the Grand River, is home to one of the world's largest annual Highland Games every July. At this time, Fergus becomes the center of Scottish life and culture in Ontario with a variety of games and events throughout the area. You can also journey a little upriver to the arts community of Elora, with its numerous galleries, pottery shops, and antique dealers, as well as the lovely Elora Mill Inn and Restaurant overlooking the dramatic waterfalls at the end of the Grand River gorge.

How to Get There: *Take Highway 401 west to the Highway 25 exit (approximately 30 miles). Take Highway 25 north for approximately 8 miles to Highway 24. Turn left and drive to Regional Road 26 (the second concession road west). Turn right and drive north approximately 6 miles to Regional Road 18. Turn left and drive 5 miles west to downtown Fergus.*

chapter five

Chinese Toronto

History

Long one of the most visible ethnic communities in the city, Toronto's Chinese community is also one of its largest and best established. North America's largest ethnic Chinese population lives in Toronto, now numbering over 250,000. It has even kept pace with the dramatic growth in the Chinese community in Vancouver.

The first Chinese settlers to Canada arrived during the 1850s and 1860s, while the Fraser and Cariboo gold rushes were going strong. Later, over 17,000 Chinese workers came to help build the Canadian Pacific Railway, settling in towns and cities along the way. This is one of the reasons almost all major cities along that railroad have at least a small Chinatown. Most immigrants went into the newly developing commercial-laundry and restaurant businesses.

Toronto's first Chinese community was in an area along York Street between Queen and King Streets, which is almost completely inhabited by skyscrapers now. At the time it was known as "the Ward" and was primarily a Jewish neighborhood. The first Chinese person listed in Toronto was a man by the name of Sam Ching, who opened a hand laundry.

"Old Chinatown," remnants of which are still visible in the area on Dundas Street West between Bay Street and University Avenue, evolved from the restaurants, laundries, and tea shops behind city hall that grew in number as Toronto's Chinese community grew in size through the 1910s and 1920s. An early focus for the community was the building of a Presbyterian church at University Avenue. It was an appropriate institution since the missionary community in Canada had played an important role in helping to bring many converted Chinese Protestants over to Canada. The *Shing Wah Daily News* began publishing in 1922, and the Chinese Benevolent Association was then set up to provide legal and social assistance.

By 1935 there were over 300 commercial Chinese hand laundries behind city hall, most operated by migrating Chinese railway workers who came to Toronto after their rail construction jobs were over. Because the railroad had a policy allowing its workers one last trip to any destination they wished after their contract was up, many Chinese workers chose to migrate to growing urban centers of Canada. In an era preceding the invention of the washing machine, Chinese hand laundries were an indispensable convenience of modern life. They were viewed, however, as a menace to property values and so were concentrated in a few districts around which Chinese people lived and worked. In Toronto the two oldest of these districts, Riverdale and the Bay/Dundas area, formed the primary focal points for the early Chinese community.

Toronto's Chinese population grew considerably between 1947 and 1960, as many Chinese students came to Toronto to go to school at the universities and stayed to work after graduation. Political instability in Southeast Asian countries like Malaysia and Vietnam also brought many ethnic Chinese to Canada. Chinese immigrants even came from countries like Uganda and Peru.

The building of a new city hall in the 1950s moved the community to the west, and a burgeoning new Chinatown formed around Dundas Street West and Spadina Avenue that remains the biggest and most important Chinatown in the Metro area. As it grew and real estate prices grew with it, new Chinese immigrants looked for less expensive areas in which to live. The area at the corner of Broadview and Gerrard Street in Toronto's East End became a focus for many of these newly arrived immigrants, and in the 1970s it became a second center for the Chinese population.

Finally, in the 1970s and 1980s, as with other established ethnic communities, the Chinese community began to look north and west, moving to the suburbs. Chinese centers sprang up around Victoria Park and Sheppard Avenue East in Scarborough and on Dundas and Hurontario in Mississauga. The arrival of moneyed Hong Kong Chinese in the 1980s also contributed to the growth in these areas because, unlike other Chinese immigrants in the past, they arrived in Canada with a relatively large amount of personal wealth.

The Chinese community remains a prominent source of population growth in Toronto and has achieved a remarkable measure of financial and political power over the years. While less than a third of the Metro Toronto Chinese population lives downtown, the area around Spadina Avenue and Dundas Street remains the economic and cultural center of the community and is active seven days a week, twenty-four hours a day. Toronto has produced a number of prominent Chinese citizens, including Susan Eng, current chairperson of the Toronto Police Commission; Gordon Chong, deputy commissioner of the Toronto Transit Commission; and Alfred Sung, fashion designer and entrepreneur.

Like many of the Mediterranean and Asian groups that live in Toronto, the Chinese community is actively urban and enjoys going out and supporting its many restaurants and nightspots. The areas are bustling and dynamic both day and night. There is a tendency among Occidentals to lump all Chinese into one cultural and ethnic group. In point of fact, that is a bit like lumping all Europeans together in one group.

The Chinese people who live in Toronto come from highly different backgrounds and cultures. Many have come from Hong Kong, Taiwan, Singapore, Malaysia, Indonesia, Vietnam, the Philippines, and even Peru, as well as from the mainland Chinese provinces of Hunan, Szechwan, Manchuria, and Kiangsu. This should be remembered when looking at the foods, crafts, and goods available in Chinatown and when enjoying what is too often seen as an undifferentiated community. Different styles of cuisine, art, and dress exist with regional variations within the great national Chinese culture.

Religion

The Chinese community is divided up among a number of Protestant, Catholic, Evangelical, and Eastern religious congregations. The majority of Christian Chinese belong to either the United Church or various Evangelical groups.

Chinese Gospel Church, *450 Dundas Street West (416-977-2530).*
Evangelical.

Chinese Presbyterian Church, *177 Beverly Street (416-977-4043).*
United Church.

Toronto Chinese Baptist Church, *78 Beverly Street (416-596-8376).*

Baptist.

Chinese Grace Baptist Church, *20 Claremount Avenue (416-363-6403).*

Baptist.

Chinese Pentecostal Church, *662 Pape Avenue (416-469-2968).*

Pentecostal.

Chinese Presbyterian Church, *4156 Sheppard Avenue East (416-299-6735).*

United Church.

Chinese United Church, *3300 Kennedy Road (416-754-7147).*

United Church.

Toronto Chinese Community Church, *2240 Birchmount Avenue (416-299-3388).*

Anglican.

Toronto Chinese Logos Baptist Church, *8 Amroth Avenue (416-690-8306).*

Baptist Church.

Toronto Chinese Mennonite Church, *1038 Woodbine Avenue (416-424-2078).*

Mennonite Church.

Toronto Chinese Methodist Church, *916 Logan Avenue (416-469-2083).*

United Church.

Our Lady of Mount Carmel Church, *184 Saint Patrick Street (416-598-3920).*

Roman Catholic.

For those interested in Eastern religious traditions, the **Chinese Buddhist Centre,** 7254 Bayview Avenue (416-881-1316), is the major Chinese Buddhist congregation in the city, although **Dharma Centre,** 16 Glen Elm Avenue (416-481-7909), **Kampo Gangra Drubgyudling and Mikyo Dorge Institute,** 200 Balsam Avenue (416-699-3801), and **Toronto Buddhist Church,** 918 Bathurst Street (416-534-4302), also have large congregations. The **Toronto Buddhist Centre** is a particularly attractive church combining naturalist design and simplicity in a quiet Oriental manner. While the **Toronto Zen Centre,** 569 Christie Street (416-766-6400), follows the Japanese Buddhist tradition, its congregation includes a large number of Chinese and Koreans as well.

Chinese communities have come to Toronto from around the world and include Chinese Hindu believers from South Asia, Malaysia, and Indonesia who worship at the **Bharat Bhavan Hindu Temple,** 754 Indian Road (416-741-1680), while Japanese-based Chinese Shinto worshippers go to the **Tenrikyo Church,** 160 Gracefield Avenue (416-247-9791).

Finally, the **Fung Loy Kok Taoist Temple,** 1376 Bathurst Street (416-656-7479), serves Toronto's Taoist community (Taoism being one of China's more ancient religions) and includes an educational and community center providing programs in Chinese language, culture, and the gentle martial art of Tai Chi.

Organizations

The Chinese community has taken an active role in developing an educational system that helps provide Chinese-language classes and programs on Chinese culture and the arts. Among these schools are:

Chinese School, *177 Beverly Street (416-977-4043).*

Chung Wah Chinese School, *701 Gerrard Street East (416-928-3499).*

Mon Sheong Foundation Chinese School, *30 Darcy Street (416-593-8512).*

There is also a wide array of groups that help provide a variety of cultural and social services for the Chinese community as a whole. This is a population with a very active tradition of self-help, educational improvement, and charitable work. Among the active groups are:

Aurora Chinese Dance Group, *51 Baldwin Street (416-598-2022).*

Provides classes and performances in the ancient arts of Chinese dance.

Cantonese Musical Club, *111 Dundas Street West (416-463-4519).*

Gives performances of Cantonese musical styles and provides classes and workshops for Cantonese music.

Cecil Community Centre, *58 Cecil Street (416-598-2403).*

The main Chinese community center with a variety of services covering education, culture, and other social services, among them the **Chinese Interpreter and Information Service,** 58 Cecil Street (416-598-2022).

Chinese Canadian Intercultural Association, *112 Huron Street, Suite 86 (416-591-6347).*

An active community services organization working toward integrating new Chinese immigrants into Canadian life.

Chinese Community Centre of Ontario, *84 Augusta Avenue (416-365-0917).*

A major community group with a variety of social, cultural, and political organizations, including the **Chinese National League** (formerly the Chinese Benevolent Association).

Chinese Cultural and Arts Centre, *1056 Gerrard Street East (416-461-9393).*

East End Chinatown's major Chinese cultural and educational center.

Great Wall Arts Chinese Arts Program/Ontario Chinese Artists Association, *76 Lippincott Road (416-968-7322).*

An organization devoted to the promulgation and development of Chinese arts and crafts in Canada.

Ontario Chinese Restaurant Association, *405 Dundas Street West (416-340-7850).*

An organization devoted to promoting Chinese cuisine and educating the public in its different tastes and styles.

Ship Toy Yen Society, *108 Beverly Street (416-593-6518).*

A benevolent and charitable society.

Taoist Tai Chi Society of Canada, *1376 Bathurst Street (416-656-2110).*

A society with a number of branches to promote Tai Chi and Taoist thought and philosophy.

Toronto Chinese Chamber Orchestra, *243 Eglinton Avenue West (416-486-2220).*

A musical organization to support and develop Chinese chamber music.

Toronto Chinese Community Services Association, *310 Spadina Avenue (416-977-4026).*

An umbrella group designed to coordinate a number of Chinese cultural and social activities.

Woodgreen Community Centre Chinese Services, *835 Queen Street East (416-469-5211).*

An east Toronto center for a variety of cultural and community services in the Chinese community.

A variety of Chinese political and fraternal groups have been formed both to fight for equality and acceptance and to push forward items of importance to the Chinese community. Benevolent and charitable organizations have a large and important role to play in the community as well. Among the more prominent organizations are:

Chinese Canadian National Council (Toronto Chapter), *500 King Street West, Suite 3423 (416-947-9541).*

Chinese Canadian National Council for Equality, *386 Bathurst Street (416-868-1777).*

Chinese Free Masons, *436 Dundas Street West (416-977-2467).*

Chinese National League, *84 Augusta Avenue (416-365-0917).*

Federation of Chinese Canadian Professionals (Ontario), *425 Queen Street West (416-591-9125).*

Mon Sheong Foundation, *30 Darcy Street (416-593-8512).*

Toronto Chinese Business Association, *405 Dundas Street West (416-595-0313).*

════ Holidays and Celebrations ════

January/February	*Chinese New Year (Gung Hee Fat Choy).* The date of the Chinese New Year changes each year (the Chinese calendar being both solar and lunar) and every thirteenth year an additional lunar month is added, so New Year's can be anywhere from January 20 to February 19. It is the biggest event of the Chinese year and is celebrated throughout Toronto, but particularly in the downtown Chinatown area around Spadina Avenue and Dundas Street West. The celebration lasts for a week, and fireworks are shot off on the seventh day.
March/April	*Festival of Ch'ing Ming,* held 106 days after winter solstice to remember the dead and visit family graves.
May/June	*Dragon Boat Festival,* on the fifth day of the fifth moon, celebrating the sacrifice made by virtuous statesman Wut Yuen, who showed his disapproval of a corrupt government by drowning himself.
July/August	*All Soul's Day,* on the fifteenth day of the seventh moon.
August/September	*Festival of the Moon,* celebrating the full moon during this lunar month, marked by dinners and dances.

December   *Kitchen God Festival,* held the last week of the
                          month before the beginning of the Chinese New
                          Year. Special foods are prepared.

≡ Restaurants, Cafés, and Nightclubs ≡

China is a country bigger in size and population than the whole of Europe
and with cuisine reflecting this variety, yet Westerners tend to lump it all together under the "Chinese cuisine" appellation. While regional cuisines like
Szechwan, Hunanese, and Mandarin have become more familiar to the
Western palate in recent years, Chinese cuisine is very geographically diverse. A general rule of thumb is that northern Chinese food is saltier,
meatier, and includes more grilled meats and noodle dishes; central Chinese
cuisine is spicy, peppery, and rice based; and southern Chinese cooking uses
sweeter sauces and includes more deep-fried specialties. Variations on this
general theme abound, as is evident in many of Toronto's restaurants.

The Metropolitan area is blessed with over 500 Chinese restaurants, and
while some Chinese restaurateurs have complained that Canada's food
preparation regulations have often gotten in the way of true culinary excellence, Toronto has more than its fair share of excellent establishments.

Bayview Garden, *350 Highway 7 West (905-882-
8333).*

One of the Toronto area's most sumptuous Chinese eating spots, located
near the growing communities of Chinese who have moved into Markham
and Richmond Hill. It serves Mandarin, Cantonese, and Szechwan specialties with what is considered by many to be the best Peking duck in the area.

Champion House, *486 Dundas Street West (416-977-
8282); 25 Watline Avenue (905-890-8988).*

One of Toronto's best Chinese restaurants, especially for Peking duck and
other Mandarin specialties, though it does produce some excellent Szechwan items as well. A no-frills low-cost setting with excellent food.

Chinatown International, *421 Dundas Street West
(416-593-0291).*

A large restaurant in the heart of downtown Chinatown, serving a wide array
of Chinese dishes and cuisines.

Chopstix and Rice, *1 Adelaide Street East (416-363-7423).*

Modern very un-Chinese decor in an airy, beautifully decorated downtown eating spot. The menu owes much to the Hugh Carpenter Pacific-flavored cookbooks, combining traditional and innovative Chinese and East Asian recipes that have proven so popular in recent years and have accounted for some superb food. Excellent but expensive.

Chung King, *428 Spadina Avenue (416-593-0101).*

Spicy Szechwanese food popular with local Chinese and college kids in the area. Cheap, casual, flavorful food heavy on the chilies and ginger.

Dynasty Restaurant, *131 Bloor Street West (416-923-3323).*

A superb new haute cuisine restaurant on the second floor of the downtown Colonade building, the Dynasty serves one of the best dim sums in the city along with a variety of other fine Chinese dishes in a very comfortable and elegant setting.

East Moon Restaurant, *2150 Steeles Avenue West (416-738-1428).*

Cantonese and Szechwan specialties, including a wide array of spicy fish dishes, as well as an excellent Sunday buffet. Very inexpensive in comfortable surroundings.

Eat Well Chinese Garden, *25 Wellesley Street East (416-924-5777).*

A lovely upscale Chinese restaurant serving Szechwan and Hunanese specialties in a very comfortable garden-like atmosphere on the second floor of an office building overlooking Wellesley and Yonge Streets.

Eating Counter, *23 Baldwin Street (416-977-7028).*

An excellent upscale seafood and barbecued-meat restaurant serving Mandarin specialties with no monosodium glutamate (MSG) added. You can see the food being cooked in the open kitchen setting, and it has excellent and inexpensive Szechwan food.

Eating Garden, *41 Baldwin Street (416-595-5525).*

Spicy combinations of southern and central Chinese cooking includes the sweetness of peanut sauces mixed with hotter Hunan and Szechwan chili sauces. A specialty is the grilled tiger shrimp in a spicy peanut sauce.

Fireplace Restaurant, *340 Jarvis Street (416-968-0071).*

Considered by many to be the best Szechwan restaurant in the city with a name appropriate to the fiery spiciness of the cooking. This is a comfortable restaurant in a large Victorian house, with a jazz-music background. Highly recommended, reasonably priced.

Garlic Pepper, *578 Yonge Street (416-323-9819); 875 Eglinton Avenue West (416-789-7079).*

Good Szechwan food in a cheerfully decorated restaurant with excellent hot-pot and stir-fry specialties. Service can occasionally be a bit slow.

Grand Restaurant, *615 Gerrard Street East (416-469-4258).*

A long-time restaurant in Toronto's East End serving a wide array of excellent noodle dishes and northern Chinese cuisine.

Grand Yatt, *9019 Bayview Avenue (416-882-9388).*

One of the best Chinese restaurants in the Metro Toronto area, catering primarily to the sophisticated upscale tastes of newly arrived Chinese immigrants. The Cantonese food served here is nothing like the North Americanized versions to which Westerners have grown accustomed, but instead emphasizes the original fresh flavor of its components. Classic Chinese items are well supplemented with nouvelle Chinese cuisine as well as Southeast Asian tastes and flavors.

Hsin Kuang, *346 Dundas Street West (416-977-1886).*

One of Toronto's largest Chinese restaurants seating almost 1,500 people, Hsin Kuang has great northern and southern Chinese food, barbecued and deep-fried, dim sum and Szechwan spiced. An eclectic testament to the varied and grand scale of Chinese cuisine. The sweet-and-sour fish, beef with ginger, and Singapore noodles are highly recommended. Modern and pleasant, but still reasonably priced.

Jade Lotus Court, *9580 Yonge Street (416-737-3222).*

A superb restaurant in the northern Toronto suburb of Richmond Hill, the Jade Lotus Court is elegant, light, and floral, with superb food served in a stylish fashion. Dim sum is available as are classic and modern Chinese dishes. Good value for the money.

Ka Hee Chinese Restaurant, *349 Broadview Avenue (416-463-6686).*

An excellent barbecue restaurant with superb pork, duck, and noodle dishes. Very inexpensive. Not the most elegant restaurant, but lively, and the food is excellent.

Lee Garden, *358 Spadina Avenue (416-593-9524).*

A large number of Chinese customers come here to enjoy what many consider to be some of the best Chinese food in the city. Crowded and barely decorated, but with good service and low prices. Licensed for beer only.

Little Tibet, *81 Yorkville Avenue (416-963-8221).*

Unique cuisine that combines the four corners of the world bordering on Tibet with allusions to Thai, Bengali, Szechwan, and northern Chinese cuisines all put together in a unique environment more like a sumptuous Indian or Afghani restaurant than a Chinese one.

Lucky Dragon, *418 Spadina Avenue (416-598-7823).*

Specializing in hot pots with intense flavors as well as excellent braised-meat dishes and interesting vegetable combinations. One of the few Chinese restaurants in the city serving brown rice.

Magic Wok, *2094 Brimley Road (416-291-7479).*

Excellent, fresh Cantonese-style cuisine in the Scarborough area. Inexpensive and unpretentious but with excellent-quality food.

Mandarin, *2200 Yonge Street (416-486-2222).*

A pretty, modern, and spacious room with a garden-like atmosphere. Good Mandarin specialties, including beef and chicken dishes as well as excellent duck. Good service and moderate prices on food, but mixed drinks can be pricey. The best location in a large chain of local Chinese restaurants.

Mandarin Club, *280 Spadina Avenue (416-979-7110).*

An élite members-only health and social club where Toronto's most powerful Chinese community members meet.

New Hunan, *4907 Yonge Street (416-730-9398).*

Hot Hunanese dishes authentically prepared with regional spices and specialties in a casual, friendly comfortable north Toronto location. Closed on weekends for lunch.

New World Oriental Cuisine, *3600 Victoria Park Avenue (416-498-1818).*

An impressive and elegant restaurant with twenty-foot-high ceilings and an imposing fountain, the New World also serves an impressive variety of Mandarin dishes and dim sum on weekends.

Pacific Restaurant, *2095 Brimley Road (416-299-3880).*

A large but plain dining room with a wide array of well-prepared dim sum specialties. Extremely crowded on weekends, especially in the afternoon for Sunday brunch. Very popular with the local Chinese community and inexpensive.

Pearl Court Restaurant, *633 Gerrard Street East (416-463-8778).*

An excellent, inexpensive seafood restaurant in Toronto's East End that is very popular with the local Chinese community. Excellent, consistent Cantonese cuisine.

Peking Man, *1110 Sheppard Avenue East (416-223-5151).*

Good Mandarin and Szechwan cuisine, including excellent Colonel Thai chicken, spring rolls, rainbow delight, and Mongolian shrimp. Service is good, if sometimes linguistically challenging, and the decor and environment is above average for an inexpensive restaurant.

Peter's Chung King, *281 College Street (416-928-2936).*

Some of the best Szechwan cuisine in town, this restaurant has preserved the tang and vigor of its seasonings with superb orange chicken and hot-and-sour soup. Cheap and simple and often quite crowded.

Sai Woo, *130 Dundas Street West (416-977-4988).*

Long well known as one of Toronto's fine Chinese restaurants, Sai Woo's remains consistent, reliable, and moderately priced, and still serves food later into the night than many other Toronto restaurants.

Sian San, *30 College Street (416-975-8823).*

One of Toronto's more stylish Chinese restaurants with excellent sweet-and-sour pickerel, crab, and beef with pineapple. The flavors are fresh and sweet in authentic Cantonese style. Good service, moderate prices, pleasant decor.

Tai Pan, *243 Eglinton Avenue West (416-482-5501).*

Excellent Cantonese food at very reasonable prices. Specialties include crab soup, phoenix nest, Peking duck, and red bean porridge. Excellent food presentation as well as taste, with good service and a pleasant unobtrusive decor.

Wah Sing, *47 Baldwin Street (416-599-8822).*

Noted for its hot pots, such as crab with bean curd or mapo bean curd with fried watercress, hot peppers, and chili. Also excellent (and an excellent value) are the lobsters or crab for two, both fried and served with either a potent ginger or black bean sauce. Eat in or take out.

Young Lok Restaurant, *122 Saint Patrick Street (416-593-9818); 4950 Yonge Street (416-225-8818).*

Long established as one of Toronto's best-known places for dim sum, Young Lok also serves a variety of Chinese foods and cooking styles from Szechwan to Cantonese. The restaurant itself is also attached to a Chinese bakery and grocery store which serves excellent and inexpensive stuffed Chinese buns (barbecued pork, curry beef, and chicken) and barbecued meats.

Food Sources

Bakeries

Chinese bakeries make a variety of excellent savory buns and pastries (barbecued pork buns, curry beef buns, and so on) and surprisingly good sweets and pastries, from more classic Chinese almond cookies to chocolate and strawberry sponge cakes. The following is a list of some of the better and more interesting bakeries.

Far East Products, *70 Huron Street (416-977-2482).*

Toronto's biggest fortune-cookie maker, producing over 100,000 cookies a day.

Kim Moon, *438 Dundas Street West (416-977-1933).*

The main Chinese bakery in the Spadina Chinatown area.

Tung Hing Bakery, *674 Gerrard Street East (416-461-1978); 428 Dundas Street West (416-593-9375); 349 ½ Broadview Avenue (416-465-9103); 880 Dundas Street East (905-270-1288).*

A chain of bakeries serving excellent pastries and savory Chinese buns.

Young Lok Dim Sum Market, *122 Saint Patrick Street (416-593-9819).*

Attached to Young Lok's Restaurant and serving a variety of Chinese pastries, savory buns, and deli specialties.

Ying Sing Pastry Shop, *22 Baldwin Street.*

Long known locally as the Baldwin Street Bakery, this Chinese pastry shop serves some of the best, freshest, and cheapest Chinese savory buns in the city. Very busy at lunchtime.

Delis/Grocers

There are over 100 Asian grocers in the city selling various Chinese sauces, food products, produce, and fruits. Some of the better ones include:

Asian Pacific Supermarket, *357 Broadview Avenue (416-465-6102).*

Dong Thanh Grocery, *484 Dundas Street West (416-977-1268).*

Hoa Tuong Trading Company, *347 Broadview Avenue (416-466-1868).*

Hong Lee Trading Company, *449 Dundas Street West (416-597-2141).*

Hope Cheung Trading Co., *482 Dundas Street West (416-977-1628).*

Hoy Kun Trading Co., *436 Dundas Street West (416-977-6010).*

Kiu Luen Co., *341 Broadview Avenue (416-465-4928).*

Shin Seng Trading Company, *358 Broadview Avenue (416-469-0751).*

Shops

As befits the growing power and economic presence of the Chinese community, a number of wholly Chinese shopping centers have opened throughout the Metro Toronto area with a large number of Chinese stores. Goods from silks, jade jewelry, rice cookers, and Chinese gifts and sculptures to oriental food and produce specialties can be bought at literally hundreds of different stores in the Metropolitan area. Some of the best shopping centers at which to find these stores include:

Chinatown Centre, *222 Spadina Avenue (416-340-9367).*

Downtown Chinatown's biggest complex with over 100 stores.

Dragon Centre, *23 Glen Watford (416-299-3810).*

Over 140 stores in the Sheppard/Victoria Park area.

Dragon City Complex, *280 Spadina Avenue (416-979-7777).*

An élite shopping center at the corner of Spadina and Dundas Street West with an excellent food fair complex in the center court.

Mandarin Shopping Centre, *4386 Sheppard Avenue East (416-299-6768).*

A shopping plaza in Scarborough with a number of Chinese restaurants, grocers, jewelry stores, and gift shops.

Milliken Wells Shopping Centre, *240 Alton Towers Circle (416-292-1211).*

Hong Kong–bazaar architecture housing a variety of modern, upscale Chinese shops, including some excellent clothing, gift, and jewelry shops.

Besides the numerous and varied retail delights of Chinese stores, a number of herbalists ply their trade throughout the city providing access to the herbal cures of Chinese medicine. Among these are:

Bo Hong Yuen Chinese Herbs, *421 Dundas Street West (416-977-5060).*

Chinese and Japanese Health Institute, *1130 Eglinton Avenue West (416-781-8888).*

Dai Kuang Wah Herb Market, *280 Spadina Avenue (416-597-2224); 595 Gerrard Street East (416-466-9207).*

Da Jung Herbal Centre, *428 Dundas Street West (416-581-1653).*

Great China Herb, *251 Spadina Avenue (416-977-8859).*

International Herbs Co., *31 Saint Andrew's (416-593-5238).*

Nam Pek Hong Kong Chinese Herb Centre, *393 Dundas Street West (416-593-8878).*

Traditional Chinese Natural Therapy Specialist,
3852 Finch Avenue East (416-298-3070).

For traditional Chinese teas that you can select from the original herbs themselves or perhaps concoct your own blend, try **Ten Ren Tea Company,** 454 Dundas Street West (416-598-7872), which has a large selection of classic Chinese teas. A **Chinese Astrologer,** 434 Dundas Street West (416-593-7032), is also available for those who wish to examine the more esoteric aspects of Chinese philosophy as well as their own futures.

Finally, a few good art galleries are available in the city that help develop local Chinese artists as well as bring in imported Chinese art. Such galleries include:

Karwah Art Gallery, *289 Dundas Street West (416-598-0043).*

Wan Po Shung Art Gallery, *198 Spadina Avenue (416-362-7548).*

A number of Chinese-language bookstores and magazine shops carrying publications in Mandarin exist throughout the area:

Chang Sheung Kee Book Company, *463 Dundas Street West (416-596-7709).*

Cheng Kong Bookstore, *2094 Brimley Road (416-293-3115).*

China Book Store, *623 Gerrard Street East (416-469-2110).*

Dundas Book Store, *421 Dundas Street West (416-596-6938).*

Dunhuang Books and Art, *328 Broadview Avenue (416-465-8266).*

First Shop, *1571 Sandhurst Circle (416-299-9475).*

Hua Hsing Bookstore, *23 Glen Watford Drive (416-299-8198).*

Kee Sam Bookstore, *3301 McNicoll Street (416-321-5090).*

Look'n'Buy Books and Art, *100 Steeles Avenue West, Thornhill (905-882-5563).*

Mandarin Book and Gift, *9019 Bayview Avenue, Markham (905-889-0383).*

Modern Books and Records, *494 Dundas Street West (416-979-1365).*

Pan Asian Publications Inc., *110 Silver Star Boulevard, Unit 109, Box 131, Agincourt Station (416-292-4468).*

A wholesaler of many Asian-language publications, including Chinese-language books, Tagalog books, and Korean-language books.

Peking Book Centre, *888 Dundas Street East, Mississauga (905-896-8707).*

People Books and Gifts, *480 Dundas Street West (416-977-8965); 273 Spadina Avenue (416-596-8709).*

S A M, *3601 Victoria Park Boulevard (416-502-3147).*

Sau Man Bookstore, *350 Highway 7 East, Markham (905-886-0959).*

Southern Bookstore, *3300 Midland (416-321-8321).*

Sun Wa Bookstore, *19 Milliken Boulevard (416-293-9438); 280 Spadina Avenue (416-596-8887).*

There are also two major distributors for Chinese-language records and tapes:

Dr. Sun Distribution, *261 Spadina Avenue (416-408-3923).*

Modern Books and Records, *494 Dundas Street West (416-979-1365).*

═══════════════ Media ═══════════════

Publications

Chinese Canadian Weekly, *100 Dynamic Drive (416-299-8229).*

A weekly magazine on the Chinese-Canadian community.

Chinese Classified Phonebooks, *3 Passmore Avenue (416-321-8794).*

A directory of people, businesses, and services within the Chinese community.

Living Times Magazine, *2250 Midland Avenue (416-292-6712).*

A monthly magazine on the Chinese community.

Modern Times Magazine, *291 Dundas Street West (416-597-1648).*

A monthly magazine on the Canadian-Chinese community.

Shing Wah Daily News, *795 Gerrard Street East (416-778-1855).*

The oldest Chinese-language newspaper in Toronto, daily news of interest to the Chinese community.

Sing Tao Jih Pao, *417 Dundas Street West (416-596-8140).*

The largest circulation Chinese daily newspaper.

Sino-Canadian Directory, *42 Pinnacle Road (416-447-3775).*

A directory of Chinese-Canadian businesses and services across Canada.

World Journal Daily News, 415 Eastern Avenue (416-778-0888).

A daily Chinese-language newspaper.

Film Theaters

A number of film theaters carry Cantonese- and Mandarin-language first-run Chinese films, as well as some revues. Most Chinese grocers and bookstores also carry Chinese-language videos.

Far East Theatre, *270 Spadina Avenue (416-977-7282).*

Golden Harvest Theatre, *186 Spadina Avenue (416-869-0046).*

Golden Princess Theatre, *608 College Street (416-532-9006).*

Pearl Theatre, *285 Spadina Avenue (416-586-0320).*

Sun Wah Theatre, *1035 Gerrard Street East (416-466-3636).*

Radio and Television

"Chinese Program," CHIN-AM 1540 (Cantonese and Mandarin), *622 College Street (416-531-9991).*

Daily from 3:00 to 8:00 PM and on Friday nights, 11:30 PM to 3:00 AM.

"Chinese Program," CHIN-FM 100.7, *622 College Street (416-531-9991).*

Sundays from 12:30 to 5:00 PM.

CFMT, Channel 47, *545 Lakeshore Boulevard West (416-593-4747).*

Carries a variety of Chinese-language television shows, including:

- **"Chinese Journal."** A highly rated nightly newscast.

- **"Chinese Movie Super Saturday Night."** Chinese movie spectaculars.

- **"Chinese Entertainment Plus."** Variety entertainment from throughout the Pacific Rim.

- **"Chinese Midnight Theatre."** Late-night Chinese-language motion pictures.

- **"Chinese Business Hour."** A weekly program covering business and financial news in the Chinese community.

- **"Chinese Tanagram."** A magazine-style news show on various cultural, political, and social issues in the Chinese community.

- **"Chinese Newsweek."** The week's top issues are examined from the Chinese perspective.

—The Four Chinatowns: The Spadina Chinatown—

The oldest of the four Toronto Chinatowns and the best known to most of Toronto's visitors is the Spadina-area Chinatown. Sprawling across Dundas Street West from McCaul Street to Augusta Street (east to west) and along Spadina Avenue (north to south) from College Street to Queen Street West, this remains *the* commercial and retail hub of the Chinese community. Hundreds of shops, grocery stores, restaurants, and businesses are crammed into this bustling area filled with Chinese-language signs and neon lights.

The area started originally as a westward extension of the original downtown Chinatown near Dundas and Bay Streets, where one can still find a number of Chinese stores and restaurants, including the well-known Sai Woo and Lichee Garden. After the building of the new city hall in 1957, the Chinese community moved westward, and with the growth of immigration in the 1960s and 1970s this area became the focal point for the community. Its proximity to the University of Toronto made it particularly attractive to the thousands of Chinese students who also come here.

This is a busy area humming with activity twenty-four hours a day, seven days a week. Barbecued pork and duck hang in the windows; an assortment of Chinese-language books, records, and videos line store shelves; and a wide array of gifts, silk clothing, and jade jewelry stores abound. Close to downtown and the Art Gallery of Ontario, a brief visit to the hub of North America's largest Chinese community is a must for any visitor to Toronto.

How to Get There: *Take the Yonge Street subway to either the Saint Patrick or Dundas Street subway station and catch a westbound Dundas Street streetcar. Get off at Spadina Avenue. You can also go to the Spadina* *subway station on the Bloor/Danforth subway line and go south to Dundas Street West.*

—The Four Chinatowns: The East End Chinatown—

At the corner of Gerrard Street East and Broadview is a second downtown-area Chinatown that is more compact than the one at Dundas and Spadina, but in some ways has more local color and is more accessible than the Spadina Chinatown. Whereas Spadina is Hong Kong, this is small-town China with a few restaurants, a couple of bakeries, an herbalist's shop, a few grocers, hairdressers, and shops, but it is very active with Chinese people from the surrounding area throughout the day.

This area doesn't attract the nighttime crowds that the Spadina Chinatown does, but it's quite lively on weekends and includes the best and least expensive Chinese restaurants in the city. The entrance to this neighborhood has a memorial to the great Chinese revolutionary leader Sun Yat-sen overlooking Riverdale Park. The nearby Riverdale Library also has a large collection of Chinese-language books, magazines, and newspapers.

This Chinatown has always had a more hardworking, everyday feel to it than the other three and attracted many of the less well-off Taiwanese and

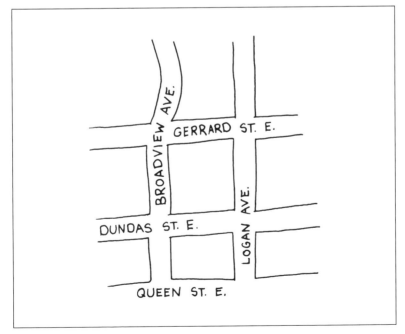

Chinatown East

mainland Chinese immigrants who couldn't afford the more expensive urban and suburban areas. In many ways it is the most authentically Chinese neighborhood in the city and is well recommended for an off-the-beaten-path excursion.

How to Get There: *Take the King Street or Dundas Street streetcar south from the Broadview subway station on the Bloor/Danforth line to Gerrard Street East or take the College streetcar east to Broadview Avenue from the College subway station on the Yonge/University line.*

—The Four Chinatowns: Scarborough— and Mississauga Chinatowns

As with many other ethnic groups, the Chinese community has moved from the downtown areas into the suburbs over the last twenty years. At first this move was made up of second-generation Chinese immigrants looking for quieter, larger accommodations in the suburbs. This trend was greatly accelerated in the 1980s as many well-heeled Chinese immigrants from Hong Kong began to move into the Toronto area and looked at buying into Toronto's expanding suburban areas.

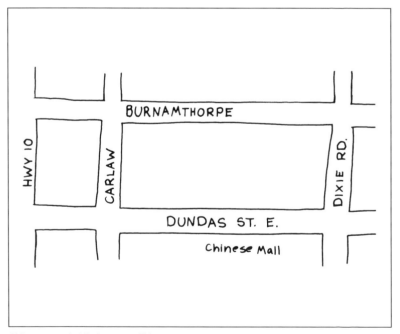

Chinatown 4: Mississauga Chinatown

In the eastern suburb of Scarborough, the community became focused around the Sheppard Avenue East and Victoria Park Avenue areas, and a large number of restaurants, shopping centers, and services for the Chinese community stretch across both roads north to Steeles Avenue, west to Warden Avenue, and east to Pharmacy Road. Population-wise, this may very well be the largest area of ethnic Chinese in the city, though movement north into the nearby suburbs of Markham, Thornhill, and Richmond Hill is occurring here as well.

In Mississauga the population is more dispersed, but a commercial center has sprung up around the Dragon's Gate shopping center on Dundas Street in Cooksville. Here there is a large Hsin Kuang restaurant, a number of grocers, bakeries, shops, and services all housed in a Chinese-motif architectural style.

How to Get There: *In Scarborough, take the Bloor/Danforth subway line east to the Victoria Park Station, then take the number 24 Victoria Park bus north to Sheppard Avenue East. Alternatively, you can take the Yonge/University subway north to the Sheppard Avenue station and then take the number 85 Sheppard Avenue East or number 139 Huntingwood bus east to Victoria Park. In Mississauga, go west to the Islington subway station on the Bloor/Danforth line and catch the number 1A Dundas Street Mississauga Transit line bus west to Carlaw Avenue.*

French Toronto

History

When thinking about the original European settlers in Toronto, the English or Scots are the ones who generally come to mind. In fact, the area had a long acquaintance with French settlement prior to the establishment by the British of Fort York and the town of York. The word "Toronto" comes from the original French name for the area, a simplification of the Native Indian word "temetegon" (carrying place), which was used to describe the Humber River valley. This was one of the major travel routes for canoeing up to the Georgian Bay, with a relative small carrying area connecting the Humber with the Holland River, and from there providing a route to Lake Simcoe and the Georgian Bay.

Francophones still make up a total of more than 300,000 people in the Greater Toronto area. Some are native Franco-Ontarians, some are from Quebec, some are from Acadia, and some are from western French-speaking areas of Canada. French immigrants from Haiti, Martinique, France, French Africa, and Belgium add to the Francophone mix.

The first European known to have stood on the soil that is now Toronto was the French explorer Etienne Brule, an interpreter to Samuel de Champlain. The sight of his landing near the Humber River is commemorated with a park. The French explorer La Salle was the first European to note that the Native Indian word "Toronto" designated this area. In the 1700s the French fur traders built a fortified trading station in what is now the west end of the city, near the grounds of the Canadian National Exhibition. Fort Rouille, commonly known as Fort Toronto, is commemorated by a boulder on the site where it once stood.

Further up the Humber River is an elite area of town known as Baby Point. This area was named after the French fur trader Jacques Baby, who opened a trading store on the banks of the Humber that was to become the origin of the Baby family estate, which at one time encompassed most of this area.

French-Canadian families were among the early prominent families of Toronto, and many French Canadians lived in the lower Cabbagetown area, between King and Queen Streets, or in Parkdale. Vestiges of the early French-Canadian presence near the Humber River can still be found in the Bloor West Village as well. French Canadians were employed in a variety of positions and included prominent business leaders and professionals as well as tailors, restaurateurs, and printers.

An early fraternal organization of the French community in Toronto was the Saint Joseph Society, a social service organization founded in 1887. The building of Sacred Heart Church also occurred at this time and formed (and still does) the heart of Catholic French Toronto. The De La Salle Institute was founded to help maintain French-language use and skills. Strangely enough, at this time many of Toronto's French-speaking residents had emigrated here, not from Quebec or France but from the United States where they were coming under increasing linguistic pressure.

In the 1960s a second French-language parish was established in the northern Toronto suburb of Don Mills. The Chasse-Galerie assumed a growing role in encouraging French art, crafts, and culture. Likewise, a French-language board of education was established to encourage the use of French in public education and to help protect the French-language base of this culture.

In 1976 **Le Conseil des Organismes Francophones du Toronto Metropolitan** was founded as an umbrella organization for French social, cultural, and political groups in the area. It has now become the Centre Francophone which, working in association with the long-established L'Alliance Française de Toronto, continues to promote French language and culture in the area.

The move toward accepting Canada as a bilingual country, as well as the pressures brought by Quebec's Separatist movement, have helped the Toronto Francophone community protect and assert its cultural and linguistic heritage in a stronger fashion over the last twenty years. As a result, French-language culture is much more readily available and accessible now than ever before.

Religion

A number of churches in Toronto hold Catholic masses in French:

Eglise de Sacre Coeur, *381 Sherborne Street (416-922-2177).*

Saint Louis de France, *1415 Don Mills Road (416-445-6433).*

Church of the Redeemer, *162 Bloor Street West (416-922-4948).*

Jarvis Street Baptist Church, *130 Gerrard Street East (416-925-3261).*

Sainte Famille, *62 Daffodil Place (905-454-4084).*

Organizations

There is a French-language school board in Toronto that promotes language classes as well as all lessons in French. The **Conseil des Ecoles Françaises de la Communauté Urbaine de Toronto,** 1 Concorde Gate (416-391-1264), is the board of education for French-language schooling in Toronto.

York University's Glendon College, 2275 Bayview Avenue (416-487-6730), is a French-language university in Toronto. Its **Maison de la Culture** also has a gallery with exhibitions of French paintings, sculptures, and books. The **Alliance Française de Toronto,** 24 Spadina Road (416-922-2014), also has regular exhibits.

There are three French-language theater groups in the city:

Théâtre Français de Toronto, *219 Dufferin Street (416-534-7303/6604).*

Performs plays for general audiences and children.

Le Théâtre Ensemble, *12 Shannon Road (416-537-5453).*

Le Théâtre du Grand Malheur, *50 Alexander Road (416-925-7592).*

Other community social and cultural organizations include:

COFTM Centre Francophone, *20 Lower Spadina Avenue (416-367-1950).*

The main center for Francophone cultural and community events, providing information on French-language services in Toronto, adult education, and counseling.

Alliance Acadienne, *381 Sherborne Avenue (416-752-7962).*

A community organization for French-speaking Acadians from eastern Canada's New Brunswick and Nova Scotia provinces. It helps preserve local folk traditions and crafts.

Alliance Française de Toronto, *24 Spadina Road (416-922-2014).*

Long one of Toronto's premier organizations for promoting the French language and culture. It has a gallery and sponsors lectures, theater programs, and films, as well as a variety of festivals.

Le Cercle Canadien, *17 Saint Joseph Street (416-925-0880).*

Centre d'Accueil Heritage, *33 Hahn Place (416-365-1354).*

Chevaliers de Colomb, *171 Cedarvale Avenue (416-423-0410).*

Club Richelieu Trilium de Toronto, *33 Hahn Place (416-365-3350).*

Federation des Clubs Sociaux Franco-Ontariens, *647 Franklin Boulevard (416-623-2822).*

An umbrella group coordinating social activities among a variety of French clubs.

Francophone de l'Ontario, *108 Spin Valley (416-393-5409).*

A community organization of Franco-Ontarians, many of whom are internal immigrants from northern and eastern Ontario.

Orientation Francophone Internationale Ontario,
150 King Street West (416-597-8811).

Union des Artistes, *2239 Yonge Street (416-485-7670.*
A union of French-speaking artists in the Metro area.

══════ Accommodation ══════

The **French Connection Bed and Breakfast,** *102
Burnside Drive (416-537-7741).*
A bed-and-breakfast near Casa Loma catering to French-speaking visitors and providing a pleasant Franco-Ontarian environment for people who don't speak French.

══════ Holidays and Celebrations ══════

February/March   *Mardi Gras* celebrations, including a masquerade ball and other social activities.

June 24   *Saint Jean Baptiste Day,* honoring the patron saint of French Canadians. *Francophone Week* takes place around this time with a variety of cultural events.

July 14   *Bastille Day.*

August 15   *Assumption Day* festival, held with an open-air festival at Harbourfront of Arts and Crafts, Singing, and Dancing.

November 25   *La Tire Sainte Catherine,* celebrating the contributions of unmarried women over the age of twenty-five, a tradition dating back to the seventeenth century in Canada when Marguerite Bourgeoys made toffee candy for her students.

═ Restaurants, Cafés, and Nightclubs ═

French cuisine is one of the world's best-known styles of cooking, and Toronto has more than its fair share of excellent French restaurants, many of which are reasonably priced. The following list gives some of the better French restaurants in the city. With the advent of cuisine minceur, French doesn't always have to be rich, and the last recession has brought prices on food in Toronto down to a very affordable level at many of these restaurants. This is by no means an exhaustive list, but these places each have a particular French flair.

À La Broche, *1505 Bayview Avenue (416-485-1111).*

A long-established French restaurant with a warm, homey atmosphere in the Bayview area of East York. Classic cuisine including excellent French onion soup, poached salmon, and crème caramel. A simple, romantic decor with reasonably priced offerings.

Arlequin, *134 Avenue Road (416-928-9521).*

A bistro and delicatessen serving modern French cuisine in a midtown location near Yorkville. The deli serves wonderful salads, sandwiches, cookies, and pastries, and restaurant specialties include an excellent cassoulet, rabbit, lamb, and seafood dishes. The wine list is good, and the restaurant is small and very active.

Auberge du Pommier, *4150 Yonge Street (416-222-2220).*

One of Toronto's premier restaurants, constantly ranked as one of the city's best. The setting is a French country home complete with stone fireplace, wood beams, and a plethora of flowers. The food presentation is particularly noteworthy, and the menu is innovative and superb. Especially recommended are the soups, desserts, and rack of lamb.

Bistro 990, *990 Bay Street (416-921-9990).*

A high-quality French-Canadian restaurant with a beautifully appointed interior, an all-Canadian wine list, and a superb array of native cuisine. Popular with nearby government workers and bureaucrats, this is a power lunch kind of restaurant.

BOBA, *90 Avenue Road (416-920-0956).*

Recently reopened in the old Auberge Gavroche location, BOBA has attained greater acclaim, presenting superb, innovative French cuisine at a reasonable price. Excellent wine list. Still retains the lovely homey atmosphere that made the Auberge such a romantic place.

Bofinger Brasserie, *1507 Yonge Street (416-923-2300).*

A large, active French bistro. The menu is diverse and very modern, with Caribbean-Asian accents to the food as well as Cajun influences, such as the blackened strip steak. A fun place but a little on the expensive side. Better for lunch than dinner, though the excellent service does make a leisurely supper a very enjoyable experience.

Brasserie Bobino, *4243 Dundas Street West (416-237-1457).*

A lovely West Toronto restaurant with excellent classic French cuisine served by a knowledgeable and helpful staff. Prices are among the most reasonable for any French restaurant in the city.

Chiaro's, *37 King Street East (416-863-9700).*

Located in the King Edward Hotel, this elegant eatery is reminiscent of a lovely French hotel restaurant, complete with a well-appointed, richly decorated room; high ceilings and white columns; and a superb array of classic French and continental cuisine. Especially recommended is the terrine of forest mushrooms with venison carpaccio, as well as the poached Dover sole and rack of lamb with hazelnuts. Expensive, but well worth it.

Corner House, *501 Davenport Road (416-923-2604).*

Long a Toronto favorite tucked away in a little neighborhood home near Casa Loma, this place has the atmosphere of a French country inn in the city. Classic French cuisine includes excellent tournedos de boeuf, veal Oscar, and duck in cognac sauce.

Hugo's, *9 Imperial Street (416-964-2440).*

An inauspicious little bistro with superb food, hidden away in a little cul de sac in the uptown Toronto area along Yonge Street just north of Davisville station. Reasonably priced with an excellent mixture of classic bistro fare and items with some modern touches to them.

Jacques Omlettes, *126 A Cumberland Avenue, 2nd floor (416-961-1893).*

Long one of the favorite restaurants of Torontonians, Jacques remains one of the most romantic, inexpensive bistros in the city. Renowned for a superb array of perfectly prepared omelets, it's located in the heart of Yorkville. This restaurant has been providing superb food at reasonable prices for over twenty years—a record in consistency hard to match.

La Maison Benoit, *1921 Avenue Road (416-782-9934).*

Madame Benoit is one of Canada's best-known cookbook writers, sort of the Julia Child of French-Canadian cuisine. This pleasant, unpretentious little restaurant in the north Toronto neighborhood along Avenue Road serves excellent and hearty French-Canadian fare at moderate prices. Good wine list that doesn't make a fetish of being Canadian.

La Maison D'Azur, *80 Front Street East (416-362-9455).*

A lovely French bistro in the heart of Toronto's Saint Lawrence market area and theater district. Good classic French cuisine with excellent duck, escargot, onion soup, and seafood. Relatively inexpensive and, unlike many French restaurants, it's hospitable and welcoming to families with children.

La Maquette, *111 King Street East (416-366-8191).*

Located downtown overlooking the Toronto Sculpture Garden, this is an excellent nouvelle cuisine restaurant with an extensive wine list. Very formal, very elegant, very French in a modern way. Among the specialties are sweetbread ravioli and salmon Wellington in phyllo pastry.

La Petite France, *3317 Bloor Street West (416-234-8783).*

A small, warm little restaurant in west Toronto's Etobicoke area, where they serve superb French food for incredibly reasonable prices. Escargots are under $4.00 as an appetizer, and there are a number of other dishes in the $3.50 to $4.50 range. Fresh trout can be as little as $7.95. The food is well cooked, interestingly put together, and graciously served. Why other restaurants can't be as innovative and inexpensive as this is beyond me, but one can certainly dine here and enjoy the difference.

Le Bistingo, *349 Queen Street West (416-598-3490).*

A funky bistro in the heart of Toronto's Queen Street West area with a bright modern look, modest prices, and a good bistro menu. Always known as having one of the best steak frites in town, but also serves interesting, innovative menu items to an upscale, artsy, professional clientele. A place to see and be seen.

Le Canard Enchaine, *12 Amelia Street (416-924-9901).*

One of Toronto's most wonderfully eccentric restaurants, Le Canard is located on a side street in Toronto's Cabbagetown area in a small house whose interior walls are covered with the intriguing art of its two owners (who also entertain guests with music). The duck served here is among the best in the city and is served a variety of ways, but there are other excellent items on the menu, such as various veal dishes. Great, friendly service; pleasant romantic atmosphere.

Le Papillon, *106 Front Street East (416-363-0838).*

Long established as one of Toronto's premier creperies, with some other bistro fare and omelets as well. Located in the Saint Lawrence market area.

Le Paradis, *166 Bedford Road (416-921-0995).*

One of my personal favorites, with an excellent inexpensive bistro menu and some well-priced specials, a good wine list, and French beer on tap, as well as imported Belgian and Alsatian beers. This was one of the first bistros in the city to open its kitchen to patrons' view. Very active and lively on weekends and in the evenings. Its Moroccan chicken is especially recommended, as is the occasional pheasant that shows up on the menu.

Le Petit Gaston, *35 Baldwin Street (416-596-0278).*

A small, unpretentious place serving excellent food in downtown Toronto's Baldwin Street Village. Classic French specialties include Coquille Saint Jacques and a lovely glazed chicken cordon bleu. Moderate prices, good wine list.

Le Rendez-vous, *14 Prince Arthur (416-961-6111).*

Large, pleasantly decorated space with a lovely outdoor patio for summertime dining al fresco. Good menu of modern-tinged classical French cuisine with an excellent and extensive wine list. Serves fondue as well.

Le Select Bistro, *328 Queen Street West (416-596-6405).*

Another consistently excellent restaurant that has been serving innovative food at affordable prices for over fifteen years. Located in the Queen Street West Village, Le Select's specialties include an excellent sweetbread and escargots in Dijon cream sauce on pasta appetizer, superb lamb chops with couscous, and other more common bistro fare, some with lovely little Asian and Thai touches. One of the best wine lists in the city with an extensive array of French and other European and Australian wines. Crowded, tiny tables are a bit annoying but contribute to the liveliness of the restaurant.

Le Soufflé, *568 Parliament Street (416-924-2934).*

A long-standing neighborhood restaurant serving excellent bistro food as well superb soufflés. This is one of the few restaurants in Toronto serving these demanding dishes and they do it superbly. Especially recommended are the chocolate dessert soufflés.

Le Trou Normand, *90 Yorkville Avenue (416-967-5956).*

Long one of Toronto's best-known restaurants for classic French cuisine, located on a quiet alleyway in Yorkville with an old-fashioned Norman French decor. Northern French country cooking at its best.

Montreal Restaurant/Bistro, *65 Sherborne Street (416-363-0179).*

A pleasant bistro with a combination of French classical favorites as well as good Quebecois cuisine, such as *tortiere* (spiced pork meat pies) and mussels in a variety of forms. Live jazz music in the evenings perfectly complements a quiet, romantic environment.

Pourquoi Pas, *63 Sheppard Avenue West (416-226-9071).*

One of the best French restaurants in North York with a long and consistent history of satisfying customers. Good classical French cuisine at reasonable prices in a homey atmosphere.

Scaramouche, *1 Benvenuto Place (416-961-8011).*

Like Auberge Pommier, this eatery is consistently chosen by Toronto patrons as one of the top restaurants in the city. Scaramouche also has one of the best views of any room in Toronto. Perched on top of Avenue Road Hill, it commands a panoramic view of downtown Toronto matched by its splendidly presented and executed meals. Specialties include lamb shank soup; veal with a rosemary cream sauce; warm sweetbread and mushroom terrine; grilled salmon with wild rice fricassee, sweet peppers, pearl onions, smoked bacon, and escarole in a horseradish white wine sauce; and pan-roasted Riesling-marinated quails. Desserts are among the best in the city.

=============== **Food Sources** ===============

Bakeries

A number of excellent French bakeries and patisseries, serving fresh croissants and brioche as well as a variety of fine pastries, are to be found in the city. Most have small cafés and delicatessens attached and carry a number of gourmet French foods as well. Some of the best are:

Daniel et Daniel, *248 Carlton Street (416-968-9275).*

A tiny little catering bakery in Cabbagetown serving excellent pastries and a lovely array of tortes, salads, breads, and sandwiches.

France Oven, *435 Midwest Road (416-752-0027).*

A wide array of French breads, baked goods, and pastries.

Genel Patisserie, *825 Denison (905-415-1459).*

Excellent French pastries, cakes, and tortes.

Le Petit Gourmet, *1064 Yonge Street (416-966-3811).*

Excellent French pastries complemented by an extensive array of salads, sandwiches, and breads.

Michel's Baguette French Bakery Café, *Eaton Centre (416-596-1094); Queen's Quay Terminal (416-203-0287); Toronto Dominion Centre (416-860-0240); Yorkdale Shopping Centre (416-789-3533).*

The best fresh croissants in the city in addition to a variety of soups, salads and sandwiches, fresh breads, and pastries.

Patachou Patisserie, *1095 Yonge Street (416-927-1105).*

Excellent French bakery and café with a wide array of luscious desserts.

Grocers/Delis

Most grocers and good food shops in Toronto carry a wide array of fine French food products. A couple of places specializing in these foods are:

Maison du Frommage, *2390 Bloor Street West (416-767-2426).*

An excellent source of French and Quebec cheese, including hard-to-find chèvres and creamy bries.

Paul's Fine Foods, *446 Spadina Road (416-483-9303).*

A large gourmet food store serving a variety of interesting deli foods and salads as well as unique condiments and imported French foods.

Shops

French Perfumes and Cosmetics, 2640 Danforth Avenue (416-678-8299), specializes in a large array of fine French perfumes and one-of-a-kind cosmetic items unavailable at department stores and pharmacies. **La Fontaine Jeuneusse,** 890 A Yonge Street (416-925-8555), specializes in French makeups and skin-care creams.

French fashions are available at good stores throughout the city, but the **French Collection,** 253 Eglinton Avenue West (416-483-4861), carries only French designer labels. The **Children's French Store,** 1486 Danforth Avenue (416-465-3015), carries fun and attractive French clothing for children, as well as books and games in French.

French chocolatiers are represented by **Le Feuvre's,** 683 Mount Pleasant Road (416-483-5512), and **Simone Marie Chocolates,** 150 Bloor Street West (416-968-7777).

Books, magazines, and newspapers in French are available from:

Maison de la Presse Internationale, *124–126 Yorkville Avenue (416-928-0418).*

Librarie Champlain, *468 Queen Street East (416-364-4345).*

Huge selection of French-language volumes with a very large collection of children's and educational books.

Librarie Renaud Bray, *912 Yonge Street (416-515-7700).*

Excellent selection of French-language books in a superstore setting.

========================= **Media** =========================

There is a variety of French-language newspapers, radio programs, and television stations in Toronto. Due to Canada's bilingual policies, French-language television and radio broadcasting is mandatory across the country, and there is a variety of programs available for those who wish to enjoy French film, music, and news shows.

Publications

Annuaire Francophone, *CFTM Centre Francophone, 20 Lower Spadina Avenue (416-367-1950).*
A Francophone annual covering French-language speakers and businesses.

L'Express, *17 Carlaw Avenue (416-465-2107).*
A French-language weekly covering local and national current events.

Le Bulletin, *20 Lower Spadina Avenue (416-367-1950).*
A monthly newspaper covering French-language cultural events and affairs produced by the Centre Francophone.

Radio and Television

La Chaine Française, *TVOntario, Box 200 Station Q (416-484-2600).*
Ontario Public Broadcasting's French-language television station.

CJBC 860 AM, *Box 5000 Station A (416-975-3311).*
French-language radio from Radio-Canada, Canadian Broadcasting Corporation's French-language service.

Société Radio-Canada, *250 Front Street West (416-205-3311).*
Canadian Broadcasting Corporation's French-language service.

MUSICPLUS, *299 Queen Street West (416-591-5757).*

Canada's French-language rock video station. Available on cable only.

German Toronto

History

The German population in Toronto is one of the city's largest communities, and its members have quietly made their mark over the years, from the design of some of the city's best-known structures—such as Eaton Centre and Toronto-Dominion Centre—to Toronto's main street (the world's longest), Yonge Street, which stretches out to the border with Manitoba 1,100 miles away.

The German presence in Toronto goes right back to the very founding of the city when John Graves Simcoe cofounded the city of York with William Moll Berczy. Berczy brought sixty-four German settlers to Canada to help clear away the bush and establish the city that was to become Toronto. He is commemorated in a lovely little parkette at the pie-shaped intersection of Front and Wellington Streets across from the Saint Lawrence Centre. The families he brought over are memorialized with German Mills Settlers Park, in Markham just north of Toronto.

German settlement in Canada goes back to 1664 when Hans Bernard purchased land in Quebec. Many German immigrants moved to Halifax and other maritime cities in the 1700s. They were joined by German loyalist farmers from the United States after the Revolution, as well as by decommissioned Hessian mercenary troops.

In the 1850s the community began organizing as a group. The first Lutheran congregation was established, and German entrepreneurs and professionals began organizing fraternal groups. By the 1890s the Germans were among the largest ethnic groups in Toronto with over 6,000 people. Commercial and industrial growth drew many who had originally gone to the United States.

The world-famous Heintzman Piano Company was founded at this time, as were many other Canadian-based businesses. Several German religious groups also arrived in the late 1800s, including the Mennonites, many of whom settled within an hour of Toronto and whose religious persuasion is similar to that of the Amish in the United States.

Over 100,000 German immigrants arrived in the years following World War I. One group, the Danube Swabians, are ethnic Germans from the Danube valley areas of Hungary, Serbia, and Romania who first came to Canada in the 1890s. When settlement areas were partitioned after the end of World War I, many joined relatives already settled in Canada. Even more arrived after expulsion from their homelands following the end of World War II. This specific German group numbers almost 20,000 and has its own club and community organization. Its members include some of the most successful entrepreneurs in the German community, owning companies like Piller's Sausages and Andres Wines, which are household names in the Toronto area.

Toronto's German community now numbers over 350,000 and has dispersed throughout the city. Among the most renowned members of the German Toronto community is John Polanyi, professor of chemistry at the University of Toronto, a Nobel prize winner, and a profound peace activist. Sir Adam Beck, a German Torontonian considered by many to be Ontario's greatest civil servant, was knighted for his work in establishing Ontario Hydro, Ontario's hydroelectricity producer. His work led to the development of Niagara Falls as a source of electricity for the area, and a bronze statue honoring him rises above University Avenue at Queen Street West. German musicians were important in establishing the Toronto Symphony and the Mendelssohn Choir.

Black Creek Pioneer Village, Jane Street/Steeles Avenue West (416-736-1733), is a popular historical reconstruction of a German immigrant's farm village. Originally the farm of Daniel Stong, who settled the area in the nineteenth century, Black Creek Pioneer Village is a fascinating excursion into Ontario's immigrant past with a particular interest to those curious about the German-Canadian community.

Another museum of interest is the **German-Canadian Heritage Museum,** Highway 10, Brampton (905-759-8879), which is also located in a restored farmhouse but possesses a wealth of information on German-Canadian settlement in the region.

Toronto also has a small but very active Austrian community. Like their German counterparts, Austrians blend into Toronto's cosmopolitan makeup, but support a variety of Austrian cultural and social organizations throughout the city. The center for the community is the **Austrian Club Edelweiss.** Founded in 1949, the club grew out of the Society for Austrian Relief, organized to provide relief for the struggling post-war Austrian economy and to help patriate Austrian immigrants to Canada.

It was during this post-war period that the largest wave of Austrian immigrants came to Canada in general and to Toronto in particular. From 1946 to 1955, Austria was divided into zones governed by the victorious Allies, and many Austrians decided to leave their homelands in pursuit of better economic opportunities elsewhere.

The first Austrians to come to Canada were the German-speaking agricultural workers from the Galicia region of what was then the Austrian-Hungarian empire. They were joined by the first mass migration of Austrians after the empire's dissolution at the end of World War I. More followed after the "Anschluss" occupation of Austria by the Nazis in 1938. Immigration slowed as the Austrian economy recovered its vitality in the 1960s and 1970s.

Today there are approximately 10,000 Torontonians of Austrian descent in the city. Their contribution and vitality belies their relatively small number. Prominent Torontonians from this community include many artists and musicians such as pianist Anton Kuerti, conductor Agnes Grossman, and sculptors Anne Kahane and Cara Popescu, as well as businessman Frank Stronach.

Religion

Toronto's German Canadians go to a variety of churches throughout the city, including Catholic, Lutheran, and other Protestant denominations. The majority of Austrians in Toronto are Roman Catholic and belong to a variety of parishes.

First Lutheran Church, *116 Bond Street (416-977-4786).*

Martin Luther Church, *2379 Lakeshore Boulevard West (416-251-8293).*

Saint George's Lutheran Church, *410 College Street (416-921-2687).*

Willowdale (Lutheran) Evangelical Church, *236 Finch Street East (416-223-3182).*

Saint Patrick's German Parish Catholic Church, *131 McCaul Street (416-598-4835).*

Christ the King/Dietrich Bonhoeffer Church, *149 Baythorn Road (905-881-9154).* Catholic.

Chapel of the Evangelical Fellowship, *778 Ossington Avenue (416-534-3030).*

Christus-Kirche, *2210 Warden Avenue (416-494-2201).*

Epiphany Church, *20 Old Kingston Road (416-284-5922).*

German Evangelical Mission Chapel, *236 Finch Avenue West (416-223-3182).*

German United Church, *20 Glebe Road East (416-484-6849).*

Humbervale Park Baptist Church, *763 Royal York Road (416-231-5314).*

Organizations

The **Austrian Club Edelweiss,** *207 Beverley Street (416-979-2048).*

The major cultural and social center of the community, which has an excellent restaurant and sponsors such activities as folk dancing, a vocal choir, a chess club, and weekend dances with Austrian bands.

The **Canadian-Austrian Society of Toronto,** *345 Adelaide Street West, #102 (416-593-2583).*

The Austrian government's **Austrian Consulate General,** *2 Bloor Street East (416-863-0649),* and **Austrian Trade Commission** *(same location).*

Both offer programs of interest to the Austrian community.

The **Goethe Institute,** *1067 Yonge Street (416-924-3327).*

Has an extensive German-language library as well as an art gallery and lecture rooms where German-language films and lectures on German culture, history, and philosophy are conducted.

The **Historical Society of Mecklenburg,** *PO Box 193, Station K (416-759-8897).*

Another influential German-Canadian cultural organization offering lectures and films throughout the year on German culture and history.

The **German Canadian Business and Professional Association,** *100 Adelaide Street West (416-863-9453).*

A highly influential association involved in political, charitable, and social activities in the German-Canadian community.

Bayern Club Canada, *68 Barkwin Drive (416-741-4787).*

Berliner Club, *3665 Flamewood Drive (905-822-5867).*

Bund Deutscher Karnevals-Gesellschaften Kanada, *41 Lakeshore Avenue (416-251-6449).*

Canadian-German Chamber of Commerce, *480 University Avenue (416-598-3355).*

Central Organization of Sudeten German CB Can, *179 Durant Avenue (416-635-6869).*

The umbrella organization for German immigrant families from the Sudeten region of Czechoslovakia.

Fredrich Schiller Foundation for German-Canadian Culture, *PO Box 406, Station K (416-488-3846).*

Kanadischer Verband Deutscher Renter EastV., *545 Sherborne Street (416-922-1565).*

Ontario Goethe Society, *360 Ridelle Avenue (416-256-0219).*

Association of Danube Swabians, *214 Main Street (416-698-3908).*

The umbrella group for a wide array of Danube Swabian groups.

Saint Michaelwerke, *131 McCaul Street (416-881-6350).*

Home to a number of Danube Swabian festivals and social events, as well as the **Saint Michael's Concert Dancers.**

German Language Schools, *6 Thurgate Crescent (905-881-0227).*

Preservation and extension of the German language is a key concern for many members of the community. These schools provide German-language training, as do many schools and universities in the area.

The **German-Canadian Congress** *(613-728-6850).*

Based in Ottawa, this is the main political lobbying group for the community and acts as an umbrella group promoting German culture in Canada.

═══ Holidays and Celebrations ═══

January/February	*Fasching Karneval (German Mardi Gras).* Masquerade parties and carnivals mark this holiday before the start of Lent.
May 1	*Mayday,* also *German Labor Day.*
May 23	Establishment of the West German constitution.
June	Annual pilgrimage of German Catholics to Mary Lake in King City on the second Sunday of the

	month to pay homage to the Germans expelled from Eastern Europe.
September 24	*Kirchweihfest,* the annual church dedication day for Saint Patrick's Church.
October	*Oktoberfest.* Large festivities are held in the nearby Kitchener-Waterloo area.
October 26	*Austrian National Day,* commemorating the return of Austrian sovereignty in 1955 and its declaration of neutrality.
December 6	*Saint Nikolaus Day.*
December 25	*Christmas.* Lighted Christmas trees were first developed by the Germans in 1781 when they were introduced by Baroness Friederike von Riedesel.

⟲ Restaurants, Cafés, and Nightclubs ⟲

A number of German restaurants are available in the Toronto area serving specialties such as *schnitzel* (fried and breaded veal and pork), *spaetzel* (little dumplings), *kassler ripchen* (smoked pork loin), sauerkraut, *sauerbraten* (sweet-and-sour marinated pot roast), sausages, and wonderful German desserts like Black Forest cake and Sacher tortes. Besides the places noted here, listings in the Hungarian, Polish, and Czech sections of later chapters may be of interest as there is a great deal of overlap in the cuisines of these central European countries.

Blackhorn Steak House, *251 Ellesmere Road (416-449-2841).*

A steak and seafood house serving a variety of German specialties such as sauerbraten and sausages with sauerkraut. Reasonable prices, featuring a family setting.

Café Bavaria and Bakery, *3244 Eglinton Avenue East (416-264-4535).*

A charming bakery café in Scarborough serving a variety of German sandwiches, salads, and other specialties, including superb German rye breads, pastries, tortes, and cakes.

Café May, *396 Roncesvalles Avenue (416-532-9218).*

An attractive, homey restaurant reminiscent of an Alpine chalet with its intricate wood work, decorative plates, and excellent German food. Specialties include *kassler rippenspeer mit weinkraut* (roast smoked pork loin with wine sauerkraut), sauerbraten, sausages cooked with sauerkraut, and German potato salad, as well as an excellent array of hearty German beers.

Fabian Café, *876 Markham Road (416-438-1561).*

Good selection of German pastries as well as luncheon specialties and sandwiches.

Graf Bobby Café Restaurant, *36 Wellington Street East (416-364-3916).*

Long a favorite of visitors to Toronto's theater district, the Graf Bobby serves a variety of Austrian delicacies, including delicious strudels, schnitzels, and dumplings as well as a variety of crisp Austrian wines.

Griffith's, *2086 Queen Street East (416-690-4022).*

A beautifully decorated restaurant in Toronto's Beaches area, filled with rich woods and the mellow smells of fine Austrian cuisine. A variety of schnitzels, excellent cheesecakes, and pastries, and a rooftop café that's open in the summer make this a popular and enjoyable culinary stop. Servers wear Austrian costume.

Old Barn Café, *1663 Bloor Street West (416-531-1311).*

Full German dinners and lunches, including a variety of schnitzels, appetizers, and desserts. Excellent array of schnapps and beers.

Old Country Inn, *198 Main Street, Markham (905-477-2715).*

Located in the tony Unionville neighborhood of the Toronto suburb of Markham, the Old Country Inn looks like an old Austrian inn and offers a superb and eclectic array of schnitzels, goulash, sausages, and pork loin. Superb desserts and pastries are available also, all in a reconverted nineteenth-century house decorated with flowers, a wintergarten, and stained-glass windows. A lovely destination for an out-of-town trip.

The Musket, *40 Advance Road (416-231-6488).*

A pleasant, formal German restaurant with a wide variety of German specialties as well as other eastern and central European foods. Live music and dancing is available, as are two outdoor patios.

Wally's Restaurant, *5088 Dundas Street West (416-234-9792).*

Excellent German food in a quiet unpretentious atmosphere. Inexpensive prices; known for excellent cabbage rolls.

Zum Rhein Restaurant, *Ontario Place (416-593-0468).*

An excellent array of German food served at the Ontario Place complex.

Food Sources

Bakeries

German bakeries serve wonderful rye breads, including rich, dark pumpernickels, as well as a variety of excellent pastries such as tortes and strudels. The following are some of the best German bakeries in the area.

Backerhaus Veit, *70 Whitmore (905-890-9229).*

Known for its sourdough ryes and whole-grain breads. Also has excellent cakes and pastries.

Dimpflmeier Bakery, *26–34 Alliance Avenue (416-239-3031).*

Rye breads and strudels are the specialties. Especially well known for the stollen, which is considered to be better than that in Germany.

Rudolph's Specialty Bakeries, *390 Alliance Avenue (416-763-4375).*

Hearty rye breads, strudels, and specialty pastries.

Butchers/Delis/Grocers

Bittner Packers, *2300 Yonge Street (416-482-0802).*

A fine array of German meats and sausages, as well as some specialty imported items.

Brandt Meats, *1878 Mattawa Avenue (905-235-2750).*

Good selection of German meats, including an excellent variety of smoked pork.

Cheese Boutique and Delicatessen, *2286 Bloor Street West (416-762-6292).*

An excellent array of German and Eastern European sausages, deli meats, cheeses, and condiments. One of the best gourmet shops in the city.

Vienna Fine Foods, *1050 Birchmount (416-759-4481).*

Producers of some of the best sausage in the Toronto area, this factory outlet store carries the best smoked sausage and bratwurst available in the city, as well as a variety of Austrian sausages, relishes, and other gourmet food items.

Vienna Gourmet Foods, *700 King Street West (416-360-0060).*

An excellent neighborhood deli and grocery selling a variety of Austrian sausages, smoked meats, imported food products, baked goods, and some gift items, as well as German-language magazines and newspapers.

Shops

A number of stores carry German-language books, gifts, records, tapes, and assorted items of interest, including:

Book Barrel, *2284 Bloor Street West (416-767-7417).*

German Book and Gift Store, *457 ½ Spadina Avenue (416-979-2725).*

Hanover Centre Records and Tapes, *375 Bloor Street West (416-535-8474).*

 **Media**

Publications

Austrian Publications, *455 Spadina Avenue (416-595-9714).*

Importers of a variety of Austrian magazines and newspapers.

Deutsche Presse, *455 Spadina Avenue (416-595-9714).*

The largest circulation German weekly in the city.

Kanada Kurier, *88 Laird Drive (416-423-9965).*

A Canada-wide German-language weekly.

Heimatbote, *1 Lyme Regis Crescent (416-267-8425).*

A Danube Swabian newsletter and bulletin.

Canadiana Germanica, *PO Box 406, Station K (416-488-3846).*

A quarterly journal of German-Canadian studies.

Radio and Television

A number of German-language music and current events shows are on radio, including:

"Continental Breakfast," CKQT-FM 94.9, *360 King Street West (905-686-1350).*

"German Continental Breakfast," CIAO-AM 790, *50 Kennedy Road South (905-453-7111).*

"German Program," CHIN-FM 100.7, *622 College Street (416-531-9991).*

"Sigi Leipold," 104.7-FM.

Danube Swabian music on Sundays.

"Austrian Program," CHIN 100.7-FM, *637 College Street (416-531-9991).*

This show plays Austrian music and provides information of interest to the Austrian community.

There is also a variety of German-language television shows:

"Drei Damen Vom Grill," Channel 47 MTV, *545 Lakeshore Boulevard West (416-593-4747).*

"Ein Erfueltes Leben," Channel 47 MTV, *545 Lakeshore Boulevard West (416-593-4747).*

"Fur Jeden Etwas," Channel 57 CITY-TV, *299 Queen Street West (416-591-5757).*

—Nearby Excursions: Saint Jacobs—

About an hour's drive from Toronto is the heart of German Mennonite country, just north of Kitchener-Waterloo. The little town of Saint Jacobs is the heart of this community, and it's been beautifully restored and developed to show off the great local food, crafts, and antiques. An information center provides background material on German Mennonite immigration, religion, and history. An excellent inn, **Benjamin's,** serves superb food and provides comfortable accommodation for visitors. Other restaurants, cafés, delis, and bakeries are also found in the area, as is one of Ontario's best country butchers.

There is a lovely walking trail along an old abandoned canal and the Conestogo River for those who wish to hike through the beautiful farmland. The town itself is full of heritage homes, and on Thursdays and Fridays the nearby Waterloo farmer's market abounds with local produce, meat, and food specialties.

Nearby towns such as Elmira, Heidelberg, and Kitchener-Waterloo also have a strong German flavor, with Kitchener-Waterloo hosting North America's largest Oktoberfest every October. A great ethnic afternoon outing.

Greek Toronto

History

Toronto's Greek community is one of the largest and most active ethnic communities in the city. Settled by the waves of Greek migrants who came here first in the post–World War II and post–Greek civil war eras (1948–1952) and later accelerated their emigration during the military junta period in the 1960s, Toronto's Greek community numbers over 125,000. It is the second largest Greek settlement outside of Greece (the largest being in the borough of Queens in New York City) and makes Toronto the fourth largest Greek city in the world.

Toronto's first known Greek settler goes back to 1864 with the arrival of Dr. Petros Constantinides, a scholar and surgeon. Some Greek immigrants came at the turn of the century to work on the building of Ontario's northern railroads. Yet fewer than twenty Greek names are present in turn-of-the-century registers, and Greek emigration to Canada as a whole, like much ethnic emigration here, didn't really take place until the upheavals of the post–World War II era.

Its first cultural presence in the city was marked in 1909 with the opening of the Saint George's Greek Orthodox church; both the Greek Orthodox and Greek Eastern Rites churches remain a strong cultural presence in the community. While the sporadic immigration of the early 1900s was primarily of rural Greeks, the waves of post-war immigrants were of a more urbanized population, who congregated in what had been the white working-class area of east Toronto known as "the Danforth."

Political, social, and philanthropic clubs grew with the more marked presence of the Greek population in the area. While many of the immigrants who came to Toronto were craftsmen and laborers looking for work in the diverse industries of the area, over 10,000 professionals also joined the migration, particularly during the era of the military junta. Among the most prominent was Andreaous Papendreaou, the current Greek Prime Minister, who taught economics for many years at Toronto's York University.

The upheavals of the late 1940s and 1960s in Greece also gave rise to many of the philanthropic and political organizations that served as a focus for community activity and cohesion here. The Greek nationalism and cultural revival following World War I and the 1919–1920 conflict with Turkey also gave rise to a community that was interested in preserving its language and culture. Canada's long-term tolerance of cultural differences and diversity has helped that interest flourish, and Greek Canadians have continued to maintain their language and interest in their homeland. They have also been active contributors to Toronto's development as an international urban center.

Religion

Greek Orthodox Church

As with the Greek population itself, many of Toronto's Greek Orthodox churches have moved into the northern and eastern suburbs of the city, but a few active ones remain in the downtown core near the Danforth.

The Greek Orthodox Diocese of Canada, 40 Donlands Avenue (416-462-0833), is the main congregation downtown and the residence of the head of the Greek Orthodox Church in Canada. Worshippers meet at the **Transfiguration of Our Lord Greek Orthodox Church** located at the same address (416-465-2345).

The oldest church remains **Saint George's Greek Orthodox Church,** 115 Bond Street (416-977-3342). Originally consecrated as the Holy Blossom Temple, the church was rededicated in 1909 and houses a number of mosaics and icons produced by monks. Other Greek churches in the Danforth area include **Saint Irene Chrisovalantou Greek Orthodox Church,** 66 Gough Avenue (416-465-8213); **Saint Anargyros Greek Orthodox**

Church, 281 Jones Avenue (416-463-9664); and the **Greek Orthodox Monastery of Saint Raphael,** 230 Glebemount Avenue (416-425-8068).

The second oldest Greek Orthodox church in the city, the **Greek Orthodox Annunciation of the Virgin Mary,** 136 Sorauren Avenue (416-537-2665), is located in one of the earlier areas of Greek settlement in Toronto, the West End Parkdale neighborhood.

One of the newest and grandest of the Greek churches is **Saint Nicholas,** 3840 Finch Avenue East (416-291-4367), whose walls and ceilings are covered in Byzantine icons painted by Father Theodore Koufas over the course of four years. It is a testament to the growth, success, and prosperity the Greek community in Toronto has experienced over the years, as well as the hard work and dedication it has shown.

Other Churches

Two non-Diocesan Greek Orthodox churches that still follow the Julian calendar for religious holidays are **The Greek Orthodox Church of the Mother of God of Proussa,** 461 Richmond Street East (416-364-8919), and **The Greek Orthodox Church of Saint Nektarios,** 1223 Dovercourt Road (416-537-7283). A **Greek Gospel Church,** 704 Mortimer Avenue (416-467-7337), preaches to an evangelical congregation of second-generation Greeks.

Organizations

The Greek community has been very active in providing a variety of organizations for community support, social action, and cultural education. Among its major accomplishments was the building of the **Hellenic Home for the Aged,** 33 Winona Drive (416-654-7700), which includes a seven-story seniors' apartment building, houses a recreational and educational center, and serves as a community center for cultural activities with a lounge which regularly shows Greek-language movies.

Another important community center is the **Hellenic Cultural Centre,** located in the **Greek Community of Metropolitan Toronto** complex at 30 Thorncliffe Park Drive (416-425-2485). It has a variety of artistic, cultural, and educational programs—including programs of Greek dance, theater, films, and music—and a large Greek-language library. It also serves as the headquarters for Greek cultural activities during Toronto's annual Caravan cultural extravaganza in June. Its social services branch is located at 760 Pape Avenue (416-469-1155).

Other cultural centers include the **All Saints Cultural Centre,** 3125 Bayview Avenue (416-221-4611), and the **Alexander the Great Youth Centre and Athletic Complex,** 1385 Warden Avenue (416-755-8867), both of which have sports clubs, soccer teams, folk dancing, and educational and cultural activities.

What the Greek Orthodox Church was for many of the Greek immigrants in the forties and fifties, the Pan Hellenic Socialist Movement (PASOK) was for the refugees from the military junta in the late sixties and early seventies. PASOK members were to have a profound influence on the politicization of the Greek community, and were instrumental in organizing the Hellenic Canadian Congress and its myriad support organizations within Toronto and in greatly expanding its other social and charitable activities. Many other Panhellenic and regional Greek social organizations are still active, including:

Arcadian Federation of Canada, *422 Danforth Avenue.*

Federation of the Aegean Islands, *PO Box 393, Station O.*

Greek Canadian Cultural Organization, *PO Box 424, Station J.*

Greek Canadian Educational Association, *1706 Danforth Avenue.*

Greek Canadian Senior Citizens Club, *918 Danforth Avenue.*

Hellenic Canadian Congress, *455 Spadina Avenue (416-971-7321).*

Also headquarters for the **Hellenic Canadian Federation of Ontario Charitable and Educational Foundation** (416-591-7382).

Rawlinson Community Organization, *231 Glenholme Avenue.*

Greek live theater has returned to the Danforth area with the opening of the **Rex J. Kallinoikis Centre,** 653 Danforth Avenue (416-461-7247). This 1,300-seat theater presents a variety of Greek movies, dramas, and musical shows. Cafés and gift shops also adorn the small mall-like complex attached to the theater, making this a major center of Greek cultural and social activity in the city.

Greek folk dancing is also performed by the **Folk Dancing Group of the Greek Community** at the Greek Community Centre, 30 Thorncliffe Park Drive. Participatory dances are held as well.

══════ Holidays and Celebrations ══════

January 1	*Saint Basil's Day* (New Year's), one of the two most important religious holidays of the season (the other being Epiphany) for the Greek Orthodox religion.
January 6	*Epiphany,* celebrated by Greeks the same way other people celebrate Christmas, with gift-giving and celebratory dinners.
January 20	*Theophany,* celebrated by Greek worshippers who follow the Julian calendar.
March 25	*Feast of the Annunciation of the Virgin Mary.* Also a celebration of Greek independence from the Ottoman Empire, annually marked by a parade down Danforth Avenue.
March/April	*Easter,* one of the Greek community's biggest holidays, marked by lamb roasts and other special foods, including *mageritsa soup* (made with lamb entrails, spring onions, and egg lemon sauce) and *tsoureki* (a sweetbread similar to Portuguese pao douce or Ukrainian bobka). Greek Orthodox churches hold a candlelight procession at midnight to mark this solemn occasion.
September 14	*Feast Day of the Holy Cross,* commemorating the finding of the Holy Cross by the Byzantine Empress Saint Helena.

Other events of profound interest to the community include Greek national elections (expatriate Canadian Greeks are able to vote in these elections) and the European and World Cup Soccer championships.

Restaurants

Toronto has long been renowned for its wide array of excellent Greek restaurants, cafés, and ouzeris, most of which are located along the Danforth. They have now been joined by a new generation of Greek restaurateurs who have brought nouvelle cuisine Hellene to the area, augmenting the classic souvlaki and spanakopita bistros that have long been a regular rendezvous for many Torontonians. Greek food by and large is peasant food, the flavors are rich and flavorful, menus are simple and similar, prices are generally inexpensive, and the atmosphere is homey.

A major upgrading and modernization of all the following restaurants has been proceeding over the last five years, and some of the newer restaurants have brought a wonderful artistic flair to the area in their decorations. Lamb, pork, chicken, calamari, and shrimp are the staples. If you prefer lamb in your souvlaki, make sure the restaurant serves it, as many of the souvlaki houses substitute pork unless you specifically request otherwise.

Astoria Shish Ke Bob House, *390–400 Danforth Avenue (416-463-2838).*

Long a Toronto favorite, the Astoria was upgraded and expanded three years ago and like many of the Greek restaurants on the Danforth, has added comfort and a better wine list to its excellent Greek food. Best known for its *souvlaki* on a bun—grilled pork or lamb served on a toasted garlic bun with tomatoes, onions, and spicy garlicky tsetskiki sauce.

Athenian Garden, *526 Danforth Avenue (416-465-4001).*

A pleasant souvlaki house, long a staple on the Danforth. Excellent home-baked *spanakopita* (spinach-and-cheese pie) and *baklava,* the sticky pistachio nut and phyllo pastry dessert that is a staple at most Greek restaurants.

Byzo's, *535 Danforth Avenue (416-778-1100).*

A big new modern Greek taverna and restaurant on the south side of the Danforth, Byzo's serves most of the classic Greek grilled and baked recipes, including excellent lamb shanks and moussaka. It also has a large array of appetizers and a lovely outdoor eating area for summertime al fresco dining and people watching right on the Danforth.

Christina's, *492 Danforth Avenue (416-463-4418).*

A very attractive ouzeria, café, and restaurant, Christina's is decorated in warm rich Mediterranean colors and has an excellent menu of Greek and Mediterranean appetizers, a fine wine list, and an array of coffees and brandies.

Ellas, *702 Pape Avenue (416-463-0334).*

One of the oldest restaurants in the area, Ellas has recently been completely refurbished. Presenting a full range of Greek specialties, Ellas also has excellent steaks and grilled fish as well as a large variety of Greek appetizers.

Epikurion Restaurant, *First Canadian Place (416-362-6761).*

As its name suggests, this is an epicurean treat encompassing the whole array of Hellenic cuisines and serving many unique specialties you won't find in other Toronto-area Greek restaurants. Unlike many other Greek restaurants, prices here can be more expensive, but the atmosphere is equally tony in keeping with its location in the heart of Toronto's financial district.

Kapilyo Restaurant, *401 Danforth Avenue (416-463-4847).*

A newcomer to the area, Kapilyo has a café atmosphere, with a large open courtyard for seating in the summertime. Bright and airy with well-cooked Greek staple items and a few new innovations for younger patrons.

Mr. Greek Shishkebobs, *568 Danforth Avenue (416-461-5470); 1033 Bay Street (416-960-8800); 1957 Kennedy Road (416-292-7788).*

Long a favorite on the Danforth, Mr. Greek has taken a successful souvlaki-house formula and brought it to all parts of the Metro Toronto area. Especially recommended is the Kennedy Road location in Scarborough, which is bright, open, airy, and inexpensive.

MYTH, *417 Danforth Avenue (416-461-8383).*

An airy, beautifully decorated modern restaurant with a large pool hall and jazz music, MYTH also serves the *best* phyllo-pastry appetizers on the Danforth. In particular, the seasoned lamb sausage in phyllo served with a light oriental sauce is a wonderful cross-cultural combination, as are many other items on the menu. The decor is a cross between Viennese modern and art nouveau with nary a white stucco wall in sight, and the menu would send a Greek traditionalist into a state of shock, but MYTH captures the spirit of a new, artistic, and more eclectic Greece and fits in well with the artier cafés along this street.

Nefelli, *389 Danforth Avenue (416-744-1411).*

An intimate new addition to the Danforth strip, Nefelli serves Greek cuisine with an Alexandrine twist combining some Helleno-Egyptian flavors into the cooking. Some grilled foods are available, but most of the menu selections are baked specialties, many with the wonderful saffron and cinnamon that mark so much good Levantine cooking.

Omonia Restaurant, *426 Danforth Avenue (416-465-2179).*

Extremely popular on the weekends with lines often stretching out of the recently expanded restaurant, Omonia has the best lamb chop and roast lamb dinners on the street. Perfectly grilled or roasted lamb served with garlic potatoes, saffron rice, a Greek salad, and bread. You can also get excellent Greek sausage here. The decor is comfortable and homey, and there is a large outdoor patio that is generally quite crowded in the summertime.

Ouzeri, *500-A Danforth Avenue (416-778-0500).*

Started by one of Toronto's legendary restaurateurs, Aris Aristedes, who loved to open interesting new restaurants but could never manage to make money from them. His ouzeria remains one of the brightest spots on the Danforth. A Greek tapas-style restaurant with a wide range of Greek appetizers and main courses and an excellent wine bar, the restaurant is decorated in an eccentrically rich, artsy manner with numerous modern and naive mosaics, paintings and murals. Aristedes has long been gone from the actual running of the restaurant, but his spirit lives on in its food and atmosphere.

Palace Restaurant, *722 Pape Avenue (416-463-3393).*

One of the most elegant of the Greek restaurants in the neighborhood, the Palace also has a long history in the area. Well known for its red snapper, scallops, and other seafood specialties, the Palace has the white stucco walls, large pine beams, and Greek paintings you associate with the best tavernas in Greece.

Pan, *516 Danforth Avenue (416-466-8158).*

My current favorite, Pan is one of the Danforth's newest restaurants and presents an interesting menu of nouvelle Greco cuisine, including beautifully prepared lamb shanks with orzo in a rich, creamy sauce; excellent grilled lamb chops coated in cinnamon and nutmeg; and a superb feta cheese-stuffed chicken breast. Make sure you get the excellent pita bread grilled in olive oil and herbs as a starter.

Pappas Grill, *440 Danforth Avenue (416-469-9595).*

Long a favorite with the denizens of this neighborhood, Pappas Grill is more Mediterranean than Greek, and its menu will remind you more of Corfu than Athens. Excellent lamb and calamari are complemented with thin-crust brick-oven pizzas, an excellent array of local microbrewery draft beers on tap, and a good array of wines by the glass.

Patris, *888 Danforth Avenue (416-466-1967).*

A little east of the main run of Danforth restaurants, Patris has some of the best Greek seafood available. In particular, the calamari is among the best in the city and the best served among the Greek restaurants on the Danforth.

Philoxenia, *519 Danforth Avenue (416-461-1997).*

A modern, beautifully decorated restaurant serving more cooked Greek specialties as opposed to the grills that permeate the Danforth. Specialties here include superb *moussaka,* the rich layered meal that includes layers of eggplant, beef, potatoes, and cream.

Cafés and Nightclubs

While the Danforth is a very active area for Toronto's nightlife, only a few local establishments still have the Greek folk music that used to permeate the neighborhood years ago. Both **Christina's** and the **Ouzeri** bring in Greek and Latin folk music performers on the weekends. The sound of the bouzouki has generally been replaced by the guitar and synthesizer for most younger Greeks, but a few clubs still play on, including the following:

Deelina, *686 Danforth Avenue (416-466-4233).*

A café that opens late and stays open till the wee hours of the morning. Not licensed; the music tends to appeal to younger Greek folk music fans.

Iliaoa Café, *Danforth Avenue (416-778-7796).*

A new addition to the Danforth, Iliaoa has an assortment of beautifully prepared Greek and European pastries, as well as fine coffees and teas, all set
in a pleasant modern room.

Kanaria Cafe, *Carlaw Avenue (416-461-4701).*

A traditional Greek café hidden away at the side entrance of a building, the
Kanaria has a very Greek clientele and superb coffee as well as late-night
Greek and Mediterranean folk music.

Playboy Bouzouky Restaurant and Tavern, *635
Danforth Avenue (416-465-1999).*

A classic old-fashioned bouzouki bar with occasional belly dancers and
stage shows.

Qunta Restaurant, *484 Danforth Avenue (416-469-
1921).*

Occasional players on weekend nights.

Yiannis Restaurant, *437 Danforth Avenue (416-462-
2575).*

Regular bouzouki and folk-music performances throughout the week.

Food Sources

The Danforth has a wide array of excellent Greek specialty bakeries, delis,
and food stores, in addition to many other fine shops in the area. Long
renowned for its twenty-four-hour market garden shops like Sunkist and
Sun Valley that have been owned and operated by local Greek families for
many years, the Danforth also has a variety of more specialized butchers,
bakers, and food purveyors.

Bakeries

A number of Greek bakeries, many with cafés serving rich Greek coffees,
are on both sides of the Danforth. While the Greeks are known mainly for
their baklava, they also make excellent chocolate cream-filled cookies, a variety of breads including the ever-present unleavened pita bread, and huge

cakes. Pies and tortes are not a Greek specialty except for savory spinach-and-cheese-filled phyllo-pastry pies, which are available hot out of the oven at many of the bakeries listed here.

Akropol Bakery, *458 Danforth Avenue (416-465-1232).*

Pastries, cookies, and savory pies make this a favorite Greek hangout.

Donlands Bakery, *1055 Pape Avenue (416-421-3010).*

European pastries and cookies as well as some of the best Greek breads in the area.

Main Greek Bakery, *2584 Danforth Avenue (416-690-6548).*

An East End Toronto center for Greek pastries and foods.

Pallas Bakery, *629 Danforth Avenue (416-461-1248).*

One of the largest Greek bakeries on the Danforth with a large dessert café, pastries, and towering wedding cakes. Recently updated and renovated.

Seven Star Bakery, *544 Danforth Avenue (416-463-9524).*

Excellent chocolate cookies, special holiday sweet breads, and spanakopita, as well as a busy café.

Stany Greek Bakery, *1015 Pape Avenue (416-423-9781).*

A small unpretentious place serving savory pitas and other Greek breads.

Butchers and Fish Markets

A number of good Greek butchers still remain on the Danforth, providing fresh lamb and other Greek specialties to their customers. Most of the lamb sold here is fresh Ontario lamb, some of the best you can buy anywhere in the world. You can also find excellent pork and Greek sausages, including specialty lamb and holiday sausages.

Athens Meat Market, *565 Danforth Avenue (416-461-7733).*

Lamb, veal, and specialty relishes.

Ellas Meat Market, *674 Pape Avenue (416-461-1211).*

A variety of Greek meats and sausages as well as other deli products.

Louis Meat Market, *449 Danforth Avenue (416-465-3364).*

Best lamb on the Danforth, cut to order.

Mister Greek Meat Market, *801 Danforth Avenue (416-469-0733).*

A general deli, including excellent Greek sausage and cheeses.

Oceans Fishmarket, *1849 Eglinton Avenue W (416-789-1497).*

A wide variety of fresh- and saltwater fish, including excellent red snapper and a variety of calamari and other seafood delicacies.

Cheeses

Greece is known for its feta cheese as well as other fine goat cheeses, and an excellent place to get a good array of these fine products is at **World of Cheeses,** tucked into the Pape subway station at the corner of Pape and Danforth Avenues (416-463-7121). Open twenty-four hours a day, seven days a week, this is *the* place to go for that special feta.

Grocers and Delis

A few shops along the Danforth serve a variety of Greek specialty foods. Many of the general grocers in the area and throughout Metro Toronto also carry many Greek specialty products along with other ethnic specialties due to the high demand from these communities as well as other residents who have grown accustomed to the many ethnic cuisines available.

Athens Toronto Wholesale and Retail Food Store,
509 Danforth Avenue (416-463-5144).

Sells a wide variety of fresh and imported Greek delicacies from fine olives to figs, special oils, squid, pastries, and fresh-baked phyllo pies.

Broadview Delicatessen, *141 Danforth Avenue (416-465-9905).*

A large European deli serving many Greek specialties to area shoppers.

Nick's Delicatessen, *2934 Danforth Avenue (416-694-2557).*

An East End center for Greek meats, produce, and special imported goods, including an array of Greek olive oils.

Shops

A variety of Greek gift shops is also present in the Danforth, which remains the central shopping area for many Greek Torontonians.

Benix and Co., *542 Danforth Avenue (416-461-6331).*
Greek gifts and jewelry, as well as some folk costumes.

Dafni Gift Shop, *511 Danforth Avenue (416-465-0709).*
A variety of Greek mementos and clothing.

Hermes, *642 Danforth Avenue (416-466-9636).*
Greek jewelry, gifts, and handmade crafts.

Parthenon Jewelry and Gift Shop, *371 Danforth Avenue (416-469-2494).*

The first Greek jewelry store in Toronto, with a wide array of jewelry designs, handmade plaques, wall ornaments, and other gifts with a Greek flavor.

Other stores in the neighborhood carry Greek books, records, tapes, and so forth:

Greek City Video Records and Tapes, *433 Danforth Avenue (416-461-6244).*

The premier location for Greek music cassettes, CDs, and Greek-language videotapes.

Platon Canadian Greek Book and Variety Store, *781 Danforth Avenue (416-469-2593).*

Provides Greek-language books, newspapers, and magazines from Greece, as well as local Canadian publications.

 Media

Publications

Enimerosis, 463 Danforth Avenue (416-461-5023).
A weekly magazine.

EVODOMAD, 867 Pape Avenue (416-461-3519).
A weekly newspaper on Greek-Canadian activities and events.

Greek Press, 777 Danforth Avenue (416-778-7607).
Covers Greek Canadian and Greek homeland events on a biweekly basis.

Hellenic Canadian Chronicles (XPONIKA), 370 Danforth Avenue (416-465-4628).
A weekly newspaper focusing on the Greek-Canadian community.

Hellenic Tribune, 1425 Danforth Avenue (416-461-7800).
A biweekly newspaper focusing on events in the Greek homelands.

Ontario's Greek Telephone Directory and Almanac, 574 Dovercourt Road (416-534-4148).
An annual publication listing Greek businesses, community groups, and services.

Patrides: A Canadian Review in Greek, *PO Box 266,*
Station O (416-921-4229).

A thoughtful, monthly alternative look at Greek art and culture.

Radio and Television

CHIN Radio FM 100.7 carries Greek music shows Monday through Friday
from 7:30 to 9:00 AM and from 9:00 PM to midnight. CHIN Radio AM 1540
presents "Greek Canadian Melodies" every Sunday night from 6:00 to 8:00
PM. CIVR Radio AM 88.7 presents Greek music shows from 6:00 to 9:00
AM and 4:00 to 6:00 PM, Monday through Friday.

Channel 47 (MTV) carries a variety of Greek-language television
throughout the week, as do CITY-TV (channel 57) and Global-TV (channel
22) on the weekends. "Greek Paradise" on channel 57 (Sunday at 11:30 AM)
is one of the most popular shows.

—The Danforth: The Greek Toronto Heartland—

Although the Greek population has spread throughout the Toronto area, the
Danforth neighborhood remains the cultural, retail, and social hub of the
city's Greek community. Originally a market-garden farming area close to
the urban center, the Danforth remained isolated from downtown Toronto
by the Don Valley until the opening of the Bloor/Danforth viaduct in the
1920s. It then became a working-class suburb with well-laid-out streets,
solid brick houses, and a long and active retail shopping street that led to
Kingston Avenue and the eastern roads to Ottawa and Montreal.

Greek settlement in the area began in the late 1940s and early 1950s but
Greek predominance in this area didn't really take place until the 1960s and
the opening of the Bloor/Danforth subway. For emigrants coming to
Toronto at that time, the subway was a vital link to jobs in other parts of the
city, just as the streetcar lines of earlier phases of Toronto's growth had fu-
eled the development of its older ethnic neighborhoods.

The heyday of the Danforth as a center of Greek population in the city
was between 1965 and 1975. By the 1980s many older Greek families had
moved to the suburbs. The Toronto real estate boom accelerated that move
as many Greek residents used the inflationary rise in real estate prices to
cash in on their homes and move to suburban condominiums and developments once their children had moved out.

The Danforth remains the hub of Greek cultural and social life, not only
for Greek Torontonians but for many other residents and visitors who have
a chance to sample the Greek way of life prevalent in this area and find it attractive and enjoyable. While the Danforth is a more eclectic neighborhood

now than it was even ten years ago, the blocks from Logan Avenue east to Pape remain visibly and vibrantly Greek with a host of restaurants, cafés, bakeries, ouzeris, and shops.

Chilean, Latin American, and East Indian restaurants, nightclubs, and institutions have also sprung up in the area, but as populations in these communities have grown their foci have moved away from the Danforth to other areas of the city.

How to Get There: *You can reach the Danforth area by taking the Bloor subway to the Broadview, Chester, or Pape subway stations or by taking the Dundas or King Street streetcars to their Broadview station terminus. It is a five- to ten-minute drive from downtown Toronto. Parking is available behind the north side shops, on the main and side streets, and at the northwest and southwest corners of Pape and Danforth Avenues.*

chapter nine

Indian and South Asian Toronto

History

The South Asian immigrants to Toronto from India, Pakistan, Afghanistan, and Sri Lanka represent one of Toronto's largest and most visible ethnic communities. The busy shopping area of Little India on Gerrard Street East is packed on Sundays with families shopping, socializing, and eating at the many establishments along the street. Toronto's association with South Asian immigration goes back many years to when India was still an imperial colony of the British Empire.

Now over 250,000 Torontonians are of South Asian background, including Sikhs, Pakistanis, Indians, Sri Lankans, and Bengalis. They have a wide variety of faiths and live in diverse areas of the city but have strong commercial concentrations in the Leslieville, Donlands Avenue, and Junction areas of town. The suburban areas of Brampton and Malton also have large Indian populations.

Immigrants to Canada began to arrive as early as the mid-nineteenth century. They were primarily professional people who came to Canada via earlier immigration to the United States or Great Britain. The major push to Toronto began in the 1960s. First there were East Indian communities from Guyana and other Caribbean countries who came to Canada. Later they were joined by an increasing number of immigrants from South Asia itself.

From 1970 to 1975, a particularly large influx of Sri Lankans came to the Metro area due to the conflicts between the Tamils and Sinhalese in their homeland. One of Canada's most prominent writers, Michael Ondaatje, is of Sri Lankan background. A small but very active Zoroastrian community resides in Toronto as well. These Parsis (Parsees) generally come from the coastal areas around Bombay.

Bengalis who come from Bangladesh and northeastern India make up another large South Asian community. Many Bengalis arrived here in the late 1960s and 1970s from Europe where they had worked, gone to school, and acquired a variety of skills. Many are well-trained technicians and skilled workers, as well as active businesspeople. Bengalis have their own language and cultural heritage and have undertaken efforts to preserve them. Writer Himani Banerjee is a prominent Torontonian of this community.

The Pakistanis are a very large component of the South Asian community. Numerous Muslim Indians are naturally affiliated with this community as well as through linguistic and religious similarities. Many of the earliest immigrants to Toronto from South Asia were Pakistanis who came in the late 1950s looking for better economic prospects and opportunities. Many were also students who decided to stay in Canada when they finished college. The **Jami Mosque** on Boustead Avenue is the Pakistanis' religious and cultural focal point.

They have a number of other community organizations and are active in maintaining many of their rich cultural and musical traditions. Some prominent Pakistani Torontonians include Masood Q. Chowdhury, a prominent lawyer; N. Ashiraf, a partner in Dunn Woody and Company; and Shamin Khan, singer and orchestra leader.

One of the most visible of the South Asian communities is the turbaned Sikhs. Sikhs first came to Canada in the 1860s. A large contingent also came in 1902 as part of the British imperial forces that traveled through Canada to the coronation of King Edward VII. The first Sikhs in Toronto emigrated here from their settlements in British Columbia. They only started arriving in large numbers in the 1960s, many coming from communities in Great Britain, and many as part of the South Asian exodus from Uganda during Idi Amin's regime.

Many more came in the 1970s, working in a variety of service-oriented jobs, from taxicab drivers and airport security guards/attendants to small business owners. Hard work and community devotion has led many Sikhs to achieve substantial success in Toronto, and they have been a generous community in giving back volunteer work to their adopted city. Almost 40,000 Sikhs now live in the Metro area, and their community today is a diverse array of laborers, professionals, ex-soldiers, academics, and businesspeople. Some prominent Sikh Torontonians include artist Hardev Singh and Avtar Singh, owner of Singh farms.

South Asian communities work to preserve their cultural and linguistic identities in a variety of languages and backgrounds. Because of the British presence in the region and the nature of international commerce, English is the "terra lingua" of the area. Pakistanis also speak Urdu; many Indians speak Hindi; and Bengali, Punjabi, and Persian are other languages common to different segments of the community.

Toronto's Afghan community has roots that go back to the immigration of British army recruits from Afghanistan to Canada in the early 1900s. The vast majority of Toronto's Afghans, however, arrived in the 1970s as refugees from the internecine political struggles that shook their mountainous kingdom, joined by a larger wave of refugees following the Russian invasion in 1980. The population numbers a little over 3,000 today and is scattered throughout the city with some concentrations in the Keele/Sheppard and Parkdale areas.

Many of the refugees who have come to Canada have professional credentials as journalists and political leaders. Members of the community speak Pushtu and Dari Persian. Most have moved into small businesses, from repair and service shops to small stores. The most visible cultural retail identification is in a few carpet and tapestry shops that some Afghan merchants started in order to sell their country's best-known export products.

Most Afghans in the city are Sunni Muslim, though some Shiite Muslim Afghans are also present. In addition some Baha'i refugees from the border areas between Iran and Afghanistan have come to the area. The major cultural meeting point for the community used to be at **Afghan House,** 1055 Bathurst Street, where Afghans gathered to speak with others in their native languages and enjoy cultural festivals. This has now been replaced by two suburban community centers in North York and Scarborough, closer to the current community.

Religion

Toronto's Pakistani community is primarily Muslim, as are other South Asians living in Toronto. Their places of worship include:

Islamic Centre of Toronto/Jami Mosque, *56 Boustead Avenue (416-769-1192).*

There are also discussions on Islam once a month with non-Muslims.

Islamic Foundation of Toronto, *441 Nugget (416-321-0909).*

A large newly built mosque, prayer hall, school, library, and community hall serving the needs of Toronto's Islamic community.

Madinah Masjid, *1051 Danforth Avenue (416-465-7833).*

Makki Masjid, *8540 Torbram Road (905-791-9260).*

Malton Islamic Association, *7344 Custer Crescent (905-671-0891).*

Masgid Farooq-I-Azam, *Eglinton Avenue/Mavis Road (905-275-2697).*

Masjide-E Noor, *277 Scott Road (416-658-6667).*

Masjide Sunnatul Jamaat of Ontario, *Ladysmith Avenue (416-462-9262).*

Rexdale Mosque, *11 Mosque Crescent (416-881-1763).*

Toronto Area Region Islamic Congregation, *PO Box 66, Station U (416-822-4320).*

The two mosques most frequented by Toronto's Afghan community are the **Medinah Mosque,** 865 Danforth Avenue (416-465-7833), and the **Jami Mosque,** 56 Boustead Avenue (416-769-1192).

There are also a number of Hindu temples, prayer halls, and religious societies in the city:

Hindu Prathana Samaj, *62 Fern Avenue (416-536-9229).*

Vishnu Temple/Voice of the Vedas, *8640 Yonge Street (905-886-1724).*

Iskcon/Hare Krishna Temple, *243 Avenue Road (416-922-5415).*

Hindu Cultural Society, *1940 Ellesmere Road #7 (416-438-6661).*

Hindu Temple Society of Canada, *10945 Bayview Avenue (905-425-8720).*

Jag Durga Hindu Society, *37 Unita Grove (416-297-1146).*

Hindu Sabha, *PO Box 2092 (905-459-7984).*

Vedic Aryan Cultural Society, *15 Applemore Road (416-291-1949).*

Ganesh Temple, *8001 Bayview Avenue, Richmond Hill (905-883-9109).*

The Parsee community, primarily from the Bombay area, are members of the ancient Persian Zoroastrian religion. They have a **Zoroastrian Temple,** 3590 Bayview Avenue (416-733-4586), which also serves as a community center.

The Sikh community worships at a number of ashrams scattered throughout the Metro area, including:

Ontario Khalsa Darbar, *7080 Dixon Road (416-670-3311).*

Shromini Sikh Society Temple, *269 Pape Avenue (416-463-3132).*

Shri Guru Singh Sabha, *331 Old Weston Road (416-656-5699).*

Shri Guru Singh Sabha, *7280 Airport Road (905-674-1662).*

The **Jain Society of Toronto,** 48 Rosemeade (416-251-8112), is the group that organizes the worship of Toronto's Jains, an Indian sect. The **Asian Presbyterian Church,** 41 Kendleton Drive (416-743-7680), ministers to the small Protestant population from South Asia.

Organizations

Two schools teach Arabic and Urdu to the Pakistani community:

Islamic Community School, *Sherway Gardens (905-272-4303).*

Rexdale Arabic School, *11 Mosque Crescent (416-881-1763).*

The **Afghan Association of Ontario (Canada)** has two suburban locations. One is in North York at 29 Pemican Court (416-744-9289), the other is in Scarborough at 1200 Markham Road (416-438-0808). Both centers provide counseling services for community members and new immigrants as well as a variety of cultural activities and events, including patriotic festivals and activities. Language courses covering English as a second language and native Afghan tongues are also conducted.

The **Islamic Community of Afghans in Canada,** 746 Warden Avenue (416-757-2553), also plays a very important role in both the social and religious affairs of the Afghan community.

The **Afghan Information & Rehabilitation Bureau of Canada,** 132 Railside (416-391-4432), is another community services organization, as are the two branches of **Afghan Women Counselling & Integrated Community Support Centres,** 3969 Chesswood (416-636-1540), and 2333 Dundas Street West (416-588-3585), set up to help Afghan women deal with integrating into the very different Canadian society. These organizations are more secular and have been developed in response to community immigration needs in Canada.

While many Afghans who arrived in Canada came here as political refugees, many were also disenchanted with the constant political shifts and continuing sporadic civil war in their home country. As a result Afghan political organizations in Toronto have remained small scale. Their biggest turnout was to celebrate the withdrawal of Soviet troops from Afghanistan.

The Bengali community's main community association is **Prabasi Bengali Cultural Association,** 140 Millwick Road (416-740-7222).

The Pakistani community has a number of different associations handling community concerns, including:

Ontario Society of Pakistani Canadian Professionals and Academics, *693 Pape Avenue (416-466-2184).*

Federation of Pakistani Canadians, *370 Winona Drive (416-652-1028).*

The **Pakistan Canada Cultural Association,** *54 Bartlett Avenue (416-532-7556).*

The umbrella organization for the promotion of Urdu-language culture and studies. Member organizations include the Pakistani Canadian Education Committee.

The **South Asian Social Services Organization,** *123 Albion Road (416-748-1798).*

A broad-based community organization providing assistance for new immigrants as well as dealing with community concerns.

EIPROC, *1262 Don Mills Road (416-447-2940).*

Canadian Council of Hindus, *PO Box 295, Station O (416-471-1211).*

Hindu Cultural Society, *1 Morningview Trail (416-284-6282).*

Jain Society of Toronto, *48 Rosemeade (416-251-8112).*

Margus Dutt Foundation, *40 Coppard Avenue (905-471-1211).*

South Asian Women's Centre, *1022 Bloor Street West (416-537-2276).*

There are two main Sikh community groups:

Sikh Foundation, *40 King Street West (416-777-6697).*

Sri-Guru-Singh Sabha, *331 Old Weston Road (416-656-5699).*

══════ Holidays and Celebrations ══════

January	*Pogal-Sankranti,* a three-day harvest festival.
	During the first week of the month, the Sikh community celebrates the birthday of Guru Gobind Singh Ji (1666–1708), tenth guru and spiritual master.
January 26	*India's Republic Day,* celebrating the day in 1950 when India became a Republic.
March	*Holi,* a boisterous Hindu festival where participants throw colored water on each other.
March 21	*Jamshedi Navroz,* a Zoroastrian festival associated with the spring solstice.
March 23	*Pakistan National Day.*
April	*Birthday of Lord Rama.*
April 13	*Basakhi* (Sikh New Year). Also celebrated by Hindus and Jains as their New Year.
May	*Buddha Purnima,* celebration of the birth, salvation, and enlightenment of Buddha.
August	*Janmashtam Festival,* held in honor of Lord Krishna.
	Pateri, Zoroastrian New Year.
	Rathyata Festival, celebrated by the Hare Krishna Temple in the middle of the month.
August 14	*Pakistani Independence Day.*
August 15	*Indian Independence Day.*
September	*Onam Harvest Festival* of Kerala.
September/October	*Durga, Puja, and Dussehra Festival,* celebrating the triumph of good over evil.
October/November	*Birthday of Guru Nanak,* founder of the Sikh religion.

══ Restaurants, Cafés, and Nightclubs ══

South Asian cuisine is an incredibly diverse mix of ethnic cooking styles and spices that go far beyond the typical curry house that is often associated with it. Tandoori, Damsak, Sri Lankan, Madras, and Bengali cooking are all represented in Toronto with many restaurants serving a variety of different foods. The spices range from mild mint and yogurt-based sauces of the northern mountain areas to the hot pepper, coriander, and turmeric spices of the south. Afghani cuisine is similar to northern Indian cuisine in its extensive use of yogurt-based sauces and curries, a variety of rices and spicy grilled kebab meats. South Asian cuisine has much to offer to vegetarians as well, with many interesting and spicy dishes.

Annapurna Restaurant, *1085 Bathurst Street (416-537-8513).*

Originally started by the followers of Indian guru Sri Chinmoy, Annapurna serves an interesting blend of spicy vegetarian cuisine.

Ariana Restaurant, *255 College Street West (416-599-2618).*

Serves a variety of full-course Afghan meals, including five different kinds of kebabs, a variety of rice dishes, and whole-wheat Afghan flat breads. A variety of vegetarian dishes are also served.

Bombay Palace, *71 Jarvis Street (416-368-8048).*

A well-known chain of restaurants, Bombay Palace is also one of the older Indian restaurants in Toronto. Serves the full array of Indian dishes as well as a very popular Indian buffet.

Chaat Hut Snack Bar, *1438 A Gerrard Street East (416-466-2264).*

Specializing in kulfi phaluda and *pani puri* (puff pastries filled with potatoes, chick peas, and mint sauce).

Indian Rice Factory, *414 Dupont Street (416-961-3472).*

One of Toronto's oldest and best-known Indian restaurants, the Rice Factory is an excellent display of Sikh cooking with a variety of excellent curries, samosas, and other Indian specialties. Highly recommended with a very pleasantly decorated and comfortable decor and reasonable prices.

Kabul Kafe, *105 McCaul Street (416-971-5852).*

Located in the Village by the Grange's Ethnic Food Festival, a wonderful location full of inexpensive ethnic fast-food treats. It serves Afghan kebab and vegetarian dishes both as sit-down meals and wrapped sandwich-style treats.

Kamal Chaad, *1427 Gerrard Street East (416-465-2953).*

A popular snack shop serving a popular specialty called *pan* (betel leaves layered with betel nuts and sweet spices).

Le Kashmir, *605 Bloor Street West (416-533-5955).*

A Pakistani restaurant serving most South Asian favorites, as well as specialties such as a beautiful *chicken Kashmir* (chicken curry with toasted almonds and raisins) and *allo dum* (new potatoes served in a sauce with lemon and onions).

Madras Durbar, *1435 Gerrard Street East (416-465-2733).*

Serves South Indian vegetarian specialties from the Madras region. Very hot and spicy food mixed with cool, refreshing sauces and condiments.

Moghul Restaurant, *563 Bloor Street West (416-535-3315); 33 Elm Street (416-597-0522).*

A long-established Toronto restaurant serving tandoori and other vegetarian and non-vegetarian Indian dishes.

Moti Mahal Restaurant, *1422 Gerrard Street East (416-461-3111).*

A good array of vegetarian foods as well as other tandoori specialties.

Oriental Indian Kitchen, *2783 Danforth Avenue (416-699-8947).*

Serves a variety of curries and Indian specialties. Known for its excellent lentil and mulligatawny soups.

Shala-Mar, *391 Roncesvalles Avenue (416-588-9877).*

An excellent Pakistani restaurant featuring cumin-scented samosas and pakoras, karahi chicken, and lamb biryani, as well as a variety of curries.

Shala-Mar, *427 Donlands Avenue (416-425-3663).*

Excellent Indian home-style cooking with good curries, vegetarian specialties, and Indian appetizers.

Shan-E-Hind Bar-be-que Hut, *1455 Gerrard Street East (416-466-2264).*

Live music on weekends accompanies some interesting tandoori clay-pot-barbecued meats, breads, and vegetables. Exotic ice creams such as saffron are also available.

Sher-E-Punjab, *351 Danforth Avenue (416-465-2125).*

Long acclaimed for its unique cuisine, which features a number of Indian dishes not normally found at other restaurants. Specialties include *lamb saag* (lamb with spinach), *palak and mattar paneer* (cottage cheese cooked with vegetables yogurt and spices), and the excellent chapatis and nan breads.

Woodlands, *177 College Street (416-593-7700); 456 Bloor Street West (416-531-2247).*

One of my favorite places for Indian food, Woodlands is comfortable and inexpensive, and has an excellent array of curries and Indian specialties. Especially recommended is the *chicken mosala,* a tandoori chicken served in a deliciously rich yogurt cream sauce. Best eaten with a side order of nan bread.

════════ Food Sources ════════

Bakeries

Indo Canada Bakery, *1002 Danforth Avenue (416-469-3753).*

Carries a variety of South Asian baked goods, including unleavened breads and pastries.

Butchers

Halaal meat products, slaughtered according to Muslim law, as well as some South Asian foods, can be purchased at the following shops:

Al Queresh, *1879 Lawrence Avenue East (416-288-0330).*

Alflah Grocers, *973 Albion Road (416-742-6824).*

Hafiz Halal Meat and Grocery, *369 Donlands Avenue (416-421-4323).*

House of Halal Meat, *803 Danforth Avenue (416-461-2839).*

Madina Halal Meat and Grocery, *1063 Danforth Avenue (416-461-0404).*

Delis and Grocers

A number of stores carry South Asian foods and spices in the Metro Toronto area. Many more are located in the Gerrard Street area from Greenwood to Coxwell, on Donlands at O'Connor, and at Dundas Street West and Bloor Street West.

Ariana Halal Meat and Groceries, *927 Danforth Avenue (416-461-7205).*

Serves a variety of halaal meat prepared to Islamic tastes and requirements as well as specialty foods and spices, including some specifically Afghan foods and treats. Baked flat breads and desserts are also available.

Indian Groceries and Spices, *1983 Lawrence Avenue East (416-752-7157).*

Indo-Canada Foods, *1391 Gerrard Street East (416-469-3662).*

Kohinoor International Foods, *1438 Gerrard Street East (416-461-4432); 455 McNicoll (416-495-0503).*

Kohinoor Supermarket, *1443 Gerrard Street East (416-461-4023).*

══════ Shops ══════

The city has a number of Indian carpet shops as well as other shops specializing in Indian imports, textiles, and crafts.

Carpets

Atlas Rug Co., *1014 Bathurst Street (416-533-9002).*

Herat Carpets, *114 Yorkville Avenue (416-920-3680).*

A very upscale shop with a variety of specialty Afghan carpets and rugs as well as Afghan figurines, artifacts, and crafts.

Indo-Iranian Rug Co., *241 Queen Street West (416-593-5870).*

Indo-Persian Rug Co., *1127 Finch Avenue West (416-736-7144).*

Karakashian Rug Gallery, *1257 Bay Street (416-964-1995).*

Taj Oriental Rugs, *8400 Woodbine Avenue (905-940-0088).*

Tapis D'Orient, *1440 Bathurst Street (416-658-7518).*

Clothing/Textiles

Kala Kendar, *1440 Gerrard Street East (416-463-3111).*

Nucreations Fashions, *1413 Gerrard Street East (416-465-1093).*

Roop Shinghar, *1404 Gerrard Street East (416-466-4111).*

Sonu Saree Palace, *1420 Gerrard Street East (416-469-2800).*

Miscellaneous

Milan's Department Store, *1460 Gerrard Street East (416-461-1456).*

The largest East Indian department store in North America, Milan's shelves are lined with unique culinary implements, statues of gods and goddesses, gift items, cloth, fashion items, jewelry, South Asian-language books, and musical instruments. The closest thing you'll find to a bazaar in Toronto.

The **ICNA Book Service,** *157 Mammoth Hall Trail (416-292-3777).*

Carries Islamic and South Asian–language books.

The **Indian Record Shop,** *1428 Gerrard Street East (416-463-6671).*

Carries a very large selection of Indian records, CDs, cassettes, and videos.

Video India, *2080 Steeles Avenue East (905-791-6221).*

Carries an even larger selection of Hindi-, Bengali-, and Urdu-language videos.

 **Media**

Publications

Sanjib Savera, *7066 Airport Road (905-677-5655).*

A weekly newspaper.

Asia Times/Bharti/Canadian Indian Star, *1433 Bloor Street West (416-445-3555).*

Perdesi Panjab, 2749 Dundas Street West (416-767-2726).

Ithias Weekly, 19 Strathearn Avenue Unit 39 (905-458-7333).

Al-Hilal, 338 Holyberry Trail (416-493-4374).

Crescent International, 300 Steelcase Road (905-474-9292).

Eastern News, 3100 Dixie Road (905-858-7525).

Jamboor/Democracy, 211 Glenholme Avenue (416-657-8529).

Imroze/Today, 5 Glamorgan Avenue (416-297-0110).

Pakeeza Urdu Magazine/Pakeeza International, 21 Lexington Avenue (416-455-9839).

The Messenger, 2 Middleport Crescent (416-283-7255).

Community Digest, 7305 Woodbine Avenue (905-283-3373).

Indo-Pak Community Voice, 264 Seaton Street (416-924-7444).

India Abroad, 8 Franca Crescent (416-740-4153).

India Calling, 41 Mabell Avenue (416-823-2541).

Canadian Times of India Newsmagazine, PO Box 2247, Station C (416-665-6547).

Voice of Immigrants, 1055 Bathurst Street (416-588-7191).

A monthly publication covering news and events in the Afghan-Canadian community as well as some broader issues of concern.

Afghan Liberation, *1055 Bathurst Street (416-588-7191).*

A monthly English-language newspaper covering political events in Afghanistan and published by the Afghan Liberation News Publications of Canada.

Radio

"Voice of Punjab," CJMR 1190-AM *(905-271-1320).*

Sikh news and music.

"Meelan," CJMR 1190-AM *(905-271-1320).*

Urdu language news and music.

"Radio Jultrung," CIAO 790-AM, *45 Highill Drive (416-494-0611).*

Indian and Pakistani music program.

"Punjabi Program," CHWO 1250-AM, *490 Wyecroft (905-845-2821).*

Weekly Sikh variety and news show.

"Voice of India," CHIN-AM 1540/FM 100.7, *622 College Street (416-531-9991).*

Indian current events.

"Sounds of Asia," CHIN-AM 1540/FM 100.7, *622 College Street (416-531-9991).*

South Asian music.

"Madhuban Radio," CJMR 1320-AM, *Box 1190, Port Credit Station (905-271-1320).*

Indian music and current affairs.

"East Indian Program," CIAO 790-AM, *50 Kennedy Road (905-453-7111).*

"Julturng, Indian and Pakistani Music Show," CIAO 790-AM, *50 Kennedy Road (905-453-7111).*

Television

"News from the Asian Subcontinent," CFMT-TV, Channel 47, *545 Lakeshore Boulevard West (416-593-4747).*

News and current events from India, Pakistan, and the South Asian area.

"Asian Horizons," CFMT-TV, Channel 47, *545 Lakeshore Boulevard West (416-593-4747).*

Movies and variety shows from India.

"Sada Punjab," CFMT-TV, Channel 47, *545 Lakeshore Boulevard West (416-593-4747).*

News, music, and current events for the Sikh Punjabi community.

"Punjabi-TV," CITY-TV, Channel 57, *299 Queen Street West (416-591-5757).*

A weekly Sikh television show.

"Islam TV," VISION TV, *1521 Trinity Drive, Unit 16 (416-672-1544).*

"Mehek," CITY-TV Channel 57, *299 Queen Street West (416-591-5757).*

"Voice of Pakistan," CHCH-TV Channel 11, *163 Jackson Street West (905-522-1101).*

"Visions of India," CHCH-TV Channel 11, *163 Jackson Street West (905-366-9688).*

"Sounds of Asia," CITY-TV Channel 57, *299 Queen Street West (416-591-5757).*

Music and video clips of South Asian musical acts.

—Little India—

The area of Gerrard Street East between Greenwood Avenue and Coxwell Avenue has become the commercial center of Toronto's Indian community. Colorful shops and street vendors, restaurants, cafés, and food stores line the area. On a Sunday, the best time to visit the area, the streets are alive with

Italian Toronto

History

In Toronto's modern era of growth, its Italian community has been one of the most visible and influential. The height of its visibility came during the street parties and celebrations that marked Italy's victory in the 1982 World Cup series. The parties along Saint Clair Avenue West, one of Toronto's main Italian neighborhoods, lasted for almost three days.

Toronto's Italian community is also its largest non-Anglo ethnic group, numbering over 650,000 and still growing. In fact, this community would be the fifth largest Italian city in the world if it existed on its own. It has spread from its early roots in the College Street area near Grace and Ossington Avenues, and there are now four major areas of commercial, cultural, and demographic concentration. The two in the city proper are the Dovercourt neighborhood, which surrounds the oldest area of Italian settlement, and the Corso Italia area along Saint Clair Avenue West between Bathurst Street and Old Weston Road. The latter area includes the upscale clothing and leather shops, cafés and restaurants that stud Saint Clair Avenue West between Dufferin and Lansdowne. There are also the suburban areas of Downsview in western North York and Woodbridge in the community of Vaughan, which has become the major destination of wealthy Italian exurbanites and has seen its population grow rapidly.

Italian involvement in Canadian affairs goes back to the exploration voyages of Giovanni Caboto (John Cabot) in 1497, when he explored the coast of Newfoundland under contract to the English. There is some evidence that two Venetian brothers may have been on an even earlier Scottish/Viking expedition in 1398 and helped guide the sailors along the coast of Nova Scotia. It is also quite possible that Columbus read of these voyages before undertaking his explorations.

The first noted Italian immigrant in Toronto was Filippo de Grassi, a retired British army officer who arrived in 1831. Today, both a street and a school bear his name. The first major wave of Italian settlers didn't come until the mid-1880s, when Italian immigration to North America increased in the wake of the Italian civil war and opportunities began to open up for seasonal laborers in Ontario's growing mining and industrial concerns. Like many other immigrants, Italians went through their share of hardships. Many early settlers, brought over by unscrupulous labor contractors, paid to come to jobs that never materialized. Many of these people were rural laborers and farmers, who were suddenly plunked down in the middle of a growing metropolis.

Toronto's first Italian district was located around College Street and University Avenue in an area known as "the Ward," where Toronto General Hospital now stands. Early settlers became miners, construction workers, small grocers, and tradesmen, with food processing such as pasta manufacturing becoming the next logical step in the area's commercial evolution.

In 1908 the first Italian parish was established at **Our Lady of Mount Carmel Church** on Saint Patrick Street. In the 1930s another wave of immigration brought the many skilled masons and building contractors who helped build much of Toronto's infrastructure. Finally, in the post–World War II years leading into the early 1950s, an even larger and more continuous wave of immigration helped make Toronto the Italian metropolis it is today. These neighborhoods became not only the center of the growing Italian population in Toronto, but also the metropolitan focus for rural Italians living in surrounding small towns, cities, and farming areas of Ontario.

Later immigrants were generally proletarian in origin coming from Italy's urbanized areas rather than the villagers who first arrived here, and they brought urban tastes, desires, and lifestyles with them. A vibrant community first grew in the College Street area between Euclid Avenue and Shaw Street with coffee bars, cafés, recreational clubs, restaurants, and specialty grocers. It had a flavor that was distinctly more European than other parts of Toronto at the time.

In the 1960s, as the community continued to grow, it moved north, colonizing the area along Saint Clair Avenue West—which has now become the cultural and commercial hub of the Italian community—and beginning its move into the suburbs. Recently second-, third-, and even fourth-generation

Italians have moved back into the original urban neighborhoods to reclaim and redevelop family properties into a thriving area of small restaurants, cafés, and nightclubs. Italian entrepreneurs control over 70 percent of the province's construction industry, with families such as the Del Zottos of Tridel and Fidanis of Orlando Corporation being as well known as their enterprises.

Italian entrepreneurs such as Johnny Lombardi and Dan Iannuzzi were instrumental in the development of multicultural media in Toronto with their establishment of CHIN radio and MTV, respectively.

A fourth-century granite Roman column rests on a grassy part of Nathan Phillips Square. It was presented in 1957 by the mayor of Rome as a token of friendship commemorating Toronto's relationship with its many Italian citizens. Another sculpture commemorating Italian-Canadian friendship is found in the plaza outside of Union Station. As far as education goes, the University of Toronto has North America's largest Italian studies program with the highest number of students. A specific chair also handles Italian-Canadian historical studies.

Religion

Catholicism remains the predominant religion among Toronto's Italian community and a number of churches have large Italian Catholic congregations. **Saint Francis of Assisi Church,** 72 Mansfield Road (416-536-8195), is the oldest church in the community. Erected in 1904, it remains the spiritual center for the Italian Catholic community with over 20,000 people attending on major holy days like Good Friday and Saint Anthony's Day. Other popular churches, many of which have some masses in Italian, include the following:

Holy Angels Church, *61 Jutland Street (416-255-1691).*

Immaculate Conception, *4 Richardson Avenue (416-651-7875).*

Italian United Church of Saint Paul-Pietro Valdo, *1120 Ossington Avenue (416-534-2562).*

Our Lady of Victory, *117 Guestville Avenue (416-769-1171).*

Saint Alfonso, *540 Saint Clair Avenue West (416-653-4486).*

Saint Ambrose, *Brown's Line Road and Evans Avenue (416-251-8282).*

Saint Anthony's Church, *1041 Bloor Street West (416-536-3333).*

Saint Augustine of Canterbury Roman Catholic Church, *98 Shoreham Drive (416-661-8221).*

Saint Bernardo's, *1789 Lawrence Avenue West (416-241-6738).*

Saint Brigid's, *300 Wolverleigh Boulevard (416-425-8072).*

Saint Catherine of Sienna, *1099 Danforth Avenue (416-466-9433).*

Saint Clare's, *1118 Saint Clair Avenue West (416-654-7087).*

Saint Helen's, *1680 Dundas Street West (416-531-8188).*

Saint John Bosco, *402 Westmount Avenue (416-651-1491).*

Saint Leo's Church, *277 Royal York Road (416-251-1109).*

Saint Mary of the Angels, *1481 Dufferin Street (416-532-4779).*

Saint Nicholas, *1277 Saint Clair Avenue West (416-654-8908).*

Saint Paschal Babylon, *92 Steeles Avenue West (416-889-9021).*

Saint Phillip Neri, *2100 Jane Street (416-241-3101).*

Saint Roch, *2889 Islington Avenue (416-749-0328).*

Saint Sebastiano, *20 Pauline Avenue (416-536-2302).*

Saint Thomas Aquinas, *640 Glenholme Avenue (416-782-8943).*

Saint Wilfred's, *1675 Finch Avenue West (416-638-0313).*

Organizations

The Italian community has always been actively involved in cultural, social, and community services and boasts a proud and extensive record of institutions and services. The **Columbus Centre,** 901 Lawrence Avenue West (416-789-7011), is one of the major centers in the Italian community and includes a seniors' center, the **Villa Colombo Home for the Aged,** 40 Playfair Avenue (416-789-2113); an excellent Italian restaurant, **Ristorante Boccacio;** the **Joseph D. Carrier Art Gallery** (416-789-7011); and lecture halls. The center hosts a variety of cultural activities and organizes heritage-language classes through the **Dante Society of Toronto** and the **Centro Scuola East Cultura Italiana,** 901 Lawrence Avenue West (416-789-7011).

The **Joseph Piccininni Community Centre,** 1369 Saint Clair Avenue West (416-392-0036), is a modern facility providing a number of community services and cultural activities, including outdoor concerts in nearby Earlscourt Park.

The **Italian Cultural Centre,** 496 Huron Street (416-921-3802), also undertakes a variety of cultural and linguistic education programs in the community.

There are over 300 social and fraternal Italian clubs in the metropolitan area. Among the largest are:

Famee Furlane Club, *7065 Islington Avenue (905-851-1166).*

Italian Social Services Community Information Centre, *34 King Street East (416-392-0505).*

Other organizations have a broader scope, encompassing many facets of Italian-Canadian life:

The **National Congress of Italian Canadians,** *756 Ossington Avenue (416-531-9964).*

An umbrella group for more than fifty-five social, cultural, and recreational groups comprising over one million Italian Canadians nationwide.

The **Italian Canadian Benevolent Corporation,** *901 Lawrence Avenue West (416-789-7011).*

A charitable organization that has overseen the building and running of the largest Italian social centers in the city—the Villa Colombo and the Columbus Centre.

COSTI-IIAS, *1710 Dufferin Street (416-658-1600).*

A nonprofit benevolent group originally established to assist Italian construction workers. It now provides a number of educational and social welfare services to Italians and other immigrant groups.

══════ Holidays and Celebrations ══════

June 2	*National Day,* celebrating the Italian decision, following the Second World War, to establish a republic.
July 1	*CHIN International Picnic,* originally an Italian celebration, this is now celebrated by all of Toronto's multicultural communities as the "largest free outdoor picnic in the world."
August	*Italian Day,* celebrating Italian culture on the third Sunday of the month. Held at Ontario Place.

══════════ Restaurants ══════════

Italian cuisine has definitely come into its own in Toronto during the past fifteen years. While many Italian restaurants have heritages that go back before this time, it is only during the past fifteen years that the quality of Italian cooking has matched the size and importance of the community. The diversity, subtlety, and freshness of Italian cuisine has been brought out in full force, with Italian restaurants rising to the forefront as some of Toronto's best.

Fine Dining

The following list covers the very best Italian restaurants. It may omit a few with broader menus, focusing on restaurants with a specific Italian flavor.

Acqua, *10 Front Street West (416-368-7171).*

One of Toronto's trendiest and most interestingly decorated restaurants, Acqua is Italian cuisine moderne with a vengeance. Specialties include rack of lamb with a rose and port wine sauce; basil mashed potatoes; goat cheese baked in pinenut sauce; and a variety of thin-crust pizzas such as prosciutto pesto, gold potatoes, arugula, and ricotta. There is a choice of pastas, such as fusilli with smoked salmon, chipotle peppers, and a tomato-vodka cream sauce. The wine list is extensive, the crowd lively.

Barolo Ristorante, *193 Carlton Street (416-961-4747).*

An elegant restaurant near Toronto's Cabbagetown with a fine array of modern Italian specialties, including excellent homemade pastas, grilled seafood specialties, and delectable stuffed chicken.

Bellini's Ristorante, *101 Yorkville Avenue (416-929-9111).*

Modern, warm, and tastefully decorated, Bellini's exudes casual elegance in a modern Italian manner. Nothing is overdone or out of place. The food is tastefully served in a pleasant but not visually overwhelming or gimmicky way. Best known for its veal and seafood dishes, particularly sautéed shrimp with baby clams, Bellini's is pricey but well worth the money if you can afford it.

Biffi Bistro, *699 Mount Pleasant Road (416-484-1143).*

A well-known establishment in Toronto's uptown Mount Pleasant area, Biffi has been providing consistently well-prepared modern Italian cuisine for many years. This is an open-kitchen-style restaurant where you can watch the chefs at work and enjoy the smells. The menu has a good range of offerings, as does the wine list.

Bindi, *3241 Yonge Street (416-487-2887).*

For those who like modern Italian cooking but can't afford some of the better-known and more costly establishments (particularly in this trendy uptown north Toronto area), Bindi offers excellent food, an interesting menu, and pleasant surroundings for a relatively low price. Veal, fish, and pasta are the specialties, but be sure to leave room for the superb chocolate bindi for dessert.

Carmen's, *26 Alexandra Street (416-924-8697).*

One of Toronto's best-known restaurants, Carmen's has long been favored by Toronto's establishment for its excellent steaks, chateaubriand, and classic Italian specialties. An old-fashioned restaurant with dark wood trim, numerous fireplaces, and stone walls, Carmen's is an élite establishment for those looking for a good Italian steakhouse.

Centro Grill and Wine Bar, *2472 Yonge Street (416-483-2211).*

Still bubbling with excitement after many successful years, Centro's remains one of Toronto's trendiest spots, with one of the best wine lists and an excellent array of classic and modern Italian cuisine. Choices range from caramelized free-range chicken and smoked capon with avocado to baked salmon with curried lentils and red onions. Food prices are moderate to expensive; wine prices can be expensive, but there are good wines by the glass, including an excellent Brolio and Barolo.

Coco Lezzone, *602 College Street (416-535-1489).*

This new restaurant is a beautifully designed, upscale addition to the Via Italia restaurant strip. Specialties include risotto with four cheeses, rack of lamb, and superb agnolotti. The wine list is diverse and well priced, the atmosphere pleasant and romantic. Service is good, but it gets very crowded on weekends.

DiSalvio's, *1959 Avenue Road (416-483-9818).*

This family-owned restaurant serves classic Italian favorites, such as mussels and shrimp in a white wine sauce, linguine with clams, and beautiful veal chops in a Madeira sauce. Prices are modest; service is warm and welcoming.

Grappa, *797 College Street (416-535-3337).*

A small, pleasantly homey restaurant at the far west end of the Via Italia where it meets Little Lisbon, Grappa has a small but interesting menu with specialties including rack of lamb with lemon and pesto; pork tenderloin with hazelnuts and tarragon; and the trademark chicken breast with grappa, spinach, pinenuts, and raisins. The cooking is excellent, the service pleasant, the atmosphere quiet and restful.

Il Posto, *148 Yorkville Avenue (416-968-0469).*

An excellent Italian restaurant in Toronto's Yorkville area with a large, lovely al fresco dining patio covered by a huge tree, Il Posto serves some of Toronto's best pastas—of particular note are its linguine, cappellini, and fettucine. The rose sauces with various mixtures are especially recommended, as are the tiger shrimp, osso bucco, saffron risotto, and excellent appetizers and desserts. Il Posto is very popular with writers and media personalities in the area.

La Bruschetta, *1325 Saint Clair Avenue West (416-656-8622).*

Long established as one of the better restaurants on the Corso Italia and one of the first of the truly fine Italian restaurants to open in Toronto, La Bruschetta continues to serve excellent northern Italian, Veronese, and Venetian specialties for reasonable prices. The tiramisu is particularly recommended.

La Fenice, *319 King Street West (416-585-2377).*

A stark, modern Italian restaurant near the theater district with one of the city's best arrays of appetizers. These are truly served à la carte—a waiter brings you the various dishes on a cart and you decide what you want—or you can make up a mixed antipasto plate from a variety of dishes. The menu itself is interesting, and pastas are well prepared, in particular the fettucine salmonate and spagettini tutto mare. This restaurant has made a wonderfully appetizing fetish of freshness in its meat and fish, as well as its pastas, prepared sausages, and hand-made desserts.

Mammina's Ristorante, *6-B Wellesley Street West (416-967-7199).*

Southern Italian cooking is the specialty in this modern brightly lit restaurant. The pastas come prepared in beautiful olive oil-based sauces, as do other superb dishes. Very popular at lunch, this is a nice quiet spot for dining in the evening. Food is reasonably priced, and the place attracts a young clientele.

Masaniello, *647 College Street (416-533-7046).*

One of the first restaurants in the Via Italia revival, Masaniello still serves superb trademark pastas in a pleasant setting with good wine and moderate prices.

Mastro's Ristorante Italiano, *890 Wilson Avenue (416-636-8194).*

A wonderfully unexpected delight, Mastro's is a great place to take someone when you are in the mood for something a bit different and unique. Located in one of the ugliest little strip malls you can find in Downsview, this restaurant is an oasis of excellent cooking and pleasant decor once you open the door. An excellent menu includes such unique dishes as pheasant, venison, and other game prepared in an array of hearty southern Italian sauces. Excellent pastas and thin-crust pizzas are also available. The wine list—the largest of any Italian restaurant I've been to in the city—is a virtual encyclopedia of Italian wines, and there is even a wine bar for tastings. Forget the neighborhood, this is a great family-owned Italian restaurant. There's even a wandering accordion player.

Paparazzi, *270 West Beaver Creek Road (416-886-6239).*

This très moderne restaurant-disco appeals to the young chic Mississauga set. An interesting, moderately priced menu and an excellent nightclub/disco provide a good setting for the modern La Dolce Vita of the Italian dance music scene.

Primavera, *1552 Avenue Road (416-782-5198).*

Although rustic, this is an excellent restaurant for Italian food, with some of the best linguine and veal in the city and a fun atmosphere with guitarists and occasional singing. Prices are moderate in a neighborhood atmosphere.

Pronto, *692 Mount Pleasant Road (416-486-1111).*

Still one of Toronto's best restaurants for superb food and service, Pronto's menu allows you to order any appetizer as a main course. Although the menu changes monthly, some of its specialties include lamb sausage with polenta and mushrooms, superb soups, grilled lamb with apples and calvados, and pork tenderloin with sweet potatoes and sun-dried sour cherries.

Rogues, *1900 Dundas Street West (416-822-2670).*

This is an outstanding, modern, and lively Italian restaurant in Mississauga, with superb appetizers (grilled peppers with asiago cheese are outstanding), excellent lamb and veal, as well as fresh seafood such as grilled pickerel with Italian seasoning. One of the best restaurants in Mississauga, it gets very crowded on weekends.

Rossini Dining Lounge, *1988 Avenue Road (416-481-1188).*

An excellent northern Italian restaurant with a classic menu, good wine list, and elegant surroundings. This is a pleasant neighborhood restaurant that is quiet and unpretentious with excellent cooking.

Sabatino's, *1144 Eglinton Avenue West (416-783-5829).*

A very European-style atmosphere in an elegantly decorated room, the food is northern Italian classic with excellent cannelloni and veal specialties, as well as fresh fish. Service is knowledgeable and friendly, and an accordionist provides atmosphere.

San Marco Restaurant, *1231 Saint Clair Avenue West (416-654-8482).*

Another stalwart restaurant on the Corso Italia strip, San Marco has an excellent array of Italian desserts to complement its wonderful pastas, pizzas, and appetizers. A pleasant covered outdoor patio turns this into an outdoor café in the summer.

Splendido's, *88 Harbord Street (416-929-7788).*

A stunningly decorated dining room perfectly capturing the spirit of modern Italy, this restaurant in a quiet part of the Annex neighborhood is one of the trendiest restaurants in the city—and deservedly so. From the bacon-wrapped shrimp hors-d'oeuvres to the beautifully prepared and marinated osso bucco, this restaurant presents some of Toronto's best and most interesting Italian food. Specialties include pistachio-crusted scallops baked in a brick oven and served with mango chutney and fermented black bean sauce, beautiful thin-crust pizzas with a variety of exotic toppings, and pastas with peppered vodka cream sauces. It's loud, it's lively, it's a place to see and be seen. In the back of the open kitchen you can watch the chefs at work and enjoy the wonderful smells of fine Italian food.

Terra, *8199 Yonge Street (416-731-6161).*

A noisy lively atmosphere more like the city than the suburb it's in, Terra serves beautiful salads on big colorful plates splashed with ground pepper, as well as the kinds of trendy modern Italian food one would find at Centro's and Splendido's. Specialties range from grilled squid with aioli on a bed of ruchetta to salmon grilled with eggplant caviar and beautiful flourless chocolate cakes served with strawberries and cream. There is an excellent if somewhat pricey wine list.

Trattoria Giancarlo, *41 Clinton Street (416-533-9619).*

This quiet and pleasant neighborhood restaurant in the Via Italia area serves excellent food at reasonable prices. The better than average wine list has reasonable markups. Service is personal and intelligent. The menu is small but ever changing, and the food is fresh and interesting.

Venezia, *1338 Lansdowne Avenue (416-654-8648).*

A family-owned restaurant serving classic Italian cuisine and long a favorite for denizens of the Corso Italia area, Venezia serves superb northern Italian and Venetian food at very reasonable prices. The atmosphere is lively, especially in the summertime, and families are welcomed. This is home cooking Italian style.

Villa Borghese, *2995 Bloor Street West (416-239-1286).*

Don't miss this excellent Italian restaurant if you are out in Toronto's West End Kingsway area. Villa Borghese is often overlooked by the downtown restaurant-going crowd because of its location, which is a shame because this beautifully decorated, sumptuous restaurant prepares some of the best Italian food available in the city for its price range. A pianist plays in the background as excellent veal, lamb, and pasta dishes are served in a variety of styles. The antipasto appetizers are particularly varied and fresh. Prices are moderate, and the service is always superb.

Cafés, Nightclubs, and Pizzerias

A number of Italian cafés, bars, pool clubs, and pizzerias are scattered throughout the city, providing the continental environment so omnipresent in Italy. Some of the more noteworthy ones include the following:

Bar Azzurri, *602 College Street (416-532-9837).*

This newly modernized and remodeled café is very popular with the Via Italia neighborhood for schmoozing, people watching, and newspaper reading. It is a typical European café with excellent coffee, a limited menu of sandwiches, some pastries, and an unhurried attitude toward its customers.

Bar Italia, *584 College Street (416-535-3621).*

The pool hall café that started the revitalizing trend in the old Via Italia neighborhood, Bar Italia is crowded throughout the week with loyal patrons eating one of the excellent daily specials, soups, salads, or thick stuffed sandwiches—and playing pool. It's also a nice place to just sip coffee with a lovely Italian pastry or dessert, read a newspaper, and watch the world go by.

Bitondo Snack Bar and Pizzeria, *11 Clinton Street (416-533-4101).*

This local neighborhood snack bar and pizzeria is in a quiet part of the Dovercourt/Via Italia area.

Camarra's Pizzeria and Restaurant, *2899 Dufferin Street (416-789-3221).*

With probably the best pizza in Toronto for thin-crust lovers, this pleasantly decorated pizzeria serves an excellent array of different homemade pizzas at very reasonable prices.

Café Diplomatic, *594 College Street (416-534-4637).*

This longtime popular neighborhood café serves sandwiches and pizza by the slice, has a limited but inexpensive wine list and, yes, a couple of pool tables and an outdoor patio as well.

Filippo's Gourmet Pizzeria, *744 Saint Clair Avenue West (416-658-0568).*

An excellent pizzeria on the Corso Italia, Filippo's serves superb thin- and thick-crust pizzas, as well as Italian café sandwiches and specialties.

La Sem, *1275 Eglinton Avenue East (416-624-8888).*

A chain of Italian bakeries located throughout Metropolitan Toronto, this is the main branch and includes a café and pizzeria.

Lombardi's, *637 College Street (416-531-1144).*

Belonging to CHIN Radio's flamboyant owner, Johnny Lombardi, this café is an interesting meeting place along the Via Italia for many denizens and personalities in the area.

Regina Pizzeria, *782 College Street (416-535-2273).*

This local pizzeria has the high quality sought by locals in the Via Italia area.

San Francesco Foods, *10 Clinton Street (416-534-7867).*

Well known for its overstuffed Italian sandwiches and pizza by the slice, San Francesco Foods has a number of locations throughout Toronto. This is the original one from which all the rest are descended.

Vesuvio's Pizzeria and Spaghetti House, *3014 Dundas Street West (416-763-4191).*

════════════ Food Sources ════════════

Bakeries

Italian bakeries abound in both the Via Italia and Corso Italia areas as well as in Downsview in North York. Often they now include cafés as well. Some of the better or more unique ones include:

Calabria Bakery, *1372 Kennedy Road (416-755-1175).*

For southern Italian breads and baked goods.

Canadian Italian Bakery and Pizzeria, *741 Danforth Avenue (416-465-7780).*

An Italian bakery and pizzeria.

Nino D'Aversa, *1 Toro Road (416-638-3271); 72
Steeles Avenue West (905-881-7393); 7960 Kipling
Avenue (905-851-2211).*

A well-known chain producing high-quality Italian breads and buns, cakes
and pastries, as well as sandwiches and pizzas.

Riviera Bakery, *576 College Street (416-537-9352).*

An Italian bakery on the Via Italia serving fresh-baked breads and overstuffed sandwiches.

Tre Mari Bakery, *1311 Saint Clair Avenue West
(416-654-8960); 41 Shorncliffe Road (416-233-3800).*

Sells breads, baked goods, and gourmet Italian specialties, including imported foods and freshly made pizzas and sandwiches. The store at 41
Shorncliffe is the wholesale outlet for bargain hunters.

Butchers

A few Italian butchers specialize in veal and baby beef, including:

Casa Del Baby Beef, *362 Old Weston Road (416-656-
7000).*

Gino Meat Market, *1203 Saint Clair Avenue West
(416-658-3643).*

Luigi Meat, *1728 Saint Clair Avenue West (416-656-
2704).*

Macelleria del Baby Beef, *1654 Saint Clair Avenue
West (416-656-7045).*

Delis/Grocers

A variety of companies produce and distribute the wide array of fine Italian
cheeses in the Toronto area. Among the more interesting and varied selections are those at:

Ferrante Cheese Manufacturing, *5732 Highway 7 (905-851-2073).*

Manufacturers of locally produced Italian cheeses.

Il Centro del Formaggio, *1255 Queensway (416-255-5682).*

L'Angolo Del Formaggio, *2984 Bloor Street West (416-690-6053).*

La Grotta del Formaggio, *930 Bloor Street West (416-531-8778); 1275 Lawrence Avenue West (416-247-7459); and 1254 Saint Clair Avenue West (416-466-5094).*

National Cheese Co., *675 Rivermede (905-669-9393).*

Manufactures other cheeses as well as Italian favorites such as parmesan, mozzarella, asiago, and ricotta.

Quality Cheese Produce Co., *459 Rogers Road (416-656-6565).*

Gourmet shops offering homemade pastas and other Italian gourmet specialties are growing in number in the metro area. Particularly noteworthy is **Sanelli's Cookery,** 348 Danforth Avenue (416-469-2330), which produces a wide array of excellent prepared foods and carries a wide array of interesting Italian specialty foods. Other gourmet pasta shops of note are:

Pasta Kitchen, *3251 Yonge Street (416-440-2850).*

Pasta Pantry, *1983 Yonge Street (416-482-4848).*

Primo Pasta, *40 Huxley Street (416-741-9300).*

Has a wholesale and retail outlet at its manufacturing plant selling fresh, inexpensive pastas.

A number of local grocers in the various Italian neighborhoods carry Italian specialties. Among the chain stores of note, **Sunkist Stores,** at 9275 Highway 48 (905-471-0777) and 4099 Erin Mills Parkway (905-820-3300), are especially unique, not simply for their wide array of Italian produce, cheeses, meats, and specialty products, but also for their excellent service and product quality that are astonishing for a grocery store chain.

Other major stores carrying a wide array of Italian food products include:

Pasquale Brothers, *217 King Street West (416-364-7397).*

Russo Foods, *5601 Steeles Avenue West (416-740-1200).*

Siena Foods Ltd., *16 Newbridge Avenue (416-239-3967).*

Gelateria

The **Sicilian Ice Cream Company,** 712 College Street (416-531-7716), is the best-known Italian gelateria in the city and produces excellent Italian gelatos as well as other ice cream treats. Its café is open twenty-four hours a day and is very busy in the summertime with an outdoor sidewalk café.

Many of the Italian bakeries noted earlier also carry extensive arrays of gelatos, as do some of the Italian cafés in both the Via Italia and Corso Italia areas.

Shops

The major shopping area for specialty Italian clothes, leather, handbags, gifts, crafts, and furnishings is the Corso Italia, the area of Saint Clair Avenue West between Ossington and Lansdowne Avenues. A huge array of shops is available here, including some particularly upscale men's clothing stores, such as:

Belissimo, *882 Eglinton Avenue West (416-782-4780).*

Provides custom-tailored Italian suits and shirts for the discerning buyer as well as imported off-the-rack designs.

The Forum, *1166 Saint Clair Avenue West (416-656-4764).*

Genesis, *1188 Saint Clair Avenue West (416-652-1386).*

La Scala, *1190 Saint Clair Avenue West (416-652-1606).*

Pal Zilieri, *87 Avenue Road (416-928-9173).*
Imports a number of exclusive Italian designer lines for men.

There are many women's clothiers in the Corso Italia area as well. Among the more noteworthy are:

Bianca Neve, *1268 Saint Clair Avenue West (416-656-9560).*
Also carries children's clothing.

Christian Boutique, *1236 Saint Clair Avenue West (416-651-2931).*

Gente Boutique, *1228 Saint Clair Avenue West (416-657-1461).*

Gianni Versace, *55 Avenue Road (416-922-1900).*
A boutique specializing in the work of this well-known Italian designer.

The **Italian Gift Store,** 1090 Saint Clair Avenue West (416-653-0930), is a large store filled with Italian jewelry, gifts, statues, and other imported items of interest.

Italian interior design and furnishing companies include a number of excellent importers of some cutting-edge furnishings and accessories for which Italy has become noted in recent years. Among the most interesting shops are:

Abitare Design, *4 Labarr (416-363-1667).*

Italinteriors, *359 King Street East (416-366-9540).*

Mobilia, *55 Bloor Street West (416-944-0461).*

For Italian-language books and magazines, you can go to **Ital Books,** 1337 Saint Clair Avenue West (416-651-3310). For records, CDs, cassettes, and videos, try **Ital Records,** 1339 Saint Clair Avenue West (416-654-8269), or **Italian Gift and Records Centre,** 755 Danforth Avenue (416-466-9228).

========================= **Media** =========================

Publications

Community Viva, *PO Box 429, Station D (416-656-2192).*
A monthly Italian-language magazine.

Corriere Canadese, *700 Caledonia Road (416-785-4300).*
The community's popular Italian-language daily.

Italian Life Newspaper, *PO Box 158, Station L (416-656-2050).*
A weekly publication.

Italian Panorama, *5125 Steeles Avenue West (416-744-8200).*
A monthly magazine.

La Parola, *33 Connie Street (416-247-8742).*
A monthly tabloid.

Lo Specchio, *166 Woodbridge Avenue, #100 (905-856-2823).*
A monthly magazine (also publishes the Italian-Canadian women's magazine *Donna*).

Viva Italiana, *Box 158, Station L (416-656-2050).*
A biweekly newspaper

Vita Sana, *10 Director Court (416-850-2404).*
A monthly magazine.

Radio and Television

CHIN Radio (AM 1540/FM 100.7), 622 College Street (416-531-9991), was originally started by Johnny Lombardi and has long carried a wide array of Italian as well as other ethnic programming. Among its current Italian offerings on CHIN-AM are:

- **"Canta Napoli,"** Southern Italian music and variety on Saturdays.
- **"Folklore Italiano,"** folk music on Saturday afternoons.
- **"Il Sabato del Villagio,"** on Saturday mornings.
- **"Italian Folklore,"** a Saturday-morning show with a Calabrese bent.
- **"L'Eco del Lazio,"** modern music on Saturday afternoons.
- **"La Voce del Vangello,"** a Pentecostal religious show on Saturday afternoons.
- **"Mosaico Musicale,"** a variety show on Saturday afternoons.
- **"Music of Your Life,"** a daily afternoon show.
- **"Per Voi Tutte,"** a daily call-in show in Italian and English.
- **"Wake Up Italian Style,"** Monday through Friday.

CHIN-FM has programs such as:

- **"La Voce Della Speranza,"** a religious show on Sunday mornings.
- **"Su Di Giri,"** a daily late-afternoon music and variety show.
- **"Voi Io E La Musica,"** a daily evening music show.
- **"Weekend Italiano,"** news, music, and entertainment from Italy on Sunday afternoons.

CIAO-RADIO (790 AM), 83 Kennedy Road South (905-453-7111), also offers a variety of Italian musical programs from 9:00 AM to 7:00 PM daily.

CFMT (channel 47), 545 Lakeshore Boulevard West (416-593-4747), carries a variety of Italian-language television shows, including:

- **"Italianissimo,"** prime-time Italian-language programming, including "Telesera," a rundown of the day's events; "Incontri," a variety of soft news and entertainment features; and "Telenovellas," top-rated dramas and serials.
- **"Viva L'Italia,"** a mixture of afternoon serial dramas and light news and entertainment.
- **"Italicine,"** feature movie classics from the Italian cinema.

- **"Windows on Italy,"** a mixture of variety entertainment, talk shows, dramas, and comedies from Italy's top-rated TV5 Berlusconi Direct.

Other Italian-language television shows on local television include:

- **"Festival Italiano—The Johnny Lombardi Show,"** Global Television Network, 81 Barber Greene Road (416-446-5311).

- **"Johnny Lombardi Show,"** CITY-TV, 299 Queen Street West (416-591-5757).

- **"Italian Panorama,"** CHCH-TV, 163 Jackson Street West (905-366-9688).

TELELATINO, 105 Carlton Street (416-591-6846), offers a variety of Italian, Hispanic, and Portuguese television programming on cable.

—Via Italia: The Old Italian Neighborhood—

The Via Italia, otherwise known as Little Italy, is the downtown area where Italian Canadians first established a commercial center for themselves. Located along College Street, the area starts at Palmerston Avenue and extends as far east as Shaw Street, where it blends into Little Lisbon or Little Portugal. Its heart is between Euclid and Grace Streets, where over two dozen cafés and restaurants line the streets.

Via Italia has undergone a considerable revival in recent years. Many of the old cafés, bars, and bakeries have been revitalized as the grandchildren and great-grandchildren of the original owners have moved into the city to run the shops and restaurants established by their ancestors. Bar Italia, the Sicilian Ice Cream Company, and CHIN RADIO are all landmarks of the area, and there are numerous restaurants, cafés/pool halls, and nightclubs for people watching and street life. This is a young area with a neighborly feeling attracting hip young families as well as the local Italian community.

How to Get There: *Take the College streetcar west from the College Street or Queen's Park subway station on the Yonge/University line to Palmerston Street and walk west along College Street. You can also take the Bathurst streetcar south from the Bathurst Station of the Bloor/Danforth subway line.*

—Corso Italia: The Current Italian Center—

This area along Saint Clair Avenue West from Oakwood Avenue to Lansdowne Avenue is the current commercial heart of the Italian community. While the Via Italia is primarily known for its cafés and restaurants, the Corso Italia is primarily known for its shops. There are, however, numerous

Japanese and Southeast Asian Toronto

Japanese, Korean, and other Southeast Asian immigrants were some of the later arrivals to the Toronto area. Although their various cultures are unique in many ways, especially due to their countries' more recent history, these peoples share numerous similarities in religion, cooking, and so on.

Nationalities

Japanese

In a world in which Japan is one of its dominant economies we often forget that at the turn of the century it was a weak, economically backward country whose major export was emigrants. Japanese emigrants settled in Brazil, Peru, the mainland United States, Hawaii, and Canada. Over 5,000 Issei arrived in the Toronto area in the years between 1890 and 1920 and were the dominant oriental group here until the rise of the Chinese community in subsequent years.

A photo taken in 1885 of a J. Kono is the earliest evidence available of a Japanese settler in the Metro Toronto area. Japanese names began appearing in Toronto directories in the 1890s. One of those names, Shigesaburo

Ubukata, remains a part of the city's heritage today in the form of the Ubukata Bursary, which was established in 1926 to help Japanese-born students attending the University of Toronto.

Growth in the Japanese community occurred not so much from immigrants from Japan as from Japanese families arriving from other parts of Canada. The forced removal of many Japanese Canadians from the west coast of Canada during World War II encouraged many immigrants to move east upon their release from the internment camps.

In the 1950s changes to Canada's immigration laws opened the way for many new Japanese middle-class immigrants to come to Canada, and the Toronto community received its first new immigrants from Japan in fifty years during this period. Prominent Japanese Canadians include the well-known television broadcaster, ecological activist, and scientist, Dr. David Suzuki; author Joy Kogawa, critic and essayist Ken Adachi; landscape artist George Tanaka; and prominent architect Raymond Moriyama, whose works include the Metro Toronto Reference Library, Ontario Science Centre, and Scarborough Civic Centre.

The **Japanese Canadian Cultural Centre,** also designed by Raymond Moriyama, is a beautiful tribute to this small but active community, capturing in its architecture and surrounding gardens much of the beauty that is a part of this rich and complex culture. A small grove of Japanese cherry trees has also been planted in High Park, in which are found two commemorative plaques from the Canada Pavillion at Expo 1970 held in Osaka. A Japanese temple bell also resides on the east island of the Toronto Islands Park and community. It was erected on the hundredth anniversary of Japanese presence in Canada. The bell is rung every New Year's Eve and on the celebration of Obon in July, which is a Buddhist remembrance day for deceased relatives.

Koreans

Like Danforth Avenue for the Greeks, Bloor Street West between Palmerston and Christie Streets remains the heart of the Korean community's commercial and entertainment area. While most Metro Koreans have dispersed throughout the city, this area still remains their center, with a high concentration of Korean restaurants, shops, karaoke bars, financial institutions, and professional services.

While South Korea itself came into existence only after World War II and opened diplomatic relations with Canada in 1963, Koreans have a long and rich cultural, linguistic, and political history. The first immigrants to Canada came in the 1880s from church missions in the Korean peninsula that sponsored converts' emigration to Canada. Korean ties to the United

Church, as well as other Protestant churches, are reflected in the fact that the current national moderator of the United Church of Canada is the Reverend Sang-chul Lee.

In the 1940s, an increasing number of Korean immigrants were students who came to study in Canadian universities and then decided to remain in Canada. An even larger wave of immigration came in the late 1960s and early 1970s, and the community as a whole now numbers over 45,000.

Many are small business entrepreneurs, but there is also a large and growing professional class of Koreans who have gone on to further themselves in the Canadian educational system or are second- and third-generation children of immigrant families. It is estimated that over 80 percent of all small grocery stores in the Metro Toronto area are owned by Koreans who have a very strong cooperative buying organization.

The Korean presence in Toronto has also contributed to close commercial ties between Canada and South Korea. Symbols of these connections include two granite pagodas donated to Victoria University at the University of Toronto in memory of Dr. O. R. Avison, a University of Toronto graduate who founded the first Western-style hospital and medical school in Seoul in 1893.

Close ties exist between Japanese and Korean cultures, as is shown in the cuisines of both countries, which have many similar dishes and some similarities in dance and theater. Linguistically, the cultures are quite different and Korea is much more than just a meeting place of oriental influences. It has many rich and unique traits and is in fact one of the more ancient oriental cultures, whose history precedes that of both Japan and southern China.

Other Southeast Asians

Toronto's Southeast Asian community has grown dramatically in recent years. Native Annamese and Cholonese from Vietnam, as well as Cambodians, Laotians, Thai, Indonesians, Malaysians, and ethnic Chinese settlers from this whole area have moved to the city in increasing numbers. The community now numbers close to 100,000, of which almost 50,000 are Vietnamese. Most came after the fall of Ho Chi Minh City in successive waves from the refugee camps outside of Hong Kong. Canada, in fact, has received more Vietnamese immigrants than the United States, with almost a third settling in the Toronto area.

Some Vietnamese originally arrived here in the 1950s and 1960s as students, and the **Saigon Star** was the first Vietnamese restaurant in the city, opening in the early 1970s. Vietnamese immigrants to Toronto have been hard-working, successful examples of the immigrant work ethic, succeeding quickly in building profitable businesses and toiling to buy houses, cars, and other accoutrements of the good life, including good educations for their children. Numerous Vietnamese restaurants, cafés, karaoke bars, and shops have opened over the years throughout the city. Most of the Vietnamese community has moved into one of the Chinatown areas, with a high concentration of Vietnamese shops and restaurants in the Spadina Avenue area.

Malaysian immigrants are also a recent addition to the Toronto community. Although smaller in number than the Vietnamese, Malaysian immigration began in the post-World War II era as Malays took advantage of their Commonwealth status to emigrate to Canada. Many Malaysian students attend local universities. Groups of clerical workers, industrial workers, and other business professionals have also come to Toronto. Some came in the late 1950s, fleeing the civil war that engulfed Malaysia just before its independence from the British Empire.

The Thai community is probably the smallest of the Southeast Asian communities in the city, though it is one of the best known because of the recent popularity of Thai cuisine. Canada-Thai trade relations have also encouraged Thai businesspeople to move to Toronto, and today over 250 Thai families live in the area.

The Indonesian community is one of the older Southeast Asian communities in the Toronto area. Some Indonesians came over in the pre-World War II era, though the majority arrived in the 1960s after the civil war that racked the islands after President Sukarno's death. Most of the community is composed of well-educated professionals and businesspeople of ethnic Chinese origin, though some Toronto Dutch have Indonesian origins.

Laotian and Cambodian refugees also arrived in Toronto in response to the upheavals that affected Southeast Asia during and after the Vietnam War. The Laotian community now numbers over 5,000 people. Many are of French-speaking background and originally moved to Quebec, only then to move on to the better economic opportunities in the Toronto area.

Immigration began in the 1960s with students from Laos staying in Canada, then a wave of immigration occurred after the Laotian king's abdication in 1975. More Laotians arrived, fleeing tension along the border with Cambodia and Vietnam in the 1980s. Laotian immigrants have included both blue-collar laborers and professionals.

Toronto's Cambodian community arrived in the wake of the horrendous massacres that racked that country during the period of Khmer Rouge control. Over 6,000 Cambodians now live in the Metro area, many having immigrated from the horrendous conditions of the refugee camps along the Thai-Cambodian border. The Riverdale Chinatown area has been their major settlement, and the community has includes a mixture of scholars, professionals, laborers, and skilled workers. Like the Vietnamese community, Cambodians have been very successful in starting and nurturing many successful small businesses in the Metro Toronto area.

Toronto's Filipino community is a large, dispersed community that has grown rapidly over the last twenty-five years. Currently there are over 60,000 members of this ethnic group in the Greater Toronto Area, with pockets in the Parkdale and Saint Jamestown areas close to the hospitals that provided much of the early employment for these immigrants.

After the close of the Second World War, Filipino nursing students first began entering the United States and later Canada, where there was a growing demand for skilled nurses and hospital workers. They were joined in this country by many domestic workers and skilled professionals who found limited opportunities in their native land. The introduction of martial law in the Philippines in the 1970s also led to many immigrants coming to Canada.

The major commercial centers for the Filipino community remain in Parkdale near Queen Street West and Lansdowne Avenue, though scattered centers do exist throughout the city. While most Filipinos in Toronto have come from the populous island of Luzon, other islanders, some with very different cultures, are also represented here.

Religion

The Japanese in Toronto belong to a variety of different churches, including Protestant, Buddhist, Shinto, and other Japanese religious sects that have establishments in the area. Among their places of worship are:

Konko Church of Toronto, *2579 Kennedy Road (416-299-6880).*

Japanese Christian Church of Grace, *310 Danforth Avenue (416-497-1017).*

Japanese Gospel Church of Toronto, *3250 Finch Avenue East (416-261-6755).*

Nichiren Shoshu Canada, *636 King Street West (416-368-0123).*

Saint Andrew Japanese Congregation, *100 Howland Avenue (416-654-5657).*

Seicho-No-Ie Canada Truth Centre, *662 Victoria Park Avenue (416-222-3097).*

Tenrikyo, *160 Gracefield Avenue (416-247-9791).*

Toronto Buddhist Church, *918 Bathurst Street (416-543-4302).*

Toronto Buddhist Temple, *20 Caithness Avenue (416-463-9783).*

Toronto Fukuin-Kyokai, *415 Broadview Avenue (416-461-1686).*

Toronto Japanese Seventh Day Adventist Church, *19 Mortimer Avenue (416-491-6750).*

Japanese United Church, *701 Dovercourt Road (416-536-9435).*

Zen Buddhist Temple, *80 Vaughan Road (416-658-0137).*

The Korean community arrived in Canada with the support of the Protestant missionaries who originally went to Korea to preach the word of God. As a result, most of Toronto's Koreans are Christian. Their churches include:

Korean Beacon Church, *177 Christie Street (416-654-9144).*

Korean Bethel Church, *22 York Mills Road (416-222-7590).*

Korean Central Presbyterian Church, *246 Westmoreland Avenue (416-535-4423).*

Korean Central United Church, *353 Sherborne Avenue (416-922-3863).*

Korean Choonghyun Presbyterian Church, *240 Manor Road East (416-487-6447).*

Korean Emmanuel United Church, *63 Dunblaine Avenue (416-488-4141).*

Korean Evangelical Fellowship Church, *20 Tuxedo Court (416-439-6004).*

Korean Mission Presbyterian Church, *1 Greenland Avenue (416-444-8002).*

Korean New Jerusalem Pentecostal Church, *5 Grenoble Drive (416-429-0808).*

Korean Peoples Church, *171 Delhi Avenue (416-633-2424).*

Korean Philadelphia Presbyterian Church, *729 Saint Clair Avenue West (416-652-3692).*

Korean Presbyterian Church, *754 Indian Road (416-762-1495).*

Korean Presbyterian Church Ministry, *1183 Davenport Road (416-532-2121).*

Korean United Church, *300 Bloor Street West (416-925-6261).*

Toronto Korean Baptist Church, *720 Ossington Avenue (416-531-7604).*

Korean Catholics worship at the **Saint Kim Dae Kun Korean Catholic Church,** 439 Dundas Street East (416-863-0415), to which is also attached the **Korean Catholic Community Centre.**

The **Korean Buddhist Temple,** 86 Vaughan Road (416-658-0137), is the main place of worship for Toronto's Korean Buddhists, and the **Korean Buddhist Society of Ontario,** 6 Wildwood Crescent (416-463-8998), acts as the overall coordinating organization.

A variety of religious institutions minister to other Southeast Asian communities. National Buddhist temples include **Cambodian Temple,** 4707 Jane Street (416-663-1104), and **Lao Buddhist Temple,** 27 Forge Drive (416-663-4638).

There also are a number of Vietnamese Buddhist temples, including **Di Da Temple,** 1120 Queen Street West (416-533-5838); **Hoa Nghiem Temple,** 1000 Queen Street West; and **Choa Hoa Nem Temple,** 1380 Gerrard Street East.

There are large Vietnamese Protestant congregations at the **Mission of the Vietnamese Martyrs,** 549 Runnymede Road (416-769-8104), and **Vietnamese Evangelical Church,** 9 Boon Avenue (416-466-7901).

There are also large Indonesian congregations at the **Indonesia Christian Centre,** 4545 Jane Street (416-736-2100), and the **Saint Joan of Arc Church,** 1701 Bloor Street West (416-762-1026).

The **Malaysian Singaporean Bible Church,** 2 Charles Street East (416-297-8355), is the main church for Toronto's Malay community.

The Filipino community is by and large of Catholic background, and many of its most frequented churches are in the areas of original Filipino settlement near Saint Jamestown.

Holy Family Catholic Church, *1372 King Street West (416-532-2879).*

Iglesia ni Cristo, *310 Burnamthorpe Road (416-231-6006).*

John XXIII Community Church, *150 Gateway Boulevard (416-429-4000).*

Our Lady of Lourdes Catholic Church, *11 Earl Street (416-924-6257).*

Saint Basil Catholic Church, *50 Saint Joseph Street (416-926-7110).*

Saint Patrick Catholic Church, *141 McCaul Street (416-598-3269).*

Evangelical and Pentecostal congregations are finding a growing reception from the community, and a number of Filipino Protestant congregations are in the Metro area as well. Protestant and Evangelical churches that have been drawing an increasing number of Filipino parishioners include:

Commonwealth Avenue Baptist Church, *83 Commonwealth Avenue (416-267-8073).*

Filipino Canadian Seventh Day Adventist Church, *788 Sheppard Avenue West (416-633-4631).*

First Filipino Baptist Church, *382 Lippincott Street (416-534-4342).*

Philipine Independent Church, *40 Pritchard (416-761-5329).*

Seventh Day Adventist Church, *555 Finch Avenue West (416-636-2471).*

═══════════ Organizations ═══════════

The **Japanese Canadian Cultural Centre,** 123 Wynford Drive (416-441-2345), is the center of the Japanese community in Toronto. It is an umbrella group that houses a number of organizations at the same address, including the **Toronto Japanese Garden Club** (416-441-2345); the **Association for Japanese Culture** (416-441-2345); and numerous arts, crafts, and discussion clubs pursuing such Japanese cultural pursuits as *ikebana* (flower arranging), calligraphy, and *shishu* (embroidery). Other cultural groups include the **Sakura Kai Dance Group,** the **Suwa Daiko Drum Group** (which has the largest collection of Japanese drums outside of Japan), and the **Toronto Go Club.** The building, designed by Raymond Moriyama, is a beautiful and inventive piece of modern architecture, blending the landscape setting of a Japanese garden with the bold, modern, minimalist lines of the building itself to create a tranquil yet powerful statement about this culture.

A number of groups act to promote Japanese-Canadian political and business interests, including:

National Association of Japanese Canadians, *192 Spadina Avenue (416-365-3343).*

Toronto Nisei Women's Group, *123 Wynford Drive (416-441-2345).*

Japanese Canadian Citizens Association, *59 Cairns Avenue (416-461-5765).*

Toronto Japanese Association of Commerce and Industry, *141 Adelaide Street West (416-360-0235).*

A number of institutions offer Korean-language training, including:

Korean Canadian Women's Association of Metro Toronto, *20 Mobile Drive (416-752-2538).*

Korean Cultural Centre for Education, *76 Three Valley Drive (416-443-8551).*

Korean Community School, *150 Madison Avenue (416-960-0074).*

The **Korean Cultural Association of Metro Toronto,** 20 Mobile Drive (416-755-9288), is the main umbrella organization for the Korean community in the city. Information on events or services can be obtained by phoning the **Korean Community Information Centre,** 146 Hallam Street (416-533-1111). **Korean Information and Social Services,** 720 Ossington Street (416-531-6701), is also a good source of information on community services. **Korean Social Services,** 162 Christie Street (416-588-6833), is the main center for accessing community and social services.

The **Ontario Korean Businessman's Association,** 1 Mobile Drive (416-285-1100), has been a very powerful and active force in the community, as many Koreans are engaged in small-business activities.

Other Southeast Asian community groups include:

Canadian Cambodian Association of Ontario, *1111 Finch Avenue West (416-736-0832).*

The main umbrella group for Cambodian community, social, and educational services. It encourages cultural exchange and integration into Canadian society.

The Indonesian Association, *4294 Fieldgate Drive (905-828-2550).*

Arranges fundraising and social events.

The Organisasi Mahasiswa Indonesia, *3390 Western Road (416-748-3529).*

An Indonesian student community and social group.

Sanggar Budaya, *239 Huntsmill Boulevard (416-363-6152).*

An Indonesian cultural association that supports a dance group and gives dance lessons.

Umat Katolik Indonesia/Catholic Society, *1858 New Street (905-831-1537).*

An Indonesian Catholic community group.

The **Lao Association of Ontario,** *1111 Finch Avenue West (416-665-3872).*

An umbrella organization for a variety of Laotian community organizations and organizations that help integrate Laotians into Canadian life.

The **Thai Business Association,** *280 Spadina Avenue (416-597-8212).*

The umbrella association of Thai business and community groups in Toronto.

The **Vietnamese Association of Toronto,** *565 College Street (416-535-5241); 1364 Dundas Street (416-536-3611).*

An umbrella group of social, cultural, and community organizations for the Vietnamese community.

Canadian Vietnamese Parents Association of Toronto, *110 Fenside Drive (416-444-7404).*

Canadian Vietnamese Student's Association of Toronto, *980 Dufferin Street (416-393-0420).*

Vietnamese Community Services, *111 Eglinton Avenue East (416-482-4933).*

Vietnamese Publications, *PO Box 310, Station W (416-249-4195).*

Vietnamese Women's Association/Vietnamese Youth and Women's Centre, *2A Olive Street (416-536-8241).*

The **Vietnamese, Cambodian, Laos Chinese Services of Ontario,** *158 Augusta Avenue (416-593-0803).*

An organization devoted to dealing with the unique needs of people of Chinese descent who have come from Southeast Asian countries to Toronto.

The **Khmer People's National Liberation Front,** *1209 Queen Street West (416-466-1302),* and

National United Front, *PO Box 63, Station G (416-465-3193).*

Both political organizations address the ongoing struggles in Cambodia.

Keluarga Masyarakat Indonesia, *40 Blackmore Avenue (905-238-2834).*

A politically nationalist Indonesian youth organization.

Kababayan Community Centre, *1444 Queen Street West (416-532-3888).*

Coordinates a number of educational, cultural, and social activities in the Parkdale community.

Silayan Filipino Community Centre, *418-B Parliament Street (416-926-9505).*

Helps provide support for new immigrants to the area as well as addressing legal and political questions for community members.

Annak Ti Batac Association, *2881 Windwood Drive (905-826-5755).*

Barangay Pilipino, *2813 Kingsberry Crescent (905-276-2264).*

Carlos Bulosan Cultural Workshop, *2926 Oka Road (905-567-4037).*

Carolinians, *1388 Queen Street West (416-532-0020).*

Culture Philippines, *2687 Kingsberry Crescent (416-276-9199).*

Supports cultural events and performance arts in the community.

Fiesta Filipina Dance Troupe, *829 Queensbridge Drive (905-566-5734).*

A very popular dance troupe performing a variety of Filipino folk dances.

Filipino-Canadian Medical Association, *600 Sherborne Street (416-968-6561).*

Filipino-jun Fan Martial Arts, *20 Baywood (416-740-5254).*

Promotes the Philippines' national form of martial arts.

Filipino Parents Association of Toronto, *260 Wellesley Street East (416-922-4414).*

Filipino Performing Arts and Culture, *251 Westlake Avenue (416-467-0612).*

Folklorico Filipino Canada, *80 Forest Manor Road (416-491-3668).*

Himig Filipino Choral Ensemble, *2653 Folkway Drive (905-820-1378).*

Kagayanon Foundation, *24 Waggoners Wells Lane (905-881-7775).*

La Famosa Nova, *135 Tyndall Avenue (416-531-8044).*

Philippine Heritage Band, *PO Box 392, Station U (416-638-1833).*

Polynesian Spectacular Dance Company, *27 Passmore (416-754-2978).*

San Lorenzo Ruiz Catholic Community Centre, *600 Sherborne Street (416-968-6561).*

Tanglaw ng Kabataan, *34 Silvercrest Avenue (416-255-7565).*

An organization devoted to advancing the playing of native string instruments among elementary school children.

Filipino organizations have been active in advancing political causes both in their home country and in Canada. Some of these include:

National Congress of Filipino Canadian Organizations in Canada, *4315 Lee Drive (905-896-6785).*

Canadian Campaign for Philipine Reconstruction,
291 Hounslow Avenue (416-222-5796).

Many Filipino immigrants to Canada have come over as household domestics, often via other countries. The **International Coalition to End
Domestics' Exploitation,** 489 College Street (416-324-8751), is an organization set up by members of the community to help deal with concerns regarding the exploitation of household domestics throughout the world,
including those of Filipino descent.

═══ Holidays and Celebrations ═══

January	*Makha Bouxa,* a Laotian Buddhist festival.
January 1	*New Year's Day,* a major holiday for Japanese people with special meals and house parties to celebrate the New Year. As for many Orientals, the beginning of the year is an important time for celebration. Most Koreans also celebrate the solar New Year, though some do celebrate the Chinese (lunar) New Year.
February	*Vixakha Bouxa* (Rocket Festival), a Laotian fes-tival commemorating Buddha's birthday.
February/March	*Boun Pha Vet,* reading of the life of Buddha.
March	*Hina-Masuri (the Doll's Festival),* otherwise known as Girl's Day in Japan, celebrated with heirloom family dolls being brought out and displayed.
	Women's Day, pays tribute to the two Trung sis-ters who fought an invading Chinese army in 40 AD.
March 1	*National Independence Day,* celebrating at-tempts by the Koreans to gain independence from Japan in 1919.
March/April	*Fatherland Founders Day,* in honor of Viet-nam's founding dynasty 4,000 years ago.

Easter, an especially festive occasion for the Filipino community as it is celebrated in conjunction with the pre-Christian festival of Salubuong. The pre-Easter Lenten season is also commemorated with great fanfare as befits the Spanish origins of Filipino Catholicism.

April
Cambodian New Year, held in the middle of the month.

April 12
Thai Monarchy Day.

April 13
Thai New Year; Water Festival.

April 30
Commemorates the fall of the South Vietnamese government.

April/May
Buddha's birthday.

May 5
Tango-Nu-Sekku, known as Boy's Day in Japan, celebrated with the flying of kites and paper streamers.

May 31
Flores de Mayo, a religious celebration honoring the Roman Emperor Constantine's mother who went on a pilgrimage searching for the cross on which Christ was crucified.

June 7
Birthday of the Malaysian monarch.

June 12
Original Philippines Independence Day, when General Emilio Aguinaldo announced the independence of the Philippines from Spanish rule. A parade and fiesta are held.

July
Khao Vassa, the festival of Patimokkha, a Buddhist festival of fasting and meditation.

July 4
Modern Philippines Independence Day, coincides with that of its last colonial ruler, the United States.

July 14
Obon Festival, the Buddhist remembrance day for deceased relatives.

August 15
Liberation Day, celebrating Korea's liberation from Japanese colonial rule. Also *Choosuk* (Korean Thanksgiving Day).

August 17
Indonesian Independence Day.

August 31	*Malaysian Independence Day.*
September	*Ho Khao Slak,* a Laotian feast.
	Vietnamese Children's Day, held mid-month.
October	*Issei Day,* honoring the first generation of Japanese settlers in Canada.
	Pchun Ben, Cambodian Thanksgiving.
October 3	*Korean Heritage Day,* commemorating the day of Korea's legendary founding over 4,000 years ago.
December	*Kohaku Uta Gassen Song Festival.*
December 5	King Bhumipol of Thailand's birthday.

═══ Restaurants, Cafés, and Nightclubs ═══

A large number of good to excellent Japanese restaurants are scattered throughout the city. Toronto was one of the cities caught in the sushi bar boom of the 1980s and as a result many fine Japanese restaurants opened here. *Sushi* (rolled rice balls in a seaweed covering with pieces of raw or cooked fish, meat, or vegetables; Japanese green mustard; and ginger) isn't the only specialty. *Tempura* (a lightly battered fish or vegetable) abounds, as do *okonomi* (a Japanese-style pizza), *soba* (buckwheat noodle soup), *teriyaki* (marinated beef and meat), and *yakiiniku* (hibachi-style grilled cooking done at your table).

Korean food is a delicious cuisine all its own with touches of Japanese spices and sauces as well as Chinese styles of cooking. Among the best-known dishes are *kim chee* (a very highly spiced pickled cabbage served with most meals as a vegetable or condiment), *bul go gee* (a delicious marinated beef dish), *kalbi ribs* (beef ribs that have been grilled and marinated in a sweet sauce), and *bibimab* (a rice-based dish in which eggs, meat, and vegetables are mixed with a sweet marinade sauce).

Southeast Asian cuisine in its various forms has been one of the trendier foods of late. It includes some spices that are exotic to the Western palate, including the ubiquitous coriander and mint, as well as Chinese basil and a variety of coconut milk-based curries. While Thai food is seen as spicy and Vietnamese as mild, Southeast Asian cuisines are actually more similar than different and constitute a very healthy and interesting alternative to more classic cuisines. Foods such as spring rolls and salad rolls are becoming better-known fast-food staples.

Filipino food is quite unique vis-à-vis both traditional Western and Asian cuisines. It combines tropical fruit and sugar cane flavors with a variety of pork (barbecued suckling pig, pork casserole), chicken (garlic chicken), and seafood as well as more exotic products like duck eggs, tripe, oxtail, and blood pudding. Philippine restaurants are generally inexpensive and unpretentious, but the food is interesting and flavorful and as yet hasn't suffered the ravages of trendiness. Filipino food is best eaten with beer such as San Miguel, the most popular one in the islands.

Many of the restaurants identified here specialize in a specific cuisine. This is by no means an exhaustive list, but it tries to present a good variety of high-quality establishments.

Bali Restaurant, *1554 Avenue Road (416-782-5928).*

Specializes in Indonesian dishes such as *rijsttafel* (rice table) and *bahmi goreng* (spicy Indonesian noodles). Long established in the Toronto area.

Bangkok Garden, *18 Elm Street (416-977-6748).*

Well known as one of the best Thai restaurants in Toronto, the Bangkok Garden is an elegant establishment complete with pond, garden, and stream. Service is good and the menu extensive.

Bon Tei, *3345 Bloor Street West (416-231-7963).*

This small restaurant in Toronto's West End has been producing some of the best Japanese food in the city for years now. Besides the tempura and teriyaki, the owners combine fresh Canadian items like fiddleheads and pickerel into unique Canadian-Japanese dishes.

Café Asia, *370 King Street West (416-408-2742).*

This cavernous restaurant in the basement of the Holiday Inn on King Street serves a variety of Asian cuisines, including Japanese and Korean foods. It has a large and excellently stocked sushi bar as well as a Korean-style barbecue grilling room where you can grill your food, including excellent thick-sliced kalbi ribs, right at your table.

Dong Il Jang, *162 Cumberland Street (416-968-7773).*

Korean.

Dr. Kim's, *4852 Yonge Street (416-221-1507).*

One of the best-known Korean restaurants in North York, Dr. Kim's also serves excellent Japanese food.

Edo, *359 Eglinton Avenue West (416-481-1370).*

A simple, elegant restaurant with very tasty Japanese food, including a full array of sushi and appetizers. Good service and good cooking are hallmarks of this small restaurant.

Emerald Thai Restaurant, *1055 Yonge Street (416-928-9288).*

Recently opened by the owners of the Golden Thai restaurant, this is an up-scale addition to the Toronto Thai restaurant scene, serving a number of unique and interesting dishes and daily specials in a cordial atmosphere.

Fiesta Manila Family Restaurant, *1620 Albion Road (416-748-7805).*

A large family-owned restaurant serving Filipino specialties like oxtail and tripe stew. A sing-along contest happens every weekend.

First Restaurant, *3–5 Oxford Street (416-598-1125).*

Floating Market Restaurant, *110 Queen Street East (416-777-9382).*

A small, intimate, pleasantly decorated Thai restaurant in downtown Toronto serving superb Thai food, including a number of interesting appe-tizers.

Fune, *100 Simcoe Street (416-599-3868).*

A modern, active sushi bar is the main highlight of this restaurant. The of-ferings are extensive and are served on little barges floating around an oval water-filled canal. There is also a large selection of udon dishes and soups as well as familiar Japanese favorites. The place turns into a lively karaoke bar after 10:00 PM.

Garuda Restaurant, *373 Eglinton Avenue West (416-487-6426).*

An Indonesian restaurant with some additional Dutch specialties.

Golden Thai, *105 Church Street (416-868-6668).*

One of the best Thai restaurants in the city, the Golden Thai presents a wide array of appetizers and main dishes. The food is fresh, served quickly and courteously; and the restaurant is quite crowded on weekends. Specialties include *shrimp fantasia* (beautifully prepared shrimp with fried coconut spires, coconut milk rice, and garlic beef).

Hoai Huong Restaurant, *420 College Street (416-929-5521).*

Hope Garden Restaurant, *379 Albion Road (416-741-7810).*

An inexpensive restaurant serving Philippine specialties like *adobo* (garlic, chicken, and pork casserole).

Ichiban Japanese and Korean Restaurant, *668 Bloor Street West (416-534-0928).*

Indochine Noodle Factory, *4 Collier Street (416-922-5840).*

The oldest and still the best Vietnamese restaurant in the city. Known for its superb lemongrass soups, as well as Vietnamese staples like fried marinated pork with rice noodles and a variety of curried chicken dishes.

Indonesia, *678 Yonge Street (416-967-0697).*

An inexpensive café-restaurant serving a variety of Indonesian foods, including fried noodles, chili shrimp, and Indonesian satays.

Jang-won, *3 Christie Street (416-537-5556).*

Specializing in bul go gee.

Jikokae, *880 Dundas Street East (416-279-1444).*

Korean.

Katsura Japanese Restaurant, *900 York Mills Road (416-444-2511).*

Set in a beautifully designed Japanese tea house overlooking the Japanese gardens in the courtyard of the Prince Hotel, the Katsura provides oriental elegance with superb food. The *robata yaki* (grilled fish) counter is extensive, and the service is gracious and classy. Expensive but good value for money.

Kim Bo, *546 Dundas Street West (416-596-8589).*

Korea House, *666 Bloor Street West (416-536-8666).*
An excellent full-menu restaurant covering the gamut of Korean dishes. It is the oldest Korean restaurant in the city and is well known for its kalbi ribs and bibimab.

Korean Barbeque Restaurant, *3280 Midland Avenue (416-754-8141).*

Korean Town Se Jong Restaurant, *658 Bloor Street West (416-535-5918).*

Korean Village, *628 Bloor Street West (416-536-0290).*
Comprehensive in its range of Korean cuisine, this place serves such specialties as *mandoo gook* (Korean won ton soup), *guhun man doo* (stuffed, fried Korean dumplings), *bindae dock* (dried green-bean floured crepes with bits of ham), cow shank soup, and *ohjung un begum* (squid in a hot chili sauce).

Luneta Filipino Barbeque, *1655 Victoria Park Avenue (416-750-4090).*
An authentic Filipino barbecue house serving *lechon* (barbecued suckling pig) and *embutido* (pork roll), as well as Filipino teriyaki barbecued ribs.

Madoka Japanese Restaurant, *252 Dupont Street (416-924-3548).*
A very pleasant little out-of-the-way restaurant serving sushi, tempura, and other Japanese favorites at a reasonable price. Neighborhood atmosphere makes for relaxed, casual dining.

Mai Thai Restaurant, *2364 Yonge Street (416-488-2250).*
An excellent north Toronto location with a wide selection of fish and seafood with a strong lemongrass and tamarind-infused flavor along with classic Thai appetizers and curries.

Manila Grill Seafood Restaurant, *304 Wilson Avenue (416-635-6522).*

Serves fish and seafood specialties from the Philippines.

Mariko, *348 Danforth Avenue (416-463-8231).*

Modern Japanese cooking with a North American look. Fresh, well-prepared, classic Japanese cuisine along with interesting specials that combine North American flavors and foods.

Masa Dining Lounge, *205 Richmond Street West (416-977-9519).*

Long an established Japanese restaurant with a full array of Japanese specialties, tatami rooms, and sushi bar.

Mayette's, *911 Danforth Avenue (416-463-0338).*

An excellent little café specializing in Filipino dishes, including crispy pata, *kara-kare* (an oxtail, tripe, and vegetable stew), *kaldereta* (goat-meat stew), and *sinigang* (stewed fish with vegetables).

Mori Japanese Café, *1280 Bay Street (416-861-9721).*

A tiny inexpensive Japanese café in the Yorkville area of Toronto. Specialties include salmon teriyaki and a large array of vegetarian teriyaki and sushi dishes.

Nami Japanese Seafood, *55 Adelaide Street East (416-362-7373).*

An extensive robata bar serving a wide range of fresh grilled fish and specialties such as bento lunches make this a popular place with local Torontonians and Japanese visitors alike. Specialties include kaki, *ebi fry* (oysters or shrimp), fish, and beef sashimi.

Okonomi House, *23 Charles Street West (416-925-6176).*

Okonomis are Japanese pizzas filled with a variety of oriental vegetables and meats. The Okonomi House also serves excellent freshly made grilled chicken and beef teriyaki at reasonable prices.

Ole Malacca, *886 Saint Clair Avenue West (416-654-2111).*

Well-known Malaysian restaurant that first helped acquaint the Toronto area with Malay cooking. Serves excellent satays and seafood specialties, such as stir-fried mussels with peanuts in chili sauce.

Osio Restaurant, *444 Yonge Street (416-599-5444).*

Korean.

Penang Island Restaurant, *1546 Bloor Street West (416-534-0461).*

Superb and diverse array of Malay food, including seafood dishes like curried shark steak, Malaysian-style mussels, and *assam redang sambal* (a kind of Malaysian seafood gumbo consisting of seafood in a tomato sauce with coconut, tamarind, onion, garlic, and sweet peppers). Banana fritters made with rice flour is a popular dessert.

Pho Hung, *200 Bloor Street West (416-963-3080).*

Considered by many to be Toronto's best-quality Vietnamese food, specialties include beautifully marinated grilled meats done over charcoal, as well complex soups bursting with spicy flavors. Very popular with local University of Toronto students.

Quanh Anh Dao, *383 Spadina Avenue (416-598-4514).*

Rasa Ria, *615 Bloor Street West (416-532-1632).*

An excellent and inexpensive Malaysian restaurant serving some unique Malaysian foods, including *goreng ikan* (a fried-noodle dish with fresh lake pickerel or grouper marinated in turmeric, then pan-fried in a ginger sauce), *goreng ayam sayur* (stir-fried chicken sautéed with vegetables and cashew nuts), and *pie tee* (hot pastry cups filled with a mixture of crab, shrimp, carrots, and other vegetables).

Saigon Palace, *454 Spadina Avenue (416-968-1623).*

Saigon Phnom Penh Restaurant, *478 Dundas Street West (416-977-5537).*

Satay Satay, *700 Bloor Street West (416-532-7489).*

A comfortable Malaysian restaurant serving some Thai dishes as well as the ubiquitous satays. Prices are inexpensive. Specialties include lemon shrimp and lamb satays.

Seoul, *3220 Dufferin Street (416-782-4405).*

Korean.

Shoko Soba, *1391 Danforth Avenue (416-465-4482).*

A small, pleasant Japanese restaurant in Toronto's East End serving good Japanese food and sushi at very reasonable prices.

South Vietnam, *444 Spadina Avenue (416-960-2032).*

A popular South Vietnamese restaurant in the heart of Chinatown serving succulent grilled meats as well as house-special butter-fried frog legs.

Sri Malaysia Restaurant, *172 McCaul Street (416-585-9052).*

Specializes in a Malaysian-style fondue in which a pot of beef broth simmers at your table and you dunk a variety of fresh meats and vegetables in to cook them. Other Malaysian specialties include *rojak* (a bean sprout-based salad) and *achat* (vegetable bits mixed with peanut, pepper sauce, and toasted sesame seeds).

Sukhothai, *136 Yorkville Avenue (416-920-0804).*

Pricier than most Thai restaurants in the city, though an excellent value for lunch in this area, Sukhothai also turns out some of the most unique and interesting cuisine. Recently renovated and improved specialties include volcano crab in the evening.

Thai Magic, *1118 Yonge Street (416-968-7366).*

Thuong Hai, *526 Queen Street West (416-360-5355).*

Restaurant and nightclub.

Toriichi, *1590 Queen Street East (416-466-6771).*

A Japanese fast-food restaurant with affordable prices for teriyakis, udon soups, and tempura dinners. Bento lunch boxes are available to take away.

Tropical Hut Foods, 1333 Danforth Avenue (416-465-6709).

Famous for its Filipino specialties such as duck eggs—either salted, pickled, dyed purple and served with sautéed tomatoes, or served as *balut* (a fertilized egg partially developed through incubation). They also serve an exotic guava and tamarind soup, anatto seeds as garnish, lechon with sauce, and a variety of other Filipino delicacies and hot sauces.

Tu Do, *669 Gerrard Street East (416-462-1255).*

Vanipha, *193 Augusta Avenue (416-340-0491).*

Located in the heart of Kensington Market, this superb and inexpensive Thai/Laotian restaurant serves a variety of dishes from *tom kha gai* (coconut-chicken soup) to *goong tod gartiem* (Laotian shrimp in garlic and chili). The Laotian dishes are hot (some very hot), the Thai dishes sweet and sophisticated. The prices are inexpensive

Vanipha Lann, *471 Eglinton Avenue West (416-484-0895).*

The same magical combination of well-cooked, well-spiced Thai and Laotian food at reasonable prices, this time in a more comfortable uptown restaurant, but with the same superb quality from the original chef and owner of Vanipha.

Vietnam House, *440 Spadina Avenue (416-962-7621).*

The only downtown Vietnamese restaurant serving coffee imported from Vietnam.

Vietnam Village Restaurant, *310 Spadina Avenue (416-598-2718).*

Yamase, *317 King Street West (416-598-1562).*

An extensive array of Japanese food is available from this excellent King Street West restaurant. Tatami rooms are available as is one of the best arrays of sushi in the city. A specialty of the house is marinated meat served with hot rocks for quick cooking at your table.

Young Thailand, *81 Church Street (416-368-1368);*
111 Gerrard Street East (416-599-9099).

A very popular spot known for its innovative Thai cuisine served at reasonable prices. The Gerrard Street location is popular with young Thailand loyalists; the Church Street location is more comfortable and upscale. Specialties include delicious pad Thai noodles and *mee krob,* a crisp fried-noodle nest with chicken, seafood, and vegetables.

Food Sources

Japanese foods and sauces can be obtained from a variety of stores throughout the city, including:

Dundas Union Store, *173 Dundas Street West (416-977-3765).*

Furuya, *460 Dundas Street West (416-977-5451).*

Japan Deli, *11 Balmuto Street (416-920-2051).*

Japan Food, *460 Dundas Street West (416-977-5451).*

Japan Food Ozawa, *135 Beaver Creek Road (905-229-6343).*

Japanese Food and Gifts, *730 Queen Street West (416-703-4550).*

Kealson, *2501 Eglinton Avenue East (416-261-2297).*

Sandown Market, *1800 Pharmacy (416-496-8093);*
221 Kennedy Road (416-261-7040).

Stores serving Korean food products and sauces, as well as the full array of Korean herbal and health remedies (such as ginseng), include:

Arirang Foods, *653 Bloor Street West (416-588-7000).*

Asian Health Food Company, *645 Bloor Street West (416-530-0522).*

Korea Bakery, *661 Bloor Street West (416-535-8605).*

Korean Red Ginseng Centre, *242 Sheppard Avenue West (416-222-6439).*

Seoul Gift Shop, *7 Drewry (416-512-6587).*

Southeast Asian products in general may be found at:

Asian Food Market, *670 A Jane Street (416-604-3342).*

Asian Foods, *1441 Queen Street West (416-536-6115).*

Asian Pacific Supermarket, *357 Broadview (416-465-6102).*

Cake Shop, *832 Sheppard Avenue West.*

Sells Filipino sweets such as mammon, enseymada, hopia, and sans rival tortes, as well as the normal array of wedding cakes and pastries.

Manila Mini Mart, *1142 The Queensway (416-255-9017).*

New Asia Supermarket, *293–299 Spadina Avenue (416-591-9314).*

Philippine Island Foods, *832 Sheppard Avenue West (416-633-7666).*

Philippine Oriental Food Market, *1033 Gerrard Street East (416-466-6938).*

Philippine Trading Centre, *1548 Queen Street West (416-536-3640).*

Philippine Tropical Food Store, *634 Saint Clair Avenue West (416-652-5542).*

Pilipino Five O Limited, *1427 Queen Street West (416-535-3676); 1198 The Queensway (416-251-2009).*

Saigon Groceries, *421 Dundas Street West (416-596-8226).*

Sun Hoa Food Market, *359 Broadview Avenue (416-463-5020).*

Viet Nam Market, *3585 Keele Street (416-631-9738).*

Shops

Japanese crafts and specialties have become popular as more and more Westerners have become aware of the beauty of this oriental culture. Among the shops specializing in Japanese gifts, ikebana, floral arts, and paper arts are the following:

Barbara Flower Shop, *1232 Danforth Avenue (416-465-9939).*

Japan Arts, *2115 Midland Avenue (416-609-2681).*

Japanese Paper Place *887 Queen Street West (416-703-0089); 207 Queen's Quay West (416-203-0687).*

Sakura Gift Shop, *4915 Bathurst Street (416-250-0691).*

Fashions and cloth from the Philippines, as well as local handicrafts and gifts, are available at a couple of locations. **Philippine Garments and Handicrafts,** 1033 Gerrard Street East (416-466-6938), has different kinds of cloth and clothing, while the **Philippine Trade House,** 111 Avenue Road (416-967-1798); 60 Bloor Street West (416-967-1788), carries a variety of gifts and handicrafts.

Other specialized stores include:

Bali Designs, *73 Forman (416-486-8185).*

A shop with clothing and textiles from Indonesia, as well as Balinese artifacts, crafts, and gifts.

Thai Lanna Siam, *939 Lawrence Avenue East (416-510-8194).*

A shop specializing in imports from Thailand.

Vientianne Trading Co., *334 Spadina Avenue (416-977-3205).*

Food, gifts, and imports from Southeast Asia.

You can find books, tapes, and records in Southeast Asian languages at the following stores:

Nippon Video Centre, *1993 Danforth Avenue (416-698-0693).*

Has a good selection of Japanese-language videos.

Wah Yue Records, *456 Dundas Street West (416-593-6827).*

Has music and videos.

Furuya, *460 Dundas Street West (416-977-5451).*

Carries a variety of Japanese-language books and magazines.

Korean Book and Video Centre, *678 Bloor Street West (416-537-6946).*

Has a wide array of Korean-language books, videos, newspapers, and magazines.

Saigon Video, *301 Spadina Avenue (416-595-5943),* and **Thai Binh Video,** *432 Dundas Street East (416-962-7292).*

Carry videos and music from Southeast Asia.

Vietnam Bookstore, *415 Spadina Avenue (416-595-5199).*

Carries Vietnamese-language books, magazines, and other publications.

========================== **Media** ==========================

Publications

Annual Korean Business Directory of Ontario, *146 Hallam Street (416-533-1111).*
Annual.

Atin Ito, *1100 Dundas Street West (416-896-2642).*
Monthly publication covering affairs of interest to the Filipino community

Balita, *PO Box 8, Station N (416-252-9954).*
Twice-monthly publication on events of interest to the Filipino community in Canada.

Ban Viet, *1364 Dundas Street West (416-536-3611).*
Vietnamese.

Cambodian Newsletter, *1111 Finch Avenue West (416-736-0832).*
Cambodian news and current events.

Canada Times, *291 Dundas Street West (416-593-2777).*
Has been published every two weeks in Japanese and English since 1907.

Chien Si Tu Do/Vietnamese Freedom Fighters Review, *PO Box 310, Station W, (416-249-4195).*
Vietnamese.

Filipiniana, *1531 Queen Street West (416-534-7836).*
A color bimonthly.

Japanese Newspaper, *312 Dundas Street West (416-593-2777).*
A weekly newspaper keeping the Japanese community up to date on events in the Toronto area.

Korea Business Information Services *(800-385-5388).*

Korea Central Daily, *488 Dupont Street (416-533-5533).*

Korea Times & Hankook il bo (Daily News), *146 Hallam Street (416-533-1111).*
Daily.

Korean (Dong-A) Daily News, *1653 Dundas Street West (416-536-6868).*
Daily.

Korean Digest, *814A Bloor Street West (416-532-0000).*
Daily.

Korean Journal, *649A Bloor Street West (416-588-4988).*

Lang Van, *PO Box 310, Station W (416-249-4195).*
Vietnamese.

Minjoong Shinmoon, *802 Bloor Street West (416-537-3473).*

New Korean Times, *720 Spadina Avenue (416-925-3259).*

Nikkei Voice, *2240 Midland Avenue (416-365-73070).*
Published bimonthly.

Pan Asian Publications Inc., *110 Silver Star Boulevard, Unit 109 (416-292-4468).*
A distributor of a variety of Asian-language books and magazines, including publications in Chinese, Vietnamese, Khmer, and Laotian.

Philippine Reporter, *14 Harvest Moon Drive (416-286-8511).*

Twice-a-month English-language publication covering events of interest in the Philippines and among the dispersed Philippine community.

Sari-Sari ATBPA, *2170 Bromsgrove Road (905-822-7954).*

Monthly Filipino publication.

Song, *PO Box 317, Station H (416-421-4073).*

Vietnamese.

The New Canadian, *479 Queen Street West (416-366-5005).*

The Nikka Times, *720 Spadina Avenue (416-923-2819).*

Thoi Bao/Vietnamese Newspaper, *PO Box 291, Station A (416-925-8957).*

Xieng Lao, *1111 Finch Avenue West (416-665-3872).*

Thrice-annual publication on events of interest to the Laotian community.

Radio and Television

"Hello Japan," CITY-TV, *299 Queen Street West (416-591-5757),* and **"Japanese Journal,"** CFMT-TV, *545 Lakeshore Boulevard West (416-260-3620).*

Weekly news and current-events television shows in Japanese.

Korean Community Radio, *458 Dupont Street (416-538-1616).*

Produces programs and music shows on Korean issues for low-power community radio as well as other radio stations in the city. For a complete list of current programs and outlets, call.

"Filipino Radio Program," CHIN-AM 1540, *622 College Street (416-531-9991).*

"TV Korea," CFMT-TV, Channel 47, *545 Lakeshore Boulevard West (416-593-4747).*

A weekly program covering issues of concern to Canadians of Korean origin.

—Koreatown—

While the Korean population has spread throughout Toronto as a whole, this four-block section of Toronto's West Annex area constitutes the heart of its commercial center. A number of Korean restaurants and karaoke bars, including **Korean Village** and **Korea House,** as well as a variety of food and gift shops, community service centers, and churches, line the streets. Visitors will find this to be a compact yet exotic area with a very different flavor from Chinatown. The restaurants are good and inexpensive, and there are a variety of interesting sights. This is also a center for the different Korean churches. The United, Baptist, and Beacon churches are all in the area.

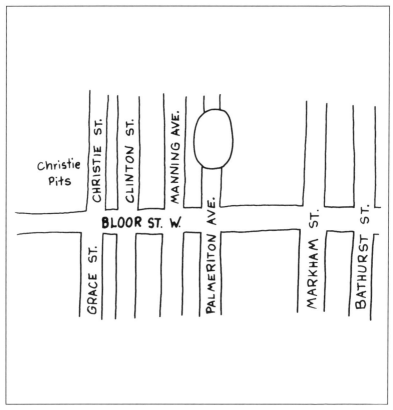

Koreatown

How to Get There: *Take the Bloor/Danforth subway line to Bathurst Street station and walk west on Bloor Street West to Palmerston Avenue. The area is located between Palmerston and Christie Avenue.*

Jewish Toronto

History

Toronto has Canada's largest Jewish population. Arrivals began in 1838 when Judah Joseph opened a jewelry shop on King Street. More Jewish families came in from England and Germany as well as the United States and Quebec, where a large Jewish community had already been formed in Montreal. In 1856 Toronto's community was large enough to finance its own congregation, and so the Toronto Hebrew Congregation was founded at the corner of Yonge and Richmond Streets. This congregation survives today as the **Holy Blossom Temple,** the largest reform synagogue in Canada.

In the 1880s a large number of Russian Jews fled the pogroms following the assassination of Czar Alexander II. Many moved to the area of town then known as "the Ward"—bounded by College and Queen Streets to the north and south, and Yonge Street and University Avenue to the east and west. Little remains of that once-thriving neighborhood except for Mount Sinai Hospital.

More synagogues were established throughout the 1880s, including **Beth Tzedec Synagogue,** now Canada's largest, and **Shomrai Shabboth,** which is the only institution in Toronto that has remained orthodox. The first lodge of the B'nai Brith Canada was also formed at this time. More schools and self-help and charitable organizations were founded in the years leading up to the turn of the century.

The Jewish neighborhood began to move east to the areas on Spadina Avenue that surround Kensington Market. While the market area has changed dramatically in the intervening years, remnants of delis, bakeries, and other Jewish shops can still be found in there, as can much of Toronto's furrier and clothing industry, in which the Jewish community still remains heavily involved.

By the 1920s over 60,000 Jewish people lived in this area, Toronto's Jewish community being its largest single ethnic enclave at the time. Following the Second World War the community doubled in size as many Holocaust refugees were allowed into Canada. The community also began to move into the then-developing suburban areas of North York along Bathurst Street from Eglinton Avenue West north to Steeles Avenue West. This remains the heart of Jewish Toronto today, though large Jewish communities have also taken up residence in the suburbs of Thornhill, Markham, and Vaughan.

Throughout the 1960s Jewish immigration continued from a more diverse range of sources, including the Middle East, Israel, North Africa, and Hungary. The Jewish community has produced an inordinate number of doctors, lawyers, educators, businesspeople, and entrepreneurs over the years, including such prominent ones as the Mirivish and Reichmann families, former Toronto mayor Phil Givens, North York mayor Mel Lastman, civil libertarian Alan Borovoy, former United Nations ambassador Stephen Lewis, actor Al Waxman, and writer Adele Wiseman.

Religion

A number of synagogues of orthodox, conservative, and reform persuasions exist in the Metro area.

Conservative Synagogues

Beth Sholom Synagogue, *1445 Eglinton Avenue West (416-783-6103).*

Built in 1947 with eighteen stained-glass windows depicting biblical scenes.

Beth Tzedec Synagogue, *1700 Bathurst Street (416-781-3511).*

The country's largest synagogue, with a sixty-foot-high mosaic wall.

Beth Emeth-Bais Yehuda, *100 Elder Street (416-633-3838).*

Beth Tikvah, *3080 Bayview Avenue (416-221-3433).*

Adath Israel Synagogue, *37 Southbourne Avenue (416-635-5340).*

Beth David B'nai Israel Beth Am, *53 Yeomans Road (416-633-5500).*

Beth Torah Synagogue, *47 Glenbrook Avenue (416-782-4495).*

Shaar Shalom Synagogue, *2 Simonston Boulevard (416-889-4975).*

Orthodox Synagogues

Anshei Minsk, *10 Saint Andrew Street (416-595-5723).*

The only orthodox synagogue in the downtown area to hold daily ceremonies.

Knesseth Israel, *56 Maria Street (416-783-5871).*

A very old-world synagogue with paintings on the ceiling and walls; housed in an historic building.

Shaarei Shomayim, *470 Glencairn Avenue (416-789-3213).*

Known for its male choir.

Baycrest Centre, *3560 Bathurst Street (416-789-5131).*

Beth Jacob V'Anshei Drildz Congregation, *147 Overbrook Place (416-638-5955).*

B'Nai Torah, *465 Patricia Avenue (416-226-3700).*

Chabad Lubavitch, *770 Chabad Gate (416-731-7000).*

Clanton Park, *11 Lowesmoor Avenue (416-633-4193).*

Magen David (Sephardic) Congregation, *10 McAllister Road (416-636-0865).*

Petach Tikvah Anshe Castilla (Sephardic), *20 Danby Avenue (416-636-4719).*

Shaarei Tzedec, *397 Markham Street (416-923-5828).*

Shaarei Tefillah, *3600 Bathurst Street (416-787-1631).*

Shomrai Shaboth, *583–585 Glengrove Avenue West (416-782-8849).*

Yavneh Zion, *788 Marlee Avenue (416-781-1611).*

Reform Synagogues

Holy Blossom Temple, *1950 Bathurst Street (416-781-9185).*

One of the largest reform temples in North America and one of the best known in Canada

Temple Emanu-El, *120 Colony Road (416-449-3880).*

A particularly lovely temple in an attractive area surrounded by trees, a courtyard, and fishing ponds.

Solel Congregation, *2399 Folkway Drive (416-820-5915).*

Temple Har Zion, *7360 Bayview Avenue (416-889-2252).*

Temple Sinai, *210 Wilson Avenue (416-487-4161).*

Other Places of Worship

The First Narayever, *187 Brunswick Avenue (416-927-0546).*

Adath Sholom Synagogue, *864 Sheppard Avenue West (416-635-0131).*

Benjamin's Park Memorial Chapel, *2401 Steeles Avenue West (416-663-9060).*

Beth Radom, *18 Reiner Road (416-633-6915).*

Beth Habonim, *12 Holloman Road (416-782-7125).*

Darchei Noam (Reconstructionist), *4140 Bathurst Street (416-638-4783).*

Lodzer Centre Holocaust Congregation, *12 Heaton Street (416-636-6665).*

Pride of Israel Synagogue, *59 Lissom Crescent (416-226-0111).*

Mikvah Society for Family Sanctity, *694 Sheppard Avenue West (416-633-4729).*

Steeles-College Memorial Chapel, *350 Steeles Avenue West (416-881-6003).*

Organizations

The community has a host of institutions that support Jewish art, history, culture, and language, including the **Lipa Green Building,** 4600 Bathurst Street (416-635-2883), which is a center for many of the community's social service institutions and houses a museum, a library, and an art gallery. It is named after a prominent Jewish builder and developer. Some of the institutions it houses include the **Albert J. Latner Jewish Public Library** (416-635-2996) and the **Holocaust Education and Memorial Centre** (416-635-2883) which accommodate a wide array of books and audiovisual materials on Holocaust history and Jewish life and culture. The **Leah Posluns Theatre** (416-636-2720) has an active schedule of plays in English and Yiddish, while the **Koffler Gallery** (416-635-2145) has works by many Jewish-Canadian artists, including William Kurelek.

The **Koffler Centre of the Arts,** 750 Spadina Avenue (416-924-6211), offers a variety of athletic, cultural, and social activities as well as dance, theater, and music schools.

Both the **Jewish Community Centre of Toronto—North Branch,** 4588 Bathurst Street (416-636-1880), and **Jewish Community Centre of Toronto—South Branch,** 750 Spadina Avenue (416-924-6211), have programs covering a wide range of cultural and artistic activities, as well as housing a swimming pool, a dance studio, and a gymnasium.

The **Beth Tzedec Museum,** 1700 Bathurst Street (416-781-3511), located in the synagogue, maintains a collection of ancient pottery, coins, spice boxes, and menorahs.

Other community groups and social organizations include:

Association of Soviet Jewry in Canada, *3456 Bathurst Street (416-636-1977).*

Canadian Council of Christians and Jews, *49 Front Street East (416-364-3101).*

Jewish Russian Community Centre, *18 Rockford Road (416-665-9600).*

Reena Foundation, *99 Cartwright Avenue (416-787-0131).*

Toronto Jewish Film Festival, *33 Prince Arthur Road (416-324-8226).*

A number of political organizations deal with Jewish concerns regarding their community and anti-Semitism, including:

Canadian Jewish Congress, *4600 Bathurst Street (416-635-2883).*

B'nai Brith Canada, *15 Hove Street (416-633-6224).*

Canadian Zionist Federation, *3910 Bathurst Street (416-633-3958).*

Hadassah-Wizo, *788 Marlee Avenue (416-789-4373).*

National Council of Women, *1111 Finch Avenue West (416-665-8251).*

══════ Holidays and Celebrations ══════

February/March	*Purim,* celebrating the defeat of evil.
March/April	*Passover.*
April/May	*Israeli Independence Day.*
May/June	*Shavuoth* (Pentecost), commemorating God giving Moses the Ten Commandments.
July/August	*Tisha B'Av,* a fasting time of reflection.
September	*Rosh Hashanah,* the Jewish New Year.
September/October	*Yom Kippur* (Day of Atonement).
	Sukkoth Festival.
October	*Haddassah-Wizo Bazaar,* one of Toronto's largest bazaars, held every year on the last Wednesday of the month at the Canadian National Exhibition grounds.
December	*Hanukkah,* feast of dedication celebrating the unwillingness of the Jewish people to convert to the religion of Antiochus IV in 165 BC.

═ Restaurants, Cafés, and Nightclubs ═

Jewish food generally follows kosher dietary laws, so no pork is used and beef is butchered in accordance with religious standards. Restaurants serve various Middle Eastern dishes, such as falafel and kebabs, or more European-Jewish dishes, such as *knishes* (deep-fried filled dumplings), chicken soup with *kneddels* (matzoh dumplings), chicken liver, smoked-meat and corned beef sandwiches, and bagels with *lox* (smoked salmon) and/or cream cheese. The following is a list of delis, dairy restaurants, and full-fledged Middle Eastern/Jewish restaurants.

Bagel Restaurant, *285 College Street (416-923-0171).*

Popular with the university crowd, serving primarily dairy and breakfast foods.

Chopstix Glatt Kosher, *3426 Bathurst Street (416-787-0345).*

Kosher Chinese food.

Dairy Treats European Café and Bakery, *3522 Bathurst Street (416-787-0309).*

A dairy café and bakery serving excellent desserts, pastries, and cookies.

Katz's Deli, *3300 Dufferin Street (416-782-1111).*

Huge deli sandwiches and big platters of kosher meats.

Lower East Side Café, *604 Spadina Avenue (416-923-3059).*

Good smoked-meat sandwiches and other delicacies.

Marky's Deli and Restaurant Glatt Kosher, *7380 Yonge Street (905-731-4800).*

Large portions of good kosher food, sandwiches, and smoked meats.

Mati's Falafel House and Pizza, *3430 Bathurst Street (416-783-9505).*

Middle Eastern-Jewish cuisine; also has kosher pizza.

Milk'n'Honey—The Dairy Restaurant, *3457 Bathurst Street (416-789-7651).*

A dairy restaurant with excellent bagels and cream cheese.

Red Pancer Deli, *6233 Bathurst Street (416-223-7870).*

One of the best places for knishes, kneddel soup, and smoked-meat sandwiches in the city.

Shopsy's, *33 Yonge Street (416-365-3333).*

A Toronto landmark in the theater district with a full deli menu, as well as a take-out deli counter for Shopsy's many specialty products.

Sonny Langer's Dairy and Vegetarian Restaurant and Bakery, *180 Steeles Avenue West (416-881-4356).*

Kosher dairy and vegetarian cuisine.

Switzer's Deli, *322 Spadina Avenue (416-596-6900).*

A long-established tradition in Kensington Market with a great 1940s atmosphere and excellent deli sandwiches.

Yitz's Delicatessen, *346 Eglinton Avenue West (416-487-4506).*

Great smoked meat and an extensive array of imported cigars.

══════════ Food Sources ══════════

Bakeries

A number of fine Jewish bakeries exist in the city, all making excellent pastries, cakes, pies, and European breads as well as the ubiquitous bagel. A few make what are known in Canada as Montreal bagels, which have a wonderfully thin dough that makes it less chewy, sweeter, and more flavorful than the fat commercial bagels generally available in supermarkets.

Gryfe's Bagel Bakery, *3421 Bathurst Street (416-783-1552).*

Hermes Bakery, *2885 Bathurst Street (416-787-1234); 3541 Bathurst Street (416-787-2611); 652 Sheppard Avenue West (416-635-1932).*

Isaac's, *3390 Bathurst Street (416-789-7587).*

My Zaidy's Bagel Bakery, *3456 Bathurst Street (416-789-0785).*

Olde Fashioned Bagel Factory, *3521 Bathurst Street (416-781-4476).*
Specializes in Montreal-style wood-oven bagels.

Open Window Bakery, *1125 Finch Avenue West (416-665-8241).*
This is the head office and warehouse sales outlet for a chain. There are many branches throughout the city.

Richman's, *4119 Bathurst Street (416-636-9710).*

Saint Urbain Bagel Bakery, *5 Glen Cameron (905-731-8305); 93 Front Street East (416-364-8305); 895 Eglinton Avenue West (416-787-6955).*

Sweet York Desserts, *1700 Bathurst Street (416-782-1798).*

Butchers

Kosher Meats, *2825 Bathurst Street (416-783-4231).*

Stroli's, *3459 Bathurst Street (416-789-5333).*

Delis and Grocers
Jewish delis, creameries, and groceries carrying kosher products include the following:

B. Goldstein Products, *308 Wilson Avenue (416-633-9642).*

Daiter's Creamery and Appetizers, *3535 Bathurst Street (416-781-6101).*

Raisins, Almonds and More, *3501 Bathurst Street (416-782-7258).*

Chocolate Charm, *3541 Bathurst Street (416-787-4256).*

Shops

The Jewish community is a very literate one, as befits a religion based on the written word. As a result, a number of bookstores cater to the needs of the community in both English and Hebrew. Many of these stores carry religious supplies, magazines, and newspapers as well.

Israel Book and Gift Shop, *897 Eglinton Avenue West (416-256-1010); 441 Clark Avenue (905-881-1010).*

Miriam's Books and Religious Supplies, *3007 Bathurst Street (416-781-8261).*

Negev Book Store and Gift Shop, *3509 Bathurst Street (416-781-9356).*

Aleph Bet Judaica, *3453 Bathurst Street (416-781-2133).*

Media

A variety of Hebrew and English-language media covering events of interest to the Jewish community exist in Toronto.

Publications

Canadian Jewish News, *10 Gateway Boulevard (416-422-2331).*

A weekly newspaper.

Jewish Standard, *77 Mowat Avenue (416-537-2696).*

Jewish Times, *2828 Bathurst Street (416-789-4503).*

Menora Hungarian Jewish Newspaper, *824 Sheppard Avenue West (416-630 4495).*

In Hungarian and English.

Kashruth Directory, *17 Sunfield (416-633-0202).*

Lists supervised retail and commercial establishments that meet the requirements of Jewish dietary law. For those who just want to phone to check on a particular establishment, try the **Kosher Information Service Hotline** (416-635-9550).

Radio and Television

"Shalom," CHIN-AM 1540/FM 100.7, *622 College Street (416-531-9991).*

A program dedicated to Jewish religious music and current events.

"Tapestry," CITY-TV, Channel 57, *299 Queen Street West (416-591-5757).*

A television program delving into the community in Canada.

—Bathurst Street North: The Heart of Jewish Toronto—

While Kensington Market still commands a soft spot in the history of Toronto's Jewish community, it is the Bathurst Street North area where the heart of its commercial, religious, cultural, and residential lives are led. This area, stretching from Glencairn Avenue North to Steeles Avenue West along the whole of Bathurst Street, is full of kosher delis, bakeries, butchers, and grocers as well as gift shops, restaurants, synagogues, and community centers.

Jewish Toronto

Starting from Holy Blossom Temple just south of Eglinton Avenue West, the community stretches past Shaarei Tefillah temple near Lawrence Avenue West. Commercially there is a long stretch of Jewish shops here all the way north to above Wilson Avenue, where you also find Adath Israel. North of Sheppard are a number of small shopping centers, as well as the Lipa Green complex, the YWHA/YMHA complex, Adath Shalom, and Earl Bates Park, the site of many festivals and celebrations.

Toronto's Jewish population has begun to move farther north into the Thornhill area, but Bathurst still constitutes the biggest part of the community and is the most active center. A shopping area on Eglinton Avenue West extending west from Bathurst Street also has a number of shops and restaurants of interest.

How to Get There: *Take the Number 7 Bathurst bus north from the Bathurst station on the Bloor/Danforth subway line or north from the Saint Clair West station on the Spadina subway line.*

Latin Toronto

Toronto's Latin community is made up of two distinct, yet not wholly dissimilar, groups: the Portuguese and the Hispanic communities. Portugal and Spain, as neighboring European countries, had various bouts of trouble over national borders throughout history. When both countries expanded, exploring and settling in South America, this tradition continued to an extent. Brazil was once a Portuguese territory (and Portuguese is still the country's official language), whereas its neighbors share a strong Spanish heritage. Despite their differences, the closeness of the cultures made some similarities between them only natural.

Nationalities

Portuguese

One of Toronto's largest and most active ethnic groups is the Portuguese community, which encompasses immigrants not only from Portugal but also from Brazil, the Azores, and Madeira. The community has grown to over 150,000 in the Metro area, with almost 100,000 in the city of Toronto itself.

The Portuguese have been coming to Canada since the first days of exploration. Portuguese fishermen fished the Grand Banks for cod, and Portuguese families were early settlers in New France. There was little immigration to Canada though until the early 1950s, when eighty-five Portuguese men were brought over to work as farm laborers then gradually moved into the cities to find factory jobs.

Other Portuguese immigrants began arriving in the same decade. Many were drawn to the opportunities of fishing in the Great Lakes. Others, from the Azores, Goa, Madeira, and the Cape Verde Islands, came to work in the food-processing and meatpacking industries. Most settled in the area around Alexandra Park and Kensington Market that still forms the nucleus of community settlement in Toronto.

The first Portuguese Canadian Club was formed in 1956, and Portuguese-language services were first held at Saint Michael's Cathedral in 1955. The first Portuguese parish was formed at Saint Mary's Church in the 1960s. The area of settlement pushed westward until today the heart of Portugal Village is around Ossington Avenue on both College Street and Dundas Street West.

Immigrants have continued to arrive primarily from the Azores; over 70 percent of Toronto's Portuguese people are of Azorean origin. The laborers and fishermen who made up the first group of immigrants have been joined by craftsmen, entrepreneurs, and skilled technicians. The Portuguese in Toronto celebrate a number of colorful festivals and hold religious processions, including the procession of Senhor Cristo do Milagres (Christ of Miracles) and the Week of Portugal celebrations.

In High Park a monument celebrates the twenty-fifth anniversary of the arrival of the Portuguese to Canada. The community here has been very supportive of efforts in their homeland, and many Portuguese Canadians hold dual citizenship. Numerous community members also contributed to the development of a Portuguese bobsledding team in the 1988 winter Olympics. At the Spadina North docks in Harbourfront Park is the *Feliz Viagem (Happy Voyage),* a Portuguese cargo vessel built in 1919 and colorfully decorated in motifs of the *canoa* (boat) native to the province of Ribatejo.

In the nearby town of Sutton, Toronto's Madeiran community has a shrine and a park dedicated to the island's spiritual protectress, Our Lady of the Mount. A procession and festival is held in the park every summer.

Toronto also has a small Brazilian population that has provided much of the music and entertainment in the Portuguese community and has contributed about 3,000 immigrants to the Toronto area since the 1970s. Originally arriving as laborers and construction workers, many Brazilians have gone on to open businesses and find work in other occupations. Artist Patricia Fisher and Dr. Tomas Antonio Salerno, the head of Saint Michael's Hospital's cardiovascular surgery unit, are two examples of prominent Brazilian Torontonians.

Hispanic

While Toronto's Hispanic-American community has grown to over 200,000 people in recent years, its actual presence has been relatively recent. Significant immigration from Hispanic areas didn't begin until the early twentieth century, and the majority of new immigrants have arrived within the last twenty-five years.

In the first years of this century, the community grew to a little over 2,000 by the end of World War I. Early settlement was around Bathurst and College Streets, and this remains the center of the Hispanic population today, although a parallel community runs along Bloor Street West at Bathurst Street.

A very large increase in the Hispanic population occurred in the 1970s coinciding with the right-wing political upheavals that affected Chile, Argentina, Uruguay, El Salvador, and other Latin and South American countries. To this day the Chilean and El Salvadorian communities remain the largest in the overall Hispanic community, numbering over 40,000 inhabitants each. Despite these numbers, however, immigrants have come to Toronto from over twenty Latin countries.

An International Hispanic Fiesta is held once a year to celebrate both the differences and similarities of the city's many Hispanic cultures. A variety of Latin shops, restaurants, and nightclubs have opened in recent years, adding an interesting new texture to Toronto's already diverse multicultural weave.

One interesting cultural group in Toronto and southwestern Ontario comprises Mexican immigrants. Most were sponsored through Canada's Mennonite religious groups, and there is in fact a considerable number of Mexican Mennonites now in this area.

Religion

Most Portuguese Canadians are Catholics, although some Protestant churches also have extensive Portuguese congregations. The main Catholic churches include:

Saint Mary's Church, *589 Adelaide Street West (416-366-2326).*

The biggest Portuguese parish in the city, this church is often decorated for a variety of saints' days and feast days throughout the year. Portugal Square, which surrounds the church, is the site of many community festivals.

Holy Name Church, *71 Gough Street (416-466-8281).*

Igreja Universal Do Reino De Deus, *1305 Dundas Street West (416-538-8923).*

Saint Agnes Church, *15 Grace Street (416-364-1715).*

Saint Anthony's Church, *1041 Bloor Street West (416-536-3333).*

Saint Clare Church, *1118 Saint Clair Avenue West (416-654-7087).*

Saint Helen's Church, *1680 Dundas Street West (416-531-8188).*

Saint Peter's Church, *659 Markham Street (416-534-4219).*

Saint Sebastian's Church, *20 Pauline Avenue (416-536-2302).*

Santa Cruz Catholic Church, *142 Argyle Street (416-533-8425).*

Other faiths are represented at the following churches:

Olivet Baptist Church, *36 Marguetta Avenue (416-535-1357).*

The main Protestant church, first organized in 1890. It has a large Brazilian and Azorean congregation.

Portuguese Seventh Day Adventist Church *(416-923-5285).*

Scarborough Baptist Church, *1597 Kingston Road (416-698-1973).*

Volunteers of Christ Centre, *2420 Dufferin Street (416-785-9327).*

Toronto's Hispanic community also worships primarily at Catholic churches, though some are members of growing Pentecostal and Evangelical congregations.

Los Franciscanos Capuchinos, *2100 Jane Street (416-241-3101).*
Provides Spanish-language masses.

Saint John the Baptist, *941 A Dundas Street West (416-366-0266).*

Saint Peter's Church, *659 Markham Street (416-534-4219).*

Saint Phillip Neri, *2100 Jane Street (416-241-3101).*

The **Pentecostal Hispanic Church,** *1292 Queen Street West (416-588-9736).*
A Pentecostal church with a large Hispanic congregation.

Tabernáculo Evangelistico, *710 Markham Road (416-293-3104).*
Conducts its services in Spanish.

Spanish Faith Cathedral, *120 Norfinch Road (416-650-0373).*

Spanish Baptist Church, *24 Birch Avenue (416-963-9073).*

=============== **Organizations** ===============

Portuguese-language courses can be found at three locations:

The **Centro de Cultura e Educação Luso-Canadiano,** *573 College Street (416-537-7288),* and

Escola Comunitaria do Clube Portuguêse Transmontano, *1659 Dundas Street West (416-537-7106).*

The city's two primary language schools.

The **First Portuguese Canadian Club,** *722 College Street (416-531-9971).*

Offers Portuguese-language courses, but is also the main umbrella group for Portuguese community, cultural, and social organizations. Its muraled outdoor facade honors the community's involvement in Canadian affairs, and a bust of Luis De Camoes, the Portuguese author and poet, adorns this garden setting at the corner of College Street and Crawford. The club includes a restaurant, lecture halls, meeting rooms, a bar, and a games room. Evenings often feature performances of fado music or dances.

Other community societies and associations include:

Alliance of Portuguese Clubs and Associations, *PO Box 66, Station C (416-536-5961).*

Organizes a number of regional sports and cultural clubs.

Federation of Portuguese-Canadian Business and Professionals of Toronto *(416-535-2500).*

A very active organization designed to help foster this busy entrepreneurial sector of the community and to work at fostering Portuguese-Canadian political interests.

Portuguese Canadian Social Service of Toronto, *84 Rusholme Road (416-533-5507); 115 College Street (416-539-9576).*

Offers counseling, social services, and immigrant aid.

Casa Do Alentejo, *646 Dufferin Street (416-537-7766).*

A regional club that sponsors an annual week-long festival featuring Portuguese food, music, and folklore, as well as exhibits, films, and lectures.

Nazare Recreative Club, *1166 Dundas Street West (416-531-0605).*

Another regional group with a library and performing arts program.

Arsenal do Minho-S.C Braga of Toronto, *1172 Dundas Street West (416-534-7919).*

One of Ontario's top soccer teams.

The **Canadian Madeira Club,** *961 College Street (416-533-2401).*

Casa Da Madeira, *295A Augusta Avenue (416-848-3214).*

Casa Do Algarve, *835 Dundas Street West (416-588-5862).*

A regional club of Portuguese from the Algarve region of Portugal.

Friends of Lisbon Cultural Association, *954 King Street West (416-537-2119).*

Vasco Da Gama Community Centre, *2101 Dundas Street West (416-534-5046).*

Casa Das Beiras, *374 College Street (416-923-8501).*

Casa Do Benefica, *62 Claremount Street (416-363-6833).*

Centro da Valorizacao da Vida, *506 College Street (416-923-5285).*

Club Transmontano, *1659 Dundas Street West (416-537-7106).*

Graciosa Community Centre of Toronto, *279 Dovercourt Road (416-533-8367).*

Organização Acores, *659 Shaw Street (416-535-5553).*

Peniche Community Centre of Toronto, *952 College Street (416-536-7063).*

Portuguese (Brazilian) Language Services, *421 Bloor Street West (416-975-5000).*

Provides translation services.

The **Portuguese-Canadian Democratic Association,** *860 College Street (416-534-3451).*

Long active in Canada, the front was originally formed to oppose the fascist Salazar regime in Portugal and has continued to work to democratize Portuguese politics. Portuguese living in Canada are allowed to vote and participate in elections in their homeland.

Conselho das Communidades Portuguêsas Do Ontario e Manitoba, *66 Sheridan Avenue (416-532-0578).*

Movimento para a Dignificação da Mulher de Cultura Portugêsa, *642 Bathurst Street (416-534-0932).*

Partido Social Democráta, *636 Dundas Street West (416-366-4703).*

The Hispanic community also has an extensive and diverse array of organizations to promote cultural and social awareness:

Spanish Complimentary School, *242 Winona Drive (416-658-7836).*

Conducts heritage language classes.

Centro Del Baile Español/Centre for Spanish Dance/School of the Paula Moreno Spanish Dance Company, *121 Avenue Road (416-924-6991),* and **Casa de España Dancers,** *559 College Street (416-760-7210).*

Offer performances and classes in various Spanish dances.

Alianza Cultural Hispano Canadiense.

A Spanish theater production group.

Centro Para Gente De Habla Hispana, *1004 Bathurst Street (416-533-8545).*

An umbrella organization for many community and cultural groups.

Chilean Social Club, *8 Milvan Drive (416-747-8142).*

Club Azuay *(416-656-5994).*

A social club.

Club Hispano/Spanish Centre, *559 College Street (416-760-7210).*

Conducts social and cultural events for the broad Hispanic community; also gives Spanish lessons.

Group Cultural Izalco de Toronto, *1004 Bathurst Street (416-533-8545).*

Works with the El Salvadorian community to help integrate immigrants into Canadian life.

Guatemala Community Network, *427 Bloor Street West (416-929-8601).*

An umbrella organization for the Guatemalan community.

Latin America Services, *1352 Kennedy Road (416-757-6036).*

Provides community and social services to the Latin American community.

Latin American Community Centre, *1280 Finch Avenue West (416-661-1104).*

A community center with a variety of services for the overall Latin American community.

Latin American Community Centre, *1300 Finch Avenue West (416-661-0806).*

A community center with a variety of services for the broad Latin American community.

Latin American Working Group, *603 ½ Parliament Street (416-966-4773).*

A political research and current events study group.

Latin American Artists Network, *96 Spadina Avenue (416-504-1594).*

Helps support the work of Latin American and Hispanic artists in Canada.

Mission Catholica Latin/Catholic Mission Centre, *941 A Dundas Street West (416-366-0266).*

Uruguay Club, *101 Freshway Avenue (905 660-2467).*

Liga Hispanamérica de Football Amateur, *Lamport Stadium, 1155 King Street West (416-588-4073).*

Represents a broad array of Latin American community soccer teams.

A number of political activist groups work to support the struggle of Hispanic Americans for democracy and human rights in their countries of origin, including:

Hispanic Council of Metropolitan Toronto, *58 Cecil Street (416-340-2552).*

Hispanic Social Development Council of Metropolitan Toronto, *950 Yonge Street.*

Inter-Church Committee on Human Rights in Latin America, *40 Saint Clair Avenue East (416-921-4152).*

══════ Holidays and Celebrations ══════

January 6	*Epiphany,* celebrating the feast of the three kings with gift-giving to children.
April/May	*Festival of Santo Cristo dos Milagres,* when churches are decorated with flowers and proces-

	sions are held to honor Christ's Ascension, on the fifth Sunday after Easter.
May	Annual festival, held by the Spanish Centre to coincide with the weekend following Ascension Day. Also, Madrid Festival is held near the end of the month.
May 24	*Ecuadorian Independence Day.*
June 10	*Day of Portugal.*
July 5	*Venezuelan Independence Day.*
July 6	*Festival of San Fermin* (coincides with the running of the bulls in Pamplona).
July 28	*Peruvian Independence Day.*
August	*Senhor Da Pedra,* a religious festival held on the first Sunday of the month.
September 7	*Brazilian Independence Day.*
October 5	*Amalia Rodrigues Day,* honoring the popular Portuguese folk and fado singer of this century.

═══ Restaurants, Cafés, and Nightclubs ═══

There are many good Portuguese restaurants in the city as befits a community as large as this one. This cuisine includes the rich seafood and pork cooked in olive oil that is one of the hallmarks of Portuguese cooking, as well as the superb Churrasqueira barbecues of Brazilian beef. Good, rich Portuguese wines are served at most restaurants, as are an array of rare ports and madeiras.

A Churrasqueira, *1168 Dundas Street West (416-534-0488).*
Brazilian barbecue and Portuguese specialties at reasonable prices.

A Churrasqueira Do Sardinha, *705 College Street (416-531-1120).*
This modern, inexpensive churrasqueira serves excellent barbecued beef and pork as well as seafood specialties.

The Boat, *158 Augusta Avenue (416-593-9218).*

One of the older Portuguese restaurants in the city, the Boat specializes in seafood platters and also presents a lively evening of entertainment. Specialties include cod with pimentos and grilled scups.

Casa Abril em Portugal, *159 Augusta Street (416-593-0440).*

This well-established restaurant serves an extensive array of seafood, including lobsters from its own aquariums and specialties such as *carne alentejana* (marinated barbecued pork) and codfish mixed with scrambled eggs, onions, and shredded potatoes. Nightly entertainment is provided by a trio of musicians.

Chiado, *864 College Street (416-538-1910).*

An elegant, upscale, modern Portuguese restaurant with a superb Portuguese wine list, as well as many seafood specialties, including marinated sardines which can be as big as lake trout, monkfish risotto, and grilled squid with coriander and garlic.

First Portuguese Restaurant, *722 College Street (416-531-9971).*

This restaurant at the Portuguese Club serves authentic and inexpensive dishes to a very demanding clientele of Portuguese-Canadian regulars.

Lisboa A Noite, *802A Dundas Street West (416-368-6522).*

Offers excellent and generously proportioned seafood platters and an excellent list of Portuguese wines. Nightly entertainment and visits from well-known Portuguese chefs are also highlights.

Ramboia Cafe-Churrasqueira, *1282 Dundas Street West (416-534-0407).*

A popular spot for lunch or dinner, this restaurant has a wide-ranging Portuguese/Brazilian menu, including specialties such as *bolhao pato* (steamed mussels in white wine and coriander) and *gambas la plancha* (steamed prawns in garlic and white wine). They also make wonderful meringue pies. A strolling guitarist entertains nightly.

Sea King Restaurant, *Galleria Mall, Dufferin and Dupont Streets (416-533-3589).*

Flamenco dancers and Latin entertainment accompany a wide array of Portuguese and Spanish specialties, including stuffed spider crab and grilled lobster.

Vasco Da Gama Dining Lounge, *892 College Street (416-535-1555).*

A long-established Portuguese restaurant serving inexpensive, well-prepared specialties and tapas at reasonable prices.

Other restaurants serving Portuguese and Brazilian specialties include:

A Tasca Restaurant, *260 Augusta Avenue (416-922-2427).*

Acor Restaurant, *923 Dundas Street West (416-363-1995).*

Amadeus Restaurant, *184 Augusta Avenue (416-591-1245).*

Banaboia Restaurant, *638 College Street (416-537-0682).*

Bolota Restaurant, *924 College Street (416-530-1050).*

Brasil Portugal Restaurant, *83 Nassau Street (416-591-6476).*

Also includes a nightly floor show and entertainment.

Cavalo Branco, *1173 Dundas Street West (416-537-9269).*

Da Guanabara Dining Room, *986 Bloor Street West (416-531-1159).*

Niagara Café's "Rio By Night," *875 Queen Street West (416-364-1690).*

Nightly entertainment and music.

Portugalia Restaurant, *630 College Street (416-532-7702).*

Verde Minho Restaurant, *940 College Street (416-533-2498).*

Portuguese cafés often include good limited prices on inexpensive Portuguese dishes, as well as an excellent arrays of coffees and desserts. *Natas* (egg custard), chocolate roulades, and almond and coconut puddings are popular items.

Bocas (Big Mouth) Café, *718 College Street (416-534-1328).*

Caffe Brazillianoe, *850 Dundas Street West (416-603-6607).*

Copacabana, *414 College Street (416-975-0375).*

Pepper Café, *189 Wallace Avenue (416-531-3146).*

Hispanic cuisine is as diverse and interesting as the many cultures it comes from. North Americans have a tendency to equate Hispanic cooking with Mexican, in particular the northern Mexican/Tex-Mex specialties of corn tortillas, tacos, burritos, enchiladas, and fajitas that have grown popular here over the years. Hispanic cuisine is in fact quite different and more diverse. Countries such as Peru, Argentina, and Colombia represent very different kinds of cooking. Latin America has a broad range of cuisine styles, as does Spain with its Catalan, Andalusian, Gallician, Basque, and Castillian varieties. Even Mexican food is far more diverse than usually thought, with central Mexican, southern Mexican, Pacific Coast, and Yucatan Peninsula cuisines offering a very eclectic array of tastes to the discerning palate. The following list tries to capture some of the diversity and excellence of Hispanic cuisine in Toronto from *tapas* (appetizers) to main courses.

Babalu, *102 Bloor Street West (416-966-9698).*

One of the most modern-looking Hispanic restaurants in the city, Babalu could have been transplanted right from the trendiest parts of Barcelona to the streets of Toronto. A tapas bar serving excellent food, its specialties include the chorizo cassoulet, garlic shrimp, and asparagus dishes. The menu contains a number of excellent Spanish wines by the glass. This is a hopping place from Thursday through Saturday, so come early and enjoy the food, and stay late and enjoy the fun.

Boulevard Café, *161 Harbord Street (416-961-7676)*.

A long-time Toronto favorite, the Boulevard serves Peruvian cuisine in a homey restaurant with a large outdoor patio for summertime dining. Specialties include appetizers like *ostras* (oysters with lime and hot sauce), *empassadas* (the Peruvian version of empañadas, dumplings with grilled meat), and *anticuchos* (marinated, charbroiled brochettes with grilled seafood).

Café Amici, *1177 Saint Clair Avenue West (416-656-5171)*.

Serves Chilean grilled meats and seafood specialties. On weekends there is entertainment, including excellent Chilean folk music.

Café Hermanos, *892 College Street (416-535-4443)*.

Ecuadorian and Peruvian specialties are available here, including delicious cornbread muffins and *huancaiana,* a spicy cheese sauce.

Casa Pepe, *1630 Bayview Avenue (416-483-5622)*.

A pleasant and homey atmosphere, with white and blue stucco walls, painted plates, and wine skins to accent the decor. Excellent paella as well as a variety of other Spanish tapas and specialties. Good, well-priced Spanish wine list.

Don Quixote Restaurant and Tavern, *300 College Street (416-922-7636)*.

One of Toronto's well-established Spanish restaurants, Don Quixote serves tapas and full-course Spanish meals, including paella, grilled calamari, and *zarazuela* (the famous Spanish fish-and-seafood stew). Accompanying dinner is complimentary cognac pâté and a Spanish floor show that includes flamenco dancing and classical guitar playing.

El Bodegon, *537 College Street (416-944-8297)*.

Very popular with the local Peruvian community, this small South American restaurant serves a variety of Peruvian and Ecuadorian specialties.

La Cumparsita, *515 Bloor Street West (416-537-7548).*

Argentina's contribution to the Latin palate is the wonderful grilled beef parilla served here, as well as beautifully marinated beef ribs and grilled *polo* (chicken). An excellent wine list includes an interesting array of Argentine, Chilean, and Spanish wines.

Plaza Flamingo, *423 College Street (416-947-9994).*

A large tapas bar with musical accompaniment on weekends, the Flamingo serves a variety of Mediterranean cuisines from pastas to tapas, but it's best known for its wide array of hot and cold tapas, spacious setting, and live entertainment on weekends.

Rancho El Restaurant and Nightclub, *430 College Street (416-921-2752).*

Mexican and Spanish foods and tapas. Live entertainment in the adjoining Borinque Room, with live Latin bands playing merengue and salsa tunes on weekends.

Restaurant Costa Azul, *574 College Street (416-533-0778).*

A variety of South American and Latin American dishes await patrons here. This is a favorite with residents of the area, many of whom have come from these countries and find the food here pleasant and reasonably priced.

Segovia, *582 Yonge Street (416-960-1010).*

A wonderful little hole-in-the-wall Spanish restaurant. Look carefully for it—it's easy to miss the entrance in the blink of an eye. Inside the door is a warm, dark room with white stucco walls, filled with lovely aromas from the delicious paella, grilled lamb, and glazed chicken. The service is always superior and hospitable from the owners/operators/chefs who also occasionally serenade guests on guitar or piano after the evening rush is taken care of. Inexpensive and consistently excellent. One of the most romantic restaurants in the city.

Serenata, *582 Yonge Street (416-929-3037).*

An unprepossessing little café on Yonge Street serving simply prepared, delicious Hispanic and Latino food, including beautiful grilled calamari, chorizo, and tripe stew and savory paellas. Inexpensive, with an interesting wine list and reasonable wine prices.

Tapas II/El Cid, *226 Carlton Street (416-323-9651).*

A great, hopping place on weekends, this tapas bar has a lovely array of hot and cold appetizers, with specialties like a red pepper-accented *tortilla* (in Spanish cuisine, this is a cold potato omelet), grilled chorizo, and flash-fried garlic shrimp, as well as an excellent Spanish wine list. Upstairs the El Cid serves more formal meals, but downstairs in the crowded little tapas bar is the place to be on weekend evenings—if you can manage to squeeze in.

Xango, *106 John Street (416-593-4407).*

Superb new Latin eclectic menu with Cuban, Brazilian, Guatemalan, and other South American specialties. A wide array of seviche dishes is complemented by superb soups (pumpkin and shrimp with cilantro and chilies), dark rich buttery-flavored Guatemalan chicken, seared double pork chops served with avocado salad and green rice, yucca, plantains, and other Latin-flavored produce. Excellent wine list. Somewhat expensive.

The following are some of the better Mexican restaurants in the city. With the exception of Chile's, none are particularly distinguishable. All serve the same blend of good, familiar northern Mexican specialties with varying degrees of consistency and about the same price range.

Chile's Mexican Flavours, *276 Carlaw Avenue (416-465-1247).*

Definitely still the best place to go for Mexican food in Toronto, with an assortment of flavors and foods that makes you realize there is a lot more to Mexican food than what's available at Taco Bell. Inexpensive and inauspicious, this restaurant depends on the quality of its cooking to bring you back for more.

Amigo's Restaurant, *81 Saint Clair Avenue East (416-323-9842).*

El Avocado Express, *642 Bloor Street West (416-588-5385).*

El Escondite, *653 Saint Clair Avenue West (416-656-0725).*

La Mexicana, *229 College Street (416-783-9452).*

Mexicali Rosa's, *545 Yonge Street (416-929-3629).*

Mickey's Hideaway, *352 Pape Avenue (416-461-2035).*

Tacos El Asador, *690 Bloor Street West (416-538-9747).*

A couple of nightclubs in the city have regular programs of Latin jazz, including:

Berlin, *2335 Yonge Street (416-489-7777).*

Judy Bar, *370 King Street West (416-599-4000).*
Underneath the Holiday Inn on King.

Food Sources

Bakeries

The Portuguese love breads and desserts, and Toronto is blessed with a wide array of Portuguese bakeries serving breads like *pao douce* (a round sweet-bread made with potato flour), *malasadas* (deep-fried doughnuts covered with sugar), marzipans, and meringues, as well as the rich, thick-crusted white breads that are a hallmark of good Portuguese bakeries.

Brasil Bakery and Pastry, *1566 Dundas Street West (416-531-2888).*
Very extensive selection in a modern setting.

Courense Bakery, *1038 Bloor Street West (416-536-1522).*

Crupi Bakery, *840 Dundas Street West (416-363-1752).*

Dundas Portuguese Bakery, *1492 Dundas Street West (416-536-5671).*

Iberica Bakery, *209 Augusta Avenue (416-593-9321);*
279 Augusta Avenue (416-593-9398).

The oldest Portuguese bakery in the city, this store also carries specialties like white cornbread, shrimp croquettes, and other deli items.

Micaelense Home Bakery, *319 Augusta Avenue (416-923-6266).*

Specializes in Portuguese wedding cakes.

Napoli Bakery, *812 College Street (416-534-2740).*

Nova Era, *1172 Dundas Street West (416-538-7700).*

Pane Vittoria Bakery, *785 Dundas Street West (416-863-0290).*

Includes an espresso bar and café as well as offering gelato and ice cream.

Portuguese Canadian Bakery, *1309-A Dundas Street West (416-532-9407).*

Sousa's Bakery, *1120 College Street (416-536-2007).*

Some of the best pao douce in the city.

Venezia Bakery, *114 Ossington Avenue (416-537-2914).*

A number of bakeries in the city prepare Spanish breads, cornbreads, empañadas, and other specialties, including the following:

Colomba Bakery, *1174 Bloor Street West (416-534-8476).*

Diaz Bakery and Delicatessen, *533 Wilson Heights Road (416-630-5843).*

Has an array of Spanish and Latin American imported foods and meats.

Harbord Bakery, *115 Harbord Street (416-922-5767).*

Carries Spanish and Latin American specialties such as empañadas in its deli shop.

Marisel's Bakery and Deli, *2708 Jane Street (416-745-7477).*

Butchers, Delis, and Grocers

Portuguese sausages are spicy affairs similar to Spanish chorizo but with a wider range of tastes and flavors. They can be obtained at a number of the bakeries already listed as well as at:

Portugal Butcher Supermarket, *558 College Street (416-924-1985).*

Portuguese Butcher, *837 Dundas Street West (416-368-0921).*

Portuguese Cheese, *2 Buckingham (416-259-4349).*

Portuguese Fish Market, *821 Dundas Street West (416-368-5198).*

Other stores carry both Spanish specialties and products common to all Latin cooking:

El Camino, *648-A Bloor Street West (416-536-5777).*
Has a wide range of Spanish and Latin American specialty foods and produce.

El Eden Eqatoriano Importers, *396 College Street (416-923-8879).*
Carries produce, imported foods, and Spanish-language magazines and newspapers.

Latin World Groceries, *252 Augusta Avenue (416-368-0011).*
Imported food products and produce from throughout the Latin world.

May's Party Shops, *984 Dundas Street West (416-537-5165).*
Sauces, meats, imported foods, and produce.

Pepe's Mexican Foods, *122 Carrier Drive (416-674-0882).*

Specialty Mexican sauces and prepared foods.

Sol de España Y Union Hispana Supermercado,
588 College Street (416-537-5002).

A market offering a variety of Hispanic products and meats.

Shops

A number of stores selling Brazilian and Portuguese specialty gifts like ceramic roosters, ornamental plates, and Portuguese and Brazilian music and tapes include:

Lisbon Import and Export, *1198 Queen Street West (416-534-3972).*

Perola Azul, *1321 Dundas Street West (416-536-5224).*

Portugal Gift Store, *703 College Street (416-536-6590).*

Portuguese Gift Store, *846 Dundas Street West (416-368-9572).*

Hildebrando's Gallery, *1078 Queen Street West (416-535-0184).*

Carries many Brazilian and Portuguese artists' paintings and sculptures.

For Portuguese-language books, magazines, and music, check **Papelaria Olhanese,** 220 Ossington Avenue (416-537-3730), or the **Portuguese Bookstore,** 86 Nassau Street (416-603-7954).

Hispanic items may also be found at a variety of stores, including:

El Pipil Crafts, *267 Danforth Avenue (416-465-9625).*

Latin American crafts and gifts.

Frida Craft Store, *39 Front Street East (416-366-3169).*

Hand-knit Ecuadorian sweaters.

Gringos, *559 Queen Street West (416-601-9534).*

Latin American and South American gifts, crafts, and clothing.

Karisma Latino, *248 Dupont Street (416-966-1698).*

Mexican crafts and furniture, as well as silver jewelry.

Spanish Books and Records, *8 Milvan Road (416-747-9740).*

Carries a variety of Spanish-language books from Spain, Argentina, and Mexico, the three publishing capitals of the Hispanic world, as well as music from these areas.

Media

Publications

Blue Pages, *1201 Dundas Street West (416-531-2021).*

A Portuguese publication.

Correio Portugues, *793 Ossington Avenue (416-532-9894).*

El Popular, *2413 Dundas Street West (416-531-2495).*

A daily Spanish-language newspaper.

El Progonero Hispano Magazine, 344 Bloor Street
West (416-962-8811).

A glossy monthly magazine.

Golo-Goal, 1282 Dundas Street West
(416-538-1788).

Portuguese.

Grafico, 2170 Bromsgrove Road, Unit 51 (905-823-
3715).

A full-color bimonthly Spanish magazine.

*Guia Commercial Portugues/Portugese
Telephone Directory,* 1278 Dundas Street West
(416-532-3167).

Nuevo Mondo, 803 Dundas Street West (416-868-
6621).

Portuguese.

Portugal Illustrado & Ves Vilda Acorano, 60 Hanson
Road (905-279-8368).

Portuguese Sun, 1282 Dundas Street West (416-538-
1788).

Spanish Directory, 1256 Bloor Street West (416-588-
1964).

An annual directory of the Spanish-language community and its services.

A Verdade, 3460 Keele Street (416-537-9386).

A Portuguese publication.

Vision Hispano Americana, PO Box 1236, Station Q
(416-537-4484).

A national Hispanic-American magazine.

Voice of Portugal, 108 Queen Street West (905-456-
3456).

A Voz Portuguese Newspaper, 428 Ossington Avenue
(416-537-3775).

Radio

"Asas do Atlantico," CPWA-FM 90.5, *62 Nassau
Street (416-596-1566).*

Portuguese programming.

"Festival Portugues," CIRV-FM 88.7, *1087 Dundas
Street West (416-537-1088).*

CHIN-AM 1540/FM 100.7, *622 College Street (416-
531-9991).*

Has a number of Brazilian and Portuguese music and current events shows
including:

- **"Brasil Na Madrugada."** Monday through Friday.

- **"Despertar."** Monday through Friday.

- **"Fim de Semana."** Saturdays.

"Dimension 85," CHIN-AM 1540, *622 College Street
(416-531-9991).*

Spanish programming.

"Ondas Hispanas," CIRV-Radio International, *1087
Dundas Street West (416-537-1088).*

"Despertar Latino," CIAO Radio, *50 Kennedy Road
South (905-851-2456).*

Spanish.

Television

"Atlantida Magazine TV," *803 Dundas Street West
(416-868-6612).*

Portuguese programming.

CFMT-TV, Channel 47, *545 Lakeshore Boulevard*
West (416-593-4747).

Offers an array of Portuguese-language programming including:

- **"Portuguese News."** Weeknights.

- **"Telenovellas."** An evening drama.

- **"Telediario."** Weekly news show on Toronto's Portuguese community.

- **"Lamine."** Saturday variety entertainment.

- **"So Desportos."** An hour-long sports program.

- **"Actualidade."** Sunday current affairs program.

Spanish-language television is available twenty-four hours a day on pay cable from **TeleLatino Pay TV,** 105 Carlton Street (416-591-6846), a Spanish- and Italian-language pay-television network. There are also some shows on regular television:

"Hispanovision," CHCH-TV, channel 11, *163*
Jackson Street West (905-591-6846).

"Matromonio Y Algo Mas," MTV, channel 47, *545*
Lakeshore Boulevard West (416-593-4747).

—Hispania: The College Street Area—

The major center for Hispanic people in Toronto has developed along College Street west of Spadina Avenue and blending into the Portuguese and Italian areas west of Bathurst Street. Shops, restaurants, tapas bars, and nightclubs abound in this neighborhood, with some extending south into the Kensington Market area.

Another area of Hispanic concentration is north on Bloor Street West at around the same junction but going all the way over to Christie Street. This area has historically been a transitional area for many immigrant communities coming to Toronto. First settled by Jewish immigrants, it has gone through its Italian, Portuguese, and Chinese phases, and is now being most intensely settled by Toronto's Hispanic population. It's a lively area with a very active nightlife, and as one proceeds westward an increasing number of small cafés and restaurants.

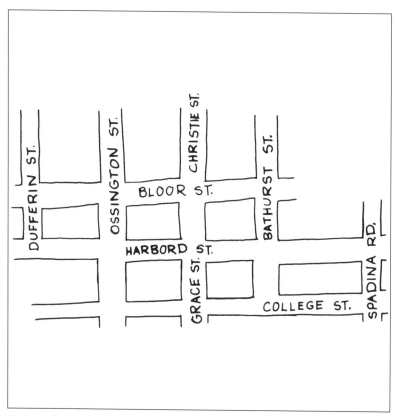

Hispanic Toronto

How to Get There: *Take the College streetcar west from the College Street or Queens Park subway stop on the Yonge/University subway line, or take the Spadina bus or Bathurst streetcar south from the Bathurst or Spadina stations on the Bloor/Danforth line.*

Russian and Eastern European Toronto

The breakup of the Soviet Union in the late 1980s has created a number of newly independent countries with predominantly Slavic backgrounds. Immigrants from these former Eastern Bloc nations—including Russia, Armenia, Poland, the Ukraine, and the Baltic countries—have come to Toronto since its early history, creating ethnic communities that are as distinct as their home countries.

Nationalities

Russians

Russian settlers in Canadian history go back to the early days of the fur trade. Russians from the port of Archangel were actively involved in the trapping and trading of furs throughout eastern Canada, and Russians from the then-Russian colony of Alaska were actively involved in the northern areas of Canada. As a fur-processing industry developed in eastern Canada, Russians were again brought in for their expertise in making fur hats and coats and eventually in developing a domesticated fur-raising industry to supplement the trapping in the wild.

These early settlers were followed in the late 1800s by a variety of Russian religious emigrants fleeing persecution, including a large segment of Toronto's Jewish population; German Mennonite Brethren from southern Russia; and the Doukhobors, infamous for undertaking public protests in the nude.

In the early 1900s these immigrants were joined by those from central and western Russia who came to Canada in search of economic opportunity or who migrated from the United States. Many of the latter were active in the Populist movement in the United States and, as the movement declined, they moved toward the Canadian prairies and the rising industrial centers of central Canada.

In the post–World War I era, refugees from the aristocratic families of Imperial Russia, as well as former army officers, came to Canada. One of the most illustrious Russian-Canadian families, the Ignatieffs, settled here at this time. Prominent in the engineering and civil service professions, the best-known family member was George Ignatieff, for whom a theater at the University of Toronto is named and who was once the university's chancellor and Canada's ambassador to the United Nations.

One community of Russians who came to Canada in the post–World War II era were the Byelorussians. This large western Russian province has often had control traded back and forth between Poland, the Ukraine, Lithuania, and Russia, interspersed with periods of independence. Its last brief period of independence before the present was in 1918.

Byelorussians' actual settlement in Canada goes back to the early 1800s, when numerous peasants moved to Canada as a reaction to their country's conquest by Imperial Russia. Many were among the first miners in Canada, while others migrated to the cities to work as industrial laborers.

The largest portion of Toronto's current Byelorussian community arrived after World War II. Many were soldiers who had fought with the Polish army and feared reprisals upon returning to the Soviet Union; others were professionals and intellectuals. The community developed its own media and social center and has worked to preserve its culture and traditions.

Armenians

Toronto's Armenian community has been an active and vocal presence in Metro life for over 70 years. With over 20,000 members, the Armenian community has taken a strong hand in tenaciously preserving its language, culture, and heritage, as well as in keeping Canada aware of events in the Armenian homelands in Turkey and the former Soviet Union.

Armenian students, sponsored by Protestant missionaries, came to Canadian universities and were among the first members of this community in the late 1800s. They were joined by many other Armenians who came over to work on the building of the Canadian Pacific Railroad and to work as temporary laborers in the farms and factories of southern Ontario.

With the beginning of the Balkan Wars in 1912, many community members remained to become permanent residents. The population swelled in 1915 when many Armenians arrived in Canada to escape the genocidal actions of the Ottoman government in Turkey. Successful Canadian-Armenian businessmen helped in the adoption of over 100 orphaned Armenian children who were subsequently cared for in the nearby suburb of Georgetown. Toronto is graced with two monuments to the 1915 massacres in Turkey. The first monument, *Revival,* is located at the Armenian cultural center in North York; the second is at the Alex Manougian Center in Scarborough.

By 1923 the center of the Armenian community focused around Church Street in the area shared by the Syrian community. Many immigrants were involved in the rug and carpet businesses, as well as other small financial and merchant operations, and Armenian-owned carpet shops, pawn shops, and stores are still to be found in this area. In the 1950s another wave of Armenian immigration occurred, primarily from sources outside of Turkey where Armenians had dispersed after fleeing their homeland. They were joined in the sixties, seventies, and eighties by more immigrants and refugees from Middle Eastern Armenian settlements.

The Armenian community in Toronto has produced more than its fair share of prominent, internationally renowned personalities, including SCTV comedy star Andrea Martin, photographer Yosuf Karsh, children's songwriter Raffi, and film director Atom Egoyan.

The Armenian community has been active in organizing aid for its homeland—in particular, earthquake relief following the 1988 earthquake—and also for encouraging an educational dialog with the general Canadian community by sponsoring annual educational awards.

Polish

Polish Canadians have long been a populous and prominent part of Toronto. Among their most distinguished early citizens was Sir Casimir Gzowski, an expatriate Polish nationalist during a time when there was no political Poland. Gzowski helped start the Grand Trunk Railway, and as a civil engineer pioneered the construction of the International Bridge at Niagara Falls, the grading and surfacing of Yonge Street, and the building of the Erie

Canal. A monument to him is located just off Lakeshore Boulevard near the heart of the Polish neighborhood along Roncesvalles Avenue.

This area, stretching along Roncesvalles from Queen Street West north to where it becomes Dundas Street West, has the majority of Toronto's Polish shops, restaurants, and grocers. It is also heavily populated by the Toronto Ukrainian community, as well as many other Eastern European and German peoples. Polish settlement in Toronto began in the 1860s with a few Polish citizens, but the majority of early immigrants didn't arrive until the 1890s, when both artisans and agricultural workers came in response to natural disasters and civil strife in Poland.

Their first settlements were in the Ward area bordered by Chestnut, Elm, and Elizabeth Streets. As the Polish population grew and moved into jobs in the burgeoning iron and steel industries as well as other types of factories, the community moved west and south to its current home in the West Parkdale area.

The Polish church was the first focus for activity within the community, and gatherings were held at **Saint Patrick's Catholic Church** on McCaul Street and **Saint Mary's Church** on Bathurst Street. In 1911 that focus moved west with the construction of **Saint Stanislaus Kostka** on Denison Avenue, which became the subsequent center for a very large Polish neighborhood.

During the years immediately following the outbreak of the Second World War, a large group of Polish engineers, technicians, and professional people moved to Canada to escape the Nazi invasion. Many Poles who fought bravely for the Allied forces in World War II came to settle in Canada after the war. A large influx of Polish refugees and ex-military personnel also arrived, including many academics, scientists, professional people, and artisans. The most recent wave of immigration occurred in the 1980s after the breakdown of the Solidarity movement in Poland, with over 6,000 refugees joining the Toronto community.

Besides the memorial to Sir Casimir Gzowski, a stark and powerful monument to the victims of the Katyn Massacre stands at the foot of Roncesvalles Avenue and Queen Street. Designed by artist Tadeusz Janowski, it is a harsh reminder of that terrible event. The 100,000-plus Polish-Canadian community has produced many prominent citizens, including broadcaster Peter Gzowski, painter and sculptor Mary Schneider, research immunologist Dr. Stanislaw Dubicki, and engineer L. Alejski.

Ukrainians

Ukrainian churches, cuppolas, and statues dot Toronto's neighborhoods showing the pervasive influence this 100,000-strong community has.

Toronto is, in fact, the second largest Ukrainian city in the world after Kiev. Its main population centers in West Toronto are along the Bloor Street West area between High Park and Jane Street; in the Parkdale area around Dundas Street West and Lansdowne Street. Metro's Ukrainians have lived in this area for over 100 years, celebrating their hundredth anniversary in 1991.

The first noted Ukrainian settler was George Horetzky, who built a house at 88 Bedford Street in 1891. Large numbers of Ukrainians settled here at the turn of the century, coming both from the old country and from Ukrainian settlements in the midwestern United States and Canadian prairie provinces. Many Midwestern American Ukrainians came to Canada after the failure of the Populist political movement, while many Russian Ukrainians fled the persecution of the Russian empire.

Numerous Ukrainians settled in downtown Toronto's Saint John's Ward, whereas later immigrants were attracted to new jobs in the growing industries of the Junction area in the 1910s. The first Ukrainian church in Toronto was erected in 1914 on Franklin Avenue; **Saint Josaphat's Ukrainian Catholic Cathedral** still stands at 143 Franklin Avenue. Toronto was the center of the Ukrainian community in Ontario, and many Ukrainians in northern Ontario and the province's farming areas were drawn to Toronto first for its cultural and religious facilities and later for its job opportunities.

In the 1920s Queen Street West, between Bathurst and Spadina Streets, was the focal point for the community and some remnant shops from that era can still be found in the area. In 1923 the Ukraine lost its newly won independence from the Soviet Union, and to provide assistance and relief efforts Toronto Ukrainians organized the Ukrainian Red Cross.

The community continued to grow in the 1930s as refugee Ukrainian families made their way to Toronto. Immigrants continued to build more churches and expand their community outreach efforts. Ukrainian bookstores and printing houses were opened; in fact, the University of Toronto Press is the largest publisher of books on the Ukraine outside of that country. The headquarters of the World Congress of Free Ukrainians was in Toronto until the Ukraine's 1991 separation from the Soviet Union.

Some local landmarks include Saint Volodymyr's statue in front of the Saint Vladimir Institute and a beautiful monument to poet Lesya Ukrainka found in High Park. There is also a memorial to Ukrainian-Canadian soldiers who fought for the Canadian army in the Ukrainian-Canadian Memorial Park at Scarlett Road and Eglinton Avenue West. Well-known Ukrainians from Toronto include CBC radio personality Luba Goy, journalist Victor Malarek, and downhill-skiing champion Steve Podborski.

Estonians, Latvians, and Lithuanians

The wide array of peoples from the Baltic Sea regions of the former Soviet Union have long played a prominent role in Toronto, with the city serving as the base for many exile organizations devoted to keeping the cultural and political spirit of these people alive. The Estonians, Latvians, and Lithuanians each have their own extensive array of cultural, religious, and political concerns.

Metro's 12,000-plus Estonian community is the largest such community outside of Estonia. Most arrived in Canada in the years following the USSR's annexation of Estonia in 1940. Coming to work as laborers initially, a long tradition of education and hard work pushed many Estonians into professional positions and made possible a variety of community efforts, such as the establishment of the **Estonia House** community and cultural center in 1960.

With over 100 different cultural, social, political, and professional organizations, Toronto's Estonian community is very active in the city. One of its proudest moments came with the establishment of **Tartu College,** an educational center and student residence on the University of Toronto campus with a special emphasis on Estonian historical and cultural studies.

A variety of churches, summer camps, youth centers, folk dance groups, and musical ensembles are supported by this community. Through the efforts of Estonian architects and developers the first Canadian co-op housing project was built in Toronto, and Estonians were instrumental in the development of the Condominium. An annual Estonian cultural festival in Seedrioru, a youth camp near the town of Elora, attracts over 5,000 people annually to its events.

A number of prominent Torontonians are from the Estonian community, including theater critic and director Urjo Kareda, architect Elmar Tampold, and artist Ruth Tulving. Tartu College has one of the most extensive Estonian studies programs in the world.

Like its Baltic neighbors, Latvia has sent Toronto a small but very active community of over 9,000 people, which has become the center for Latvian cultural, social, and political activities in Canada. This group's settlement goes back to the 1890s, when Latvian farmers emigrated to the western farming regions of Canada. They eventually moved into the eastern cities as opportunities for work in these urban areas grew during the ensuing years.

The largest wave of emigration to Canada didn't occur until after World War II, when Latvia was annexed by the Soviet Union. Over 110,000 Latvians fled their homeland, with 15,000 coming to Canada and the vast majority of these to Toronto. Most of the community remains settled in the West Toronto areas around High Park, which are home to much of Toronto's Polish, Russian Ukrainian, and German populations. The community has also spread into Riverdale and the suburbs of York and North York.

The first Latvian community organization centered around the First Evangelical Lutheran Congregation, which was established in 1949. Eventually the group joined with the Estonian congregation and formed a joint congregation and community group. This later evolved into two separate community organizations: The Latvian House and Latvian Canadian Cultural Centre are two impressive and active organizations aimed at fostering and cultivating Latvian culture in Canada.

Like other Baltic peoples, the Latvians pride themselves on their musical heritage. Every five years Toronto is honored to present the Dainas, a celebration of Latvian choral singing, dance, and rhythmic gymnastics that was first transplanted to Toronto in 1952. Some well-known Latvians in the city include Karlis Irbitis, an aviation designer and award-winning author of books on aviation; sculptor Uga Drava; and playwright and scholar Banuta Rubess.

The third of the three Baltic Republics to send immigrants to Canada, Lithuania has sent the largest number to Toronto with over 15,000 Lithuanians living in the city. A Lithuanian heritage is also claimed by many resident Polish and Ukrainian families since during Lithuania's long and rich history it at times encompassed large areas of these two countries. The central focus of the community revolves around Park Lithuanian in the North York area near Keele Street and Glenlake Avenue.

Lithuanian emigration to Canada goes back to the early nineteenth century when Lithuanian soldiers are recorded as having served with the British army in Canada. The first major wave of immigration, which included many Polish and Ukrainian immigrants, occurred during the famines of the early 1900s. Many were also fleeing mandatory service in the czar's army or were looking to earn money in Canada to buy a farm back in their homeland.

Early settlers found work in Toronto factories as well as in construction trades. Toronto's first Lithuanian organization, the Saint Joseph's Society, was also formed around this time, as was the Saint John the Baptist Relief Society, which grew from the first Lithuanian parish in Toronto. In 1928 the church purchased a site that would become the first site of the **Lithuanian Cultural Community Centre,** with language classes, social groups, and offices for a variety of organizations.

After World War II the already burgeoning Lithuanian community became host to a large population of refugees escaping the Russian occupation of their homeland. Of the 20,000 who came to Canada, over 5,000 settled in Toronto, with many families in other areas later moving to this area to pursue the better opportunities afforded by Toronto's growing economy.

A number of prominent Lithuanians have contributed to Toronto over the years, including Leo Rautins, the first Canadian to play in the revived National Basketball Association; sculptors Juozas Bakis and Jacob Dagys; and opera singer Rimas Strimatis.

Religion

Russian Canadians worship at a number of churches. The largest percentage go to Russian Orthodox churches:

Christ the Saviour Russian Orthodox Cathedral,
102 Follis Avenue (416-534-1763).

A reconverted Anglican church with stained glass and icons from Russia. The altar includes icons of the first Russian Orthodox saint from North America. Connected with the Russian Orthodox Church in North America.

Russian Orthodox Holy Trinity Church, *23 Henry Street (416-979-2990).* Bookstore ?

Connected with the Russian Orthodox Church outside of Russia, Holy Trinity conducts masses in Russian, holds language classes and folk dancing, and supports a Slavic-language choir.

Russian Orthodox Church of the Holy Resurrection, *213 Winona Drive (416-651-3226).*

The **Russian Ukrainian Church of Evangelical Christians,** 24 Carr Street (416-363-0105), is the main Protestant congregation.

Many Byelorussians belong to the Greek Orthodox or Byzantine tradition. The main church with a large Byelorussian congregation is **Belarusan Orthodox Church,** 524 Saint Clarens Road (416-530-1025).

Armenians have long been proud of the fact that their nation was the first in the world to adopt Christianity as its official religion. Nearly 90 percent of all Armenians belong to the Armenian Apostolic Church; the rest are divided between the Armenian Catholic and Armenian Evangelical churches. The main religious center in the city is the **Armenian Apostolic Church of Saint Mary,** 45 Hallcrown Place (416-493-8122), which also houses the **Armenian Community Centre** (see separate listing in next section).

The Armenian Catholic community is served by the **Armenian Catholic Church of Saint Gregory the Illuminator,** 46 Yardley Avenue (416-751-0803). The **Armenian Evangelical Church,** 34 Glenforest Road (416-489-3188), is the primary church for the Armenian Protestant-Evangelical community. Other churches with primarily Armenian congregations include the **Armenian Brotherhood Bible Church,** 2755 Victoria Park Avenue (416-492-3300), and the **Holy Trinity Armenian Church,** 20 Progress Court (416-431-3001).

Most Polish Canadians are Catholic, although there are some Protestants in the community as well. The Catholic churches serving the Polish community include:

Saint Casimir's, *156 Roncesvalles Avenue (416-532-2822).*

The largest Polish church in the Metro area, with over 5,000 parishioners. Seven of eight Sunday masses are in Polish. There are also Polish-language, cultural, and dance classes held throughout the week.

Saint Stanislaus Roman Catholic Church, *12 Denison Avenue (416-368-2633).*

The oldest Polish Catholic church in the city, it also holds language and dance classes.

Saint Maximillian Kolbe, *4260 Cawthra Road (905-848-2420).*

A large new Polish church in Mississauga.

Saint Mary's Queen of Poland Roman Catholic Church/Polish Roman Catholic Mission, *2661 Kingston Road (416-289-0505).*

Saint Mary's Roman Catholic Church, *1996 Davenport Road (416-656-3130).*

Saint Theresa's Roman Catholic Church, *123 11th Street (416-259-2933).*

Polish National Catholic Cathedral of Saint John, *186 Cowan Avenue (416-532-8249).*

Saint Judy Tadeuza Apostles, *1747 Victoria Park Avenue (416-537-8157).*

The **Polish Baptist Church,** 2611 Dundas Street West (416-239-3305), is the major Polish Protestant church in the area.

Although the Ukraine has been Christian since 988 when King Volodymyr (Vladimir) first adopted that religion, the area's shifting political winds have created a situation in which Ukrainians are evenly divided between the Catholic Church, influenced by the Polish and Lithuanian rulers, and the Orthodox Church, influenced by Russian conquest and Byzantine missions. The result is that Toronto is chock-full of beautiful, ornate churches of both denominations. Neighborhood Catholic churches include the following:

Saint Josaphat's Ukrainian Catholic Cathedral,
143 Franklin Avenue (416-535-9192).

The community's oldest church, with an historic altar brought from Lvov and decorated with eight large religious paintings.

Saint Demetrius the Great Martyr Ukrainian Catholic Church, *135 La Rose Avenue (416-244-5333).*

The dome here is an eight-foot-wide skylight with depictions of Christ and seven angels. A traditional resurrection scene glows through a large stained glass window. The church is also home to a folk dance ensemble called the **Yavir Dance Ensemble.**

Holy Eucharist Ukrainian Catholic Church, *515 Broadview Avenue (416-465-5836).*

Saint Basil the Great Ukrainian Catholic Church, *449 Vaughan Road (416-656-3772).*

Saint Mary's Ukrainian Catholic Church, *18 Leeds Street (416-531-9944).*

Saint Mary's Dormiton Ukrainian Catholic Church, *276 Bathurst Street (416-364-8049).*

Saint Michaels Ukrainian Catholic Church, *182 Sixth Street West (416-274-6845).*

Saint Nicholas Ukrainian Catholic Church, *770 Queen Street West (416-364-2774).*

Saint Peter and Paul Ukrainian Catholic Church, *1490 Markham Road (416-291-7401).*

The Ukrainian Orthodox Church, the other great religious force in the Ukraine, also has a number of churches in the Metropolitan area:

Ukrainian Orthodox Cathedral of Saint Vladimir,
404 Bathurst Street (416-366-3224).

Besides being a center for religious life in the area, this church is also home to a wide range of community and cultural groups, including the **Ukrainian War Veterans League,** the **Ukrainian Democratic Youth Association of Canada,** the **Vesnianka Dance Ensemble,** the **Ilarion Dance Ensemble,** the **Moloda Ukraina Choir,** the **Hnat Khotkotkevych Bandurist Ensemble,** the **Desna Choir,** and **The Ukrainian Canadian Women's Association.**

Saint Andrew Ukrainian Orthodox Church, *1630 Dupont Avenue (416-766-9069).*

Saint Anne's Ukrainian Orthodox Church, *525 Morrish Road (416-284-9642).*

Saint Demetrius Ukrainian Orthodox Church,
3338 Lakeshore Boulevard West (416-255-7506).

Saint Vladimir's Ukrainian Orthodox Church, *404 Bathurst Street (416-366-3224).*

Ukrainian Protestant congregations have been growing in popularity. A few of the larger ones are:

First Ukrainian Pentecostal Church, *557 Bathurst Street (416-922-2038).*

Ukrainian Evangelical Baptist Church, *148 Tecumseth Street (416-368-3744).*

Ukrainian Seventh Day Adventist Church, *555 Finch Street West (416-636-2471).*

Estonians are by and large Protestants, with a large established Lutheran church. Among the churches with large national congregations are

Saint Andrew's Estonian Evangelical Lutheran Church, *383 Jarvis Street (416-923-5172).*

Saint Peter's Estonian Evangelical Lutheran Church, *817 Mount Pleasant Road (416-483-5847).*

Estonian Emmanuel Evangelical Church, *240 East Manor Road (416-488-1754).*

Toronto Estonian Baptist Church, *883 Broadview Avenue (416-465-0639).*

The Lutheran church is the major religious institution in Latvia and a variety of churches have large Latvian congregations including:

Saint Andrews Evangelical Lutheran Latvian Church, *383 Jarvis Street (416-924-1563).*

This is an historic church and is home to the famous Latvian Choir of Saint Andrews.

Saint John's Evangelical Lutheran Latvian Church, *200 Balmoral Avenue (416-921-3327).*

The first church built by Latvians in Canada.

Barnabas Church, *361 Danforth Avenue (416-463-1344).*

Latvian Evangelical Lutheran Church of Canada, *5 Valleymede Road (416-767-2310).*

Toronto East Evangelical Lutheran Church, *47 Lord Roberts Drive (416-267-3507).*

Latvian Baptist Church of Toronto, *30 McDairmid Road (416-299-8545).*

The main church for Latvian Baptists.

The **Latvian Canadian Catholic Association,** *330 Dixon Road (416-248-5856).*

Also has social and cultural activities.

Lithuanians are both Catholic and Protestant as befits the varying influences of both the German Reformation and Catholicism.

The **Lithuanian Church of the Resurrection,** *999 College Street (416-533-0621).*

Adorned with traditional Lithuanian crosses; has one of the best collections of Lithuanian art in the country.

Lithuanian Lutheran Church of the Redeemer, *1691 Bloor Street West (416-766-1424).*

The main church for the Lithuanian Lutheran community.

Lithuanian Martyrs Church, *494 Isabella Avenue (416-277-1270).*

══════ Organizations ══════

There are many community organizations that support the Russian community. These include:

The **Russian Canadian Cultural Aid Society,** *91 Kersdale Avenue (416-653-1361).*

The community's main cultural group sponsors Russian-language lectures, language classes, dinners, and dances. Other groups affiliated with it include the

Polyanka Dancers, the **Literary Circle,** and the **Drama Circle.**

The **Russian Academy of Classical Ballet,** *935 Bloor Street West (416-532-2993).*

Conducts classes in classical Russian ballet.

The **Federation of Russian Canadians,** *6 Denison Avenue (416-368-8101).*

The main political lobbying group for Russian Canadians.

The **Bayavaya Uskalos/Byelorussian Literary Association,** *24 Tarlton Road (416-488-0048).*

The main cultural group in the Byelorussian community.

The **Byelorussian Canadian Alliance,** *524 Saint Clarens Road (416-530-1025).*

The main Byelorussian political group.

The **Azeri Community Centre,** *5000 Dufferin Street (416-665-7669).*

Just completed by the Azeri community, this center supports a number of cultural and community groups.

There is a wide variety of Armenian cultural organizations, among them:

The **Armenian Community Centre,** *45 Hallcrown Place (416-493-8122).*

Acts as the cultural focal point of the community, with an Armenian-language library and bookstore and a gallery showing art work by local Armenian artists. It has an excellent restaurant and cafeteria serving Armenian specialties like khorovatz, otherwise known as shish kebab.

The **Alex Manougian Centre,** *30 Progress Court (416-431-2428).*

Operates a number of community services as well as another Armenian-language library, and serves traditional Armenian foods on Sundays. Dance groups and discussion groups also meet at both community centers.

The **Hamazkain Cultural Association,** *45 Hallcrown Place (416-491-2900).*

Maintains a choir of over 130 members and sponsors a theater group, dance group, music group, and literary discussion.

The **Armenian Folk Dance Ensemble,** *3180 Bathurst Street (416-781-1620).*

The **Tekeyan Cultural Association,** *20 Progress Court (416-431-2428).*

The **Nor Serount Armenian Cultural Association,** *174 Shropshire Drive (416-429-7948).*

The Armenian community has been particularly active in promoting education regarding its unique thirty-six-letter alphabet-based language, as well as in taking a very strong role in relief, aid, and political efforts to help

Armenians living in the original homelands. The **AGBU Day School,** 30 Progress Court (416-439-3900); **Holy Cross Armenian Day School,** 1641 Pharmacy Avenue (416-441-2152); and the **ARPI Nursery School,** 3180 Bathurst Street (416-781-1620), each offer education in English, French, and Armenian, as well as special Armenian-language classes for students from other schools.

The **Armenian Relief Society,** 45 Hallcrown Place (416-491-2900), located in the Armenian Community Centre has helped coordinate fundraising and political education efforts on behalf of the community. Also active are the **Armenian National Committee** at the same address, the **Armenian Senior Citizens Club,** and the **Armenian Youth Federation.**

Other politically active organizations include:

Armenian General Benevolent Union, *30 Progress Court (416-431-2428).*

Armenian Democratic Liberal Organization, *20 Progress Court (416-431-2428).*

Armenian Revolutionary Federation, *45 Hallcrown Place (416-429-2900).*

Social Democrat Hentchag Party, *174 Shropshire Drive (416-429-7948).*

Zorian Institute for Contemporary Armenian Research and Documentation, *101 Duncan Mills Road (416-449-7171).*

This organization also sponsors lectures and educational events.

The umbrella group for many Polish community, social, cultural, and political groups is the **Canadian Polish Congress—Toronto District,** 206 Beverly Street (416-979-9634). It houses a wide range of community groups, including the **Polish Immigrant Aid Centre,** the **Polish Engineers Association,** and the **Polish Society of Music.**

Another center of Polish cultural activity is the **Polish Cultural Centre,** 2282 Lakeshore Boulevard West (416-252-9519), a beautiful old mansion overlooking Lake Ontario that is the site for many music, dance, and performing arts affairs in the community.

Other Polish-Canadian community and social groups include:

Canadian Polish Business Council, *95 Saint Clair Avenue West (416-961-0101).*

Lechowia (Polish Canadian Folk Dance Company), *PO Box 53, Station D (416-622-3387).*

N.S.Z.Z. Canadian Representative of Solidarity, *155 Jarvis Street (416-441-3714).*

Polish Alliance Centre (Polish Cultural Centre), *2282 Lakeshore Boulevard West (416-252-9519).*

Polish Canadian Action Group, *PO Box 55, Station V (416-747-6034).*

Polish Canadian Community Services, *2333 Dundas Street West (416-533-9471).*

Polish-Canadian Society of Music, *2 Dermott Place (416-421-7416).*

Polish Canadian Women's Federation, *25 Henry Lane (416-362-5110).*

Polish Institute of Arts and Sciences in America, *14 Duncairn Road (416-444-6940).*

Polish National Hall/Polish National Union of Canada, *905 Queen Street West (416-366-0667).*

Polish National Union Mutual Benefit Society, *31 Indian Trail (416-767-9538).*

Polish Veteran's Association, *783 College Street (416-534-7231).*

Royal Canadian Legion, *905 Dovercourt Road (416-366-8667).*

White Eagle-Polish Dance Group, *2282 Lakeshore Boulevard West (416-252-9519).*

The **Canadian Polish Congress,** *288 Roncesvalles Avenue (416-532-2876),* and **Polish Alliance of Canada,** *1640 Bloor Street West (416-531-4826).*

The major political lobbying groups for issues concerning Poland and Polish Canadians.

The **Polish National Hall,** *905 Queen Street West (416-504-8667).*

Active as the head office of the **Polish National Union** and **Credit Union.**

Organizations within the Ukrainian community include the following:

The **Ukrainian Canadian Committee,** *2118A Bloor Street West (416-762-9457).*

The central coordinating body and umbrella organization for most Ukrainian-Canadian groups. The **Ukrainian Canadian Art Foundation** is headquartered here.

The **Saint Vladimir Canadian Ukrainian Institute,** *620 Spadina Avenue (416-923-3318).*

This community and cultural institute is also home to the **Canadian Ukrainian Opera Association, The Ukrainian Opera Company, The Ukrainian Canadian Woman Writers Association,** the **Ukrainian-Canadian Women's Council,** and the **Ukrainian Librarians of Canada.** The Institute contains an art gallery, library, theater, and bookstore with a special collection of over 20,000 volumes devoted to Ukrainian studies.

The **Ukrainian Central Information Centre,** *83 Christie Street (416-531-3610).*

Member groups include the **Ukrainian Youth Association,** the **Dilrova Women's Choir,** the **Prometheus Men's Choir,** and the **Zahrava Ukrainian Drama Ensemble.** This building also houses the **Ukrainian Cultural Centre,** with a library and lecture hall.

Ukrainian National Federation of Canada, *297 College Street (416-921-0231).*

Member groups include the **Ukrainian National Youth Federation,** the **Boyan Choir,** the **Ukrainian Canadian Women's Organization,** the **Ukrainian War Veterans** Association, the **Kalyna Girls Choir,** and the **Kalyna Dance Ensemble.** The Federation also houses a library of over 11,000 volumes on Ukrainian history, language, and culture.

Other community and cultural groups include:

Canadian Shevchenko Cultural Society, *314 Oriole Parkway (416-480-2440).*

Canadian Ukrainian Immigrant Aid Society, *2150 Bloor Street West (416-767-4595).*

Plast Ukrainian Youth Organization, *2199 Bloor Street West (416-769-9998).*

Shevchenko Scientific Society, *140 Bathurst Street (416-366-9350).*

Shevchenko Ukrainian Community Centre, *482 Horner Avenue (416-255-6249).*

Ukrainian Academy of Dance, *4 Morningside (416-760-0228).*

Ukrainian Association of Creative Artists in Canada, *19 Brule Crescent (416-363-0961).*

Ukrainian Historical Association, *215 Grenadier Road (416-536-0402).*

Ukrainian Labour Temple, *300 Bathurst Street (416-368-9144).*

Ukrainian Music Festival, *209 Riverside Drive (416-762-9158).*

Ukrainian Professional and Business Club of Toronto, *620 Spadina Avenue (416-762-4858).*

Ukrainian Theatrical Ensemble and Art Society, *79 Ulster Street (416-922-5355).*

Ukrainian Youth Ensemble, *7142 Tamai Road (905-821-0662).*

The Ukrainian community also has its own museum. The **Ukrainian Museum of Canada—Ontario Branch,** 620 Spadina Avenue (416-923-3318), displays Ukrainian religious and historic artifacts, decorated Easter eggs, embroidered regional costumes, icons, and heirlooms. Another museum, **Ukrainian Arts and Crafts Museum,** 404 Bathurst Street (416-366-3224), is devoted to Ukrainian costumes, folk art, and embroidery and has a number of wonderful examples of these aspects of the Ukrainian heritage. Another excellent place to visit is the **Ukrainian Canadian Art Foundation,** 2118 A Bloor Street West (416-766-6802), which has a permanent collection of over 500 works of art from four generations of Ukrainian-Canadian artists.

Toronto is also an important center of studies in Ukrainian history and culture, with major programs at both the University of Toronto and York University. Lessons in Estonian language and history are available from:

Eesti Kodu, *50 Old Kingston Road (416-281-1792).*

Estonian Schools, *958 Broadview Avenue (416-461-1344).*

Tartu College, *310 Bloor Street West (416-925-9405).*

Has one the most extensive libraries on Estonian subjects in the world and also provides the community with an extensive array of lectures and other programs.

Estonian House, 958 Broadview Avenue (416-461-7963), is the umbrella center for many organizations in the Estonian community, including the **Estonian Arts Centre,** the **Estonian Folkdance Group,** the **Estonian Ethnographical Society,** the **Estonian Central Council in Canada,** the **Estonian Federation in Canada,** the **Estonian Canadian Festival Foundation,** the **Estonian Choir of Mixed Voices** and **The Estonian Association of Toronto.**

A number of other musical groups are active in the community also:

The **Estonian Concert Band,** *34 Woolton Crescent.*

Lyra Borealis, *334 Wellesley Street East.*

A chamber orchestra.

The **Toronto Estonian Male Choir,** *15 Cotman Crescent.*

Kalev-Estienne, 3 Pebble Beach Gate (905-889-4167), is a rhythmic gymnastics organization (one of the major Estonian cultural physical fitness pursuits), as is **Ritmikia,** 14 Oaken Gateway.

The **Estonian Central Council in Canada,** 958 Broadview Avenue (416-461-7963), remains the governing political organization representing Estonian Canadians. It also provides support for the **Estonian Relief Committee** the community's major charitable organization.

The Latvian community has undertaken a number of programs to help preserve their native language, which is considered one of the oldest surviving Indo-European languages still spoken. Among the programs available are those at:

Latvian High School, *491 College Street (416-922-2551).*

Valodina Latvian School, *4 Credit Union Drive (416-759-4900).*

Toronto Latvian School, *61 Davenport Avenue (416-922-7725).*

Other Latvian organizations include:

Latvian House, *491 College Street (416-922-255).*

The cultural home of the Latvian community, housing a variety of community and cultural organizations, including a book and handicrafts store, an extensive library, and meeting rooms.

The **Latvian Canadian Cultural Centre,** *4 Credit Union Drive (416-759-4900).*

Holds concerts, dances, lectures, films, and other events throughout the year, including a display of historic costumes, artifacts, and Latvian art in its art gallery. There is also a library, gift shop, and bookstore. A lounge and restaurant called **Umurumurs** is open in the evening for members and guests.

The **Daugavas Vanagi House,** *125 Broadview Avenue (416-465-5225).*

A community center in Toronto's Riverdale area.

Baltic Veteran's Association in Canada, *18 Shaver Avenue North.*

Camberchoir Dzirkists, *6 Browning Avenue (416-463-6613).*

Latvian Business Association, *123 Overland Drive (416-444-5201).*

The main political organizations promoting both Latvian and Latvian-Canadian issues are:

The **Latvian National Federation in Canada,** *4 Credit Union Drive (416-755-2353).*

Latvian Relief Society, *125 Broadview Avenue (416-465-5225).*

Lithuanian language classes are held at:

Lithuanian Sunday School, *240 Church Street (416-364-5577).*

Vilnius Manor, *1700 Bloor Street West (416-762-1777).*

Other Lithuanian cultural and social societies and associations include:

Anapilis Hall, *2185 Stavebank Road (905-566-8755).*
Located opposite the Lithuanian cemetery, a pretty and peaceful place with a number of very artistic headstones.

Lithuanian House, *1573 Bloor Street West (416-534-8214).*
The main community center for the Lithuanian community in Toronto. It houses a variety of community and social groups, including a little café called **Club Lokys** and a library. It also holds regular bingo games. For information on community activities, call 416-532-3312.

The **Lithuanian Museum and Archives,** *2185 Stavebank Road (905-566-8755).*
Exhibits books, letters, art, historic documents, folklore, costumes, and militaria from Lithuanian history.

The **Lithuanian Canadian Community National Executive,** *1011 College Street (416-533-3292).*

The main political body for Lithuanians' concerns about Lithuania as well as about their community in Canada.

Holidays and Celebrations

January 6	*Epiphany,* the Armenian Apostolic Church's main holiday, celebrating the birth and baptism of Jesus.
January 7	*Epiphany* (Russian holiday).
January 13	*Russian Orthodox New Year.*
	Ukrainian New Year's Eve.
January 19	*Jordan Day,* a combination Ukrainian Christmas and Epiphany.
January 22	Declaration of Independence for the Ukraine in 1919.
January 28	*Cultural Appeal Day* recognizes the day in 1935 when then-president of Latvia Dr. Karlis Ulmanis called on all Latvians to preserve and defend their cultural heritage.
February/March	*Maslyanitsa* (Butter Week), Russian festivities preceding the start of Lent. Pancake Tuesday marks the day before the start of Lent.
	Vartan's Day, a moveable feast celebrating the Battle of Avarair, which the Armenians lost to the Zoroastrian Persians but through which they still retained their faith and attained victory thirty years later.
February 16	*Lithuanian Independence Day,* celebrating the day in 1918 when Lithuania became an independent nation.
February 24	*Estonian Independence Day,* celebrating Estonia's independence in 1918.

March 4	*Saint Casimir's Day,* honoring Lithuania's patron saint.
March 6	Honors Colonel Oskar Kalpaks, a hero of the Latvian War of Liberation, who was killed in fighting in 1919.
March 9	Birthday of the great Ukrainian poet, Taras Shevchenko.
March 14	*Remembrance Day* of Slovak Independence.
March 25	*Byelorussian Independence Day,* celebrating the day in 1918 when Byelorussia declared its independence.
March/April	*Easter,* the most important holiday in the Russian Orthodox Church.
April 24	*Martyr's Day,* commemorating the day the Turkish genocide of Armenians began in 1915.
Early May	*Sadarabad Day,* a moveable feast celebrating a victory over the Turkish army at the battle of Sadarabad which took place May 22–26, 1918.
May 3	*Polish National Constitution Day,* commemorating the establishment of the constitution of 1791.
May 11	*Saint Kryla (Cyril) Day,* honoring the bishop of the Eastern Orthodox Church who did missionary work among the Byelorussians.
May 28	*Independence Day,* marking the declaration of independence of the Armenian Republic in 1918.
June	*The Talinn Festival,* an annual cultural festival held at Estonia House at the end of June.
June 5	Honors Saint Euphrasinia, the patron saint of Byelorussia.
June 14	*Remembrance Day* for the Lithuanians deported to Siberia by the Russians between 1941 and 1948.
	Commemoration Day, in remembrance of the thousands of Estonians deported to Siberia.

Commemoration Day, held in memory of the thousands of Latvians exiled to Siberia in 1941.

June 24 — *Saint John's Day,* a summer solstice festival honoring Estonia's patron saint; also *Midsummer's Day.*

July 5 — Commemoration of Saints Cyril and Methodius.

July 17 — Russian day of mourning for the death of Czar Nicholas II.

July 28 — *Saint Vladimir's Day,* honoring the saint who brought Christianity to Russia in the tenth century.

August — *Pilgrimage to the Cathedral of the Transfiguration,* on the first Sunday of the month.

August — *Ukrainian Heritage Day.*

August 15 — *Assumption Day* for Polish Catholics; also commemorates the 1920 Polish victory over Soviet troops at the Vistula River.

August 23 — *Black Ribbon Day,* a day commemorating the inclusion and occupation of the Baltic states by the Soviet Union in 1939.

September 7 — *Ukrainian Canadian Day.*

September/October — *Lithuanians in Canada Day,* celebrated annually with a conference and social and cultural functions.

October — A month of cultural activities at the Alex Manougian Center.

October 14 — Veneration of the icon of Pokrov (the mother of God), patron saint of the Cossacks.

November 11 — *Polish Independence Day,* first recognized when occupying forces were expelled from Poland. Also commemorates the reinvigoration of the Polish nation in 1945.

November 18 — *Latvian Independence Day.*

November 23	*Armed Forces Day,* commemorating when the Lithuanian armed forces were reconstituted in 1918.
November 29	*Memorial Day,* remembering the Russian victims of the Slucak Uprising in 1918.
December	Armenian Christmas bazaar.
December 13	*Saint Andrew Day,* honoring the patron saint of the Ukraine.
December 19	*Saint Nicholas Day,* honoring the saint renowned for his kindness to children and charitable deeds.

═══ Restaurants, Cafés, and Nightclubs ═══

Only a couple of restaurants in the city serve Russian cuisine, though similar items can be found at many Polish restaurants. Russian cooking includes as its basic staple a variety of hearty, grainy rye breads; *kasha* (a buckwheat porridge); beef stroganoff; *blinchiki* (crepes filled with cottage cheese and preserves); and *chakhombili* (chicken casserole with tomatoes and onions).

There are two main Armenian cuisine restaurants and two other prominent restaurants owned by Armenians that serve some Armenian foods, such as grilled meat kebabs, *mesashot* (a pizza-like dish made with ground lamb and pattotz), and grape vine leaves stuffed with rice.

Polish cuisine is served in a number of restaurants, often with other Eastern and Central European cuisines, including Baltic, German, and Hungarian dishes. Polish specialties include the creamy paprika-laden stews called *paprikashes,* the ever-present *pierogis* (potato- or cheese-filled dumplings), *borscht* (creamy beet soup with dill), *kielbassa* (Polish sausage), *kasza* (buckwheat groats or barley served with potatoes), *bigos* (hunter's stew), and *zony schab* (marinated roast pork loin). Polish beers such as Krakus are available at most restaurants, as are Polish vodkas such as Wyborowa, Baltic, and Winiak.

Ukrainian cooking is a robust Eastern European cuisine similar to Polish and Russian styles of cooking. Specialties include *holubtsi* (cabbage roles stuffed with rice and sometimes ground meat), *perohy* (Ukrainian pierogis or stuffed dumplings), *borscht* (red beet soup), and *makivnyk* (poppy seed cake rolls). As with Russians, vodka is the alcoholic beverage of choice.

Latvian cuisine is a combination of Swedish, Polish, German, and Lithuanian influences, with many local seafood and meat specialties.

Lithuania's cuisine is very similar to that of Poland and the Ukraine, and many Polish and Ukrainian restaurants in the city serve Lithuanian specialties. The **Lithuanian House** has a small café called **Club Lokys,** which features Lithuanian specialties such as *barsciai* (cold beet soup), *suris* (a cooked cheese dish), and *cepiliniai* (meat-filled potato pierogis).

Amber European Restaurant, *2372 Bloor Street West (416-763-6164).*

This pleasantly decorated, country-style restaurant serves a variety of Polish, Russian, and Baltic foods, including specialties like *nalesniki* (Polish crepes) and *kotlety* (meatballs). Service is friendly; prices are modest.

Arax Restaurant, *1979 Lawrence Avenue East (416-288-1485).*

Dishes here are a mixture of Armenian and Middle Eastern specialties and include fried eggplant, falafel, meat-and-onion soup, and grilled lamb. Also available is *hoom kufteh,* an Armenian-spiced steak tartare, as well as an array of Armenian wines and liqueurs. The owner is generally on hand and personally involved in helping customers through the large menu. There are over fifteen appetizers to choose from, including what many consider to be the best fried eggplant in Canada.

Armenian Kitchen, *1646 Victoria Park Avenue (416-752-8122).*

Home cooking Armenian style with a variety of other Levantine specialties. An excellent *herresh* (lamb stew thickened with oats) is available, as is *beureg* (cheese turnover), *garmroug* (hot red pepper with bread crumbs), and *tertanoush* (a flaky pastry dessert made with walnuts).

Café Mediterranee, *2655 Yonge Street (416-488-3976).*

A lovely new restaurant serving a variety of Mediterranean specialties. Owned by an Armenian family, it offers some Armenian dishes.

Café Polonez, *195 Roncesvalles Avenue (416-532-8432).*

One of the best and longest existing Polish restaurants in the city, the Café Polonez serves a wide array of Polish specialties, as well as a Polish-style French toast filled with custard that's one of the best in Toronto. Potato pancakes, pierogis, and borscht are among the specialties, as are such unique items as beef tripe soup and schnitzel Polonez with fried mushrooms.

Café Sava, *2219 Dundas Street West (416-588-4563).*

This small restaurant serves a number of Polish specialties, including excellent *flaczki* (roast pork loin), beef goulash, cabbage, and cucumber and beet soups.

Chopin Restaurant, *52 Lakeshore Road East (905-891-8100).*

An elegant restaurant serving Polish and central European specialties in upscale surroundings, along with a full array of Polish appetizers and desserts. Piano entertainment is provided.

Dancing Spoon Restaurant, *353 Roncesvalles Avenue (416-531-3360).*

Another well-established Polish restaurant serving pierogis, marinated herring, cabbage rolls, pork dishes, and wiener schnitzel. This cozy little room is reminiscent of a small country restaurant in central Europe.

Future Café Bakery, *483 Bloor Street West (416-922-5875); 2199 Bloor Street West (416-769-5020); 1535 Yonge Street (416-944-1253); 735 Queen Street West (416-504-8700); 95 Front Street East (416-366-7259).*

This formerly sleepy little Ukrainian bakery has been transformed in recent years into a chain of some of the city's hippest cafés. Still serving Ukrainian specialties in a cafeteria-style arrangement along with an excellent array of pastries, breads and sweets, Future Café is a must for tourists. It may not have the Ukrainian atmosphere you are expecting, but the food is excellent—as are the prices.

Izba (Wooden Cottage), *648 The Queensway (416-251-7717).*

A clean, well-maintained chalet-style exterior opens into a lovely cottage-style interior filled with Polish dolls and wall ornaments. The kitchen serves Polish specialties such as roast pork served with fried cabbage, dumplings, pierogis, and schnitzel. Piano and violin music accompany dinner.

Kungla Restaurant/Estonian House Restaurant, *958 Broadview Avenue (416-463-3321).*

This restaurant in Estonia House serves a variety of Estonian specialties, including fish, seafood, pork, and sauerkraut dishes that represent the strong Swedish and German influence in Estonian cuisine.

The Poles, *206 Beverly Street (416-979-9634).*

Rooneem's Bakery and Café, *484 Queen Street West (416-366-1205).*

The owners may now be Chinese, but the traditions of producing Estonian breads, baked goods, and hearty Estonian deli food such as specialty sausages and cheeses, continues.

Round Window Seafood Restaurant, *729 Danforth Avenue (416-465-3892).*

Long a favorite with Torontonians for its wide variety of seafood dishes, the Round Window also serves some Armenian seafood recipes.

Samovar Barmalay Restaurant, *505 Mount Pleasant Road (416-480-0048).*

Long a popular restaurant serving a wide array of Russian foods in a country-style setting with folk-music entertainment. Specialties include *satsivi* (cold chicken with a spicy nut-and-garlic sauce, chicken tabak, and caucasus *shashlik* (marinated lamb). The owner can at times be charming and helpful and at other times overbearing and rude (a duality often associated with the Russian temperament).

Sir Nicholas Restaurant, *91 Roncesvalles Avenue (416-535-4540).*

The oldest and best-known Polish restaurant in the city is modeled after the famous Krokodyl restaurant in Warsaw. Decorated with many Polish artifacts, this restaurant has a large buffet serving a variety of Polish specialties. Musical entertainment is provided on weekends.

Staropolska (Old Poland), *299 Roncesvalles Avenue (416-537-8850).*

Traditional Polish cuisine, including cheese and apple crepes, breaded pork chops, and cabbage rolls, is available here.

Ukrainian Caravan Restaurant, *5245 Dundas Street West (416-231-7447).*

Offers a dinner dance show with Ukrainian specialties, shish kebobs, and other grilled meats, as well as folk dancing in the "cossack" style.

Umurkumurs, *4 Credit Union Drive (416-759-4900),*

This lounge and restaurant in the Latvian Canadian Cultural Centre serves a variety of Latvian foods and drinks.

Winter Palace, *123 Queen Street West (in the Sheraton Centre Hotel) (416-361-1000).*

An elegant if pricey restaurant. The resplendent decor is matched by superb Russian food. This romantic spot has an extensive menu, beautiful surroundings, and, in winter, a view reminiscent of Moscow or Saint Petersburg.

Food Sources

Most Russian specialty foods and baked goods can be found at Ukrainian or Polish outlets, as well as at some of the Jewish bakeries in North York, north of Finch Avenue West on Bathurst Street, where a large Russian-Jewish community lives.

Several bakeries in the Metro area carry Armenian baked specialties, including fresh lahmajoon, beureg, and various pastries such as nut and syrup pahklava (baklava):

Ararat Bakery, *1800 Avenue Road (416-782-5722).*

Armenian Bakery, *1646 Victoria Park Avenue (416-757-1559).*

Beirut Bakery, *369 Wilson Avenue (416-630-6163).*

Meat and food specialties, such as *soujoukh* (Armenian sausage), *sisser* (specially prepared chick peas), and basterma are available from the following deli/grocers:

Arax Meat Products, *3905 Chesswood Drive (416-636-6143).*

Grande Cheese Co. Ltd., *175 Milvan Drive (416-740-8847); factory outlet, 468 Jevlan Drive (905-856-6880).*

This place produces the special white Armenian stretch cheeses.

Shirak Delicatessen and Meat, *1375 Danforth Road (416-266-7519).*

The Roncesvalles Avenue area of Toronto is often filled with the wonderful smells of Polish bakeries, butchers, and delicatessens. Most Polish bakeries and many delis include cafés and offer wonderful homemade ice creams in addition to their excellent breads (particularly recommended are the large, sweet, round egg breads), cakes, sausages, and pastries.

Anna's Bakery and Deli, *2394 Bloor Street West (416-769-8065).*

Astra Meat Products, *2238 Bloor Street West (416-763-1093).*

Benna's Fine Foods, *135 Roncesvalles Avenue (416-534-0031).*

Copernicus Meat Products, *97 Roncesvalles Avenue (416-536-4054).*

Cracovia Deli, *3261 Lakeshore Boulevard West (416-253-5966).*

Granowska's, *175 Roncesvalles Avenue (416-533-7755).*

This well-known institution on Roncesvalles includes a lovely café, an excellent and inviting array of pastries and desserts, and an ice cream stand.

K B Deli, *131 Roncesvalles Avenue (416-533-7054).*

Karl's Butcher, *105 Roncesvalles (416-531-1622).*

Kingsway Meat Products, *2342 Bloor Street West (416-762-5365).*

Krokus Meat Deli, *1570 Bloor Street West (416-534-2033).*

An incredible array of Polish meats, sausages, imported foods, and baked goods.

Polonez Meat Products, *2436 Lakeshore Boulevard West (416-251-0942).*

Polonia Meat Market and Deli, *129 Roncesvalles Avenue (416-533-5475).*

Quality Sausage, *78 Six Points (416-231-8679).*

Roncesvalles Bakery, *173 Roncesvalles Avenue (416-535-7143).*

Super Kolbasa and Deli, *83 Roncesvalles Avenue (416-588-3759).*

Warszawianka, *363 Roncesvalles Avenue (416-532-8762).*

Ukrainian food specialties can be found at a variety of stores in the community, including the following:

Astra Meat Market, *2238 Bloor Street West (416-763-1093).*

Ukrainian meat specialties, including kobassa, head cheese, blood pudding, and *studzienna* (jellied pig's knuckles).

Durie Meat Products, *2302 Bloor Street West (416-762-4956).*

Ukrainian sausages, homemade pierogis, cabbage rolls, and other Ukrainian specialties.

Future Bakery, *483 Bloor Street West (416-922-5875); 2199 Bloor Street West (416-769-5020); 1535 Yonge Street (416-944-1253); 735 Queen Street West (416-504-8700); 95 Front Street East (416-366-7259).*

Excellent Ukrainian rye breads, cookies, and pastries. The family who owns the chain has been baking Ukrainian specialties since the time of the last czar. They came to Canada after World War II and have been here ever since.

Shops

Troyka Ltd., 799A College Street (416-535-6693), and the **Ukrainska Book and Gift Store,** 2282 Bloor Street West (416-534-7551), carry Russian gifts, crafts, books, and magazines.

The Armenian community has long produced and supported an inordinate number of talented visual artists in Toronto. Some of the galleries where the works of these artists are shown include:

Armen Art Gallery, *16 Wellesley Street West (416-924-5375).*

Sevan Art Gallery, *364 Yonge Street (416-597-0368).*

Zaven Art Gallery, *2300 Yonge Street (416-483-1504).*

Armenian carpets and rugs are also extremely well known for their high quality and artistic merit. Carpet importing and retailing was an early profession among the Armenian community in Toronto. Some of the stores where Armenian carpets are available include:

Adourians Rug Galleries, *89 King Street East (416-362-6713).*

Alexanian Carpet, *1855 Dundas Street East (905-624-0844).*

Armenian Rug Company, *476 Davisville Avenue (416-483-3300).*

Karakashian Rug Gallery, *1257 Bay Street (416-964-1995).*

Selyan's Oriental Rugs, *1764 Avenue Road (416-781-2030).*

The **Armenian Community Center,** 45 Hallcrown Place (416-491-2900), also has a bookstore selling Armenian-language publications and recordings.

Three shops specializing in Polish goods and services are:

Cepalia, *139 Roncesvalles Avenue (416-536-2738).*

Has a wide array of Polish crafts, gifts, and imported goods.

PEKAO Trading Co., *1610 Bloor Street West (416-588-1414).*

Has many imported Polish linens, glassware, and china, as well as gifts.

Polimex Parcels to Poland, *215 Roncesvalles Avenue (416-537-3496).*

Handles services for shipping to Poland as well as importing Polish crafts and goods.

There is also a range of stores carrying Ukrainian goods, from artwork to Ukrainian-language publications:

Arka Canadian Book Store, *575 Queen Street West (416-703-2752).*

More than a bookstore, Arka also carries gifts, magazines, handicrafts, art work, and Ukrainian religious items.

Trypillia Arts, *2285 Bloor Street West (416-766-0113).*

A gallery displaying Ukrainian and ceramic art.

Ukrainska Knyha, *962 Bloor Street West (416-534-7551).*

Ukrainian fabrics, folk art, crafts, banduras, language books, and periodicals, as well as some food specialties.

West Arka Gift Store, *2282 Bloor Street West (416-762-8751).*

Specializes in imported handicrafts, such as decorated Easter eggs, patterned ceramics, and embroidered tablecloths, as well as Ukrainian music, art, and jewelry.

===================== **Media** =====================

Publications

Annual Ukrainian Directory, *380 Dixon Road (416-247-0424).*

Armenian Cause Newsletter, *45 Hallcrown Place (416-491-2900).*
Published every three months, it covers issues regarding the Armenian homelands.

Batkivschyna (Our Country), *PO Box 308 Station M (416-769-1231).*
Publishes for the Ukrainian community.

Beacon, *447 Vaughan Road (416-656-3772).*
A Ukrainian publication.

Byelorussian Voice, *24 Tarlton Road (416-488-0048).*
A Byelorussian monthly.

Canadian Armenian Press, *34 Glenforest Road (416-485-4336).*
A quarterly publication following the concerns of Toronto's Armenian community.

Echo Tygodnia, *124A Manville Road (416-759-7771).*
Polish.

Echo-Tygodnik Polski, *51A Thistledown Boulevard (416-747-6034).*
Published for the Polish community.

Gazeta, *215 Roncesvalles Avenue (416-531-3230).*
A Polish publication.

Glos Polski (Polish Voice), *390 Roncesvalles Avenue (416-533-9469).*

Homin Ukrainy (Ukrainian Echo), *140 Bathurst Street (416-368-3443).*

Khosnag, *30 Progress Court (416-431-2428).*

A bimonthly newsletter on the Armenian-Canadian community.

Latvija Amerika (Latvia in America), *125 Broadview Avenue (416-465-7902),*

The main publication covering issues of concern to Latvian Canadians.

LRADU, *45 Hallcrown Place (416-491-2900).*

A monthly newsletter published in Armenian.

Meia Elu, *958 Broadview Avenue (416-466-0951).*

A weekly newspaper published in association with Estonia House and covering news of interest to the Estonian community.

Nasha Meta (Our Aim), *278 Bathurst Street (416-368-3519).*

A Ukrainian Catholic newspaper.

Nepriklausoma Lietuva (Independent Lithuania), *75 Graydon Hall (416-447-4128).*

A monthly publication.

Novy Shliakh (New Pathway), *297 College Street (416-960-3424).*

Ukrainian.

Plastovy Shliakh (Plast Way), *2445-A Bloor Street West (416-769-7855).*

A Ukrainian publication.

Polish Business Directory–Phone Book, *251 Sorauren Avenue (416-761-9659).*

Polish Canadian Courier, *PO Box 161, Station B (416-255-6486).*

Polish Weekly Chronicle, *330 Roncesvalles Avenue (416-533-9469).*

Promyk, *25 Saint Denis Drive (416-425-4776).*
A Polish publication.

Rozmaitosci, *87 Jameson Avenue (416-532-4065).*
Polish.

Teviskes Ziburiai (Light of the Homeland), *2185 Stavebank Road (905-275-4672).*
A weekly newspaper on Lithuanian affairs published since 1949.

Vaba Eestlane, *120A Willowdale Avenue (416-733-4550).*
A biweekly newspaper covering political events in Estonia.

Vestnik, *799 College Street (416-536-7330).*
A Russian-language weekly.

Visnyk, *2118A Bloor Street West (416-762-1108).*
Ukrainian.

Women's World, *18 Leland Avenue (416-233-5762).*
A Ukrainian publication.

Yunak Magazine (Youth), *2199 Bloor Street West (416-769-9998).*
Publishes for the Ukrainian community.

Zhyttia i Slovo (Life and Word), *962 Bloor Street West (416-534-8635).*
Ukrainian.

Zwiazkowiec (Polish Alliance Press), *1638 Bloor Street West (416-531-2491).*

Radio and Television

"Armenian Program," CHIN-FM 100.7, *622 College Street (416-531-9991).*
Broadcast on Sunday afternoons.

"Polish Studio," Channel 57 CITY-TV, *299 Queen Street West (416-591-5757).*

"Radio Kalejdoskop," CIAO 790-AM, *PO Box 55, Station V (416-249-1887).*

Polish.

"Radio Polonia," CHIN-AM 1540/FM 100.7, *622 College Street (416-531-9991).*

Polish.

"Rozmaitosci," CFMT-TV, Channel 47, *545 Lakeshore Boulevard West (416-593-4747).*

Polish.

"Moloda Ukraina (ODUM)," CHIN-AM 1540/FM 100.7, *622 College Street (416-531-9991).*

"Pisnia Ukrainy/Song of the Ukraine," CHWO-1250 AM, *PO Box 1 Station V (416-536-4262).*

"Prometheus," CHIN-AM 1540/FM 100.7, *622 College Street (416-531-9991).*

"Svitohliad," CFMT-TV, Channel 47, *545 Lakeshore Boulevard West (416-593-4747).*

An hour-long weekly show with news and events of interest to the Ukrainian community.

"Titka Kvitka," Graham Cable 10, *35 Scarlett Road (416-762-3631).*

A Ukrainian children's television program.

"Ukrainian Orthodox Show," CHIN-AM 1540/FM 100.7, *622 College Street (416-531-9991).*

"Latvian Voice," CHIN-AM 1540/FM 100.7, *622 College Street (416-531-9991),*

A radio show offering Latvian music, as well as current events and news regarding Latvia.

The **"Lithuanian Program,"** CHIN-AM 1540/FM 100.7, *622 College Street (416-531-9991).*

Covers news, music, and current events in Lithuania.

—Bloor Street West Village—

The Bloor Street West Village is home to a number of Eastern European groups, including large Ukrainian, German, Polish, Lithuanian, Bulgarian, and Macedonian communities. In this area the Ukrainians predominate with their cultural centers, ethnic shops, bakeries, and grocers. The whole area has a very Eastern European flair with outdoor cafés, small grocers, produce stands, and a variety of unique and interesting gifts shops. Many of the shops, museums, and centers noted in this section are located along this strip.

The surrounding streets are quiet and dignified with well-kept brick houses, trees. and an orderly atmosphere. High Park borders this community on one side, the Humber River on the other, and in between on Bloor Street West is one of Toronto's most active and interesting urban shopping and entertainment areas. This is a great place to go anytime during the week as it is always bustling with activity and old-world charm. Not overrun with tourists, the area gives you a good feeling of what urban ethnic Toronto is all about.

How to Get There: *Take the Bloor Street West subway west to either the Runnymede or the Jane Street Station. The community is right along the Bloor Street corridor.*

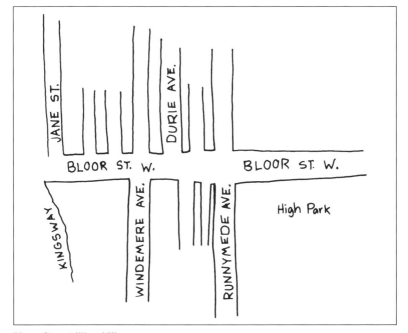

Bloor Street West Village

Western and Central European Toronto

Many European immigrants from the western, central, and northern parts of the continent have settled in Toronto and formed distinctive ethnic communities of their own. These immigrants arrived from Belgium; Holland; Switzerland; Hungary; the Czech Republic; and the Scandinavian nations of Norway, Sweden, Finland, Denmark, and Iceland.

Nationalities

Dutch and Belgians

The Dutch were among the earliest settlers to Canada and have had a long and friendly relationship with both the country as a whole and the city of Toronto. In World War II the Dutch royal family lived in exile in Canada, and it was Canadian troops who were among the first liberators of Holland near the end of the war. Dutch settlers in the Toronto area were among the first wave of United Empire Loyalists to settle the Upper Canadian region in the years following the American Revolution.

These were the boat people of the Revolution who fled to Canada fearing reprisals from the victorious revolutionaries. Among them was Egerton Ryerson, a prominent educator of Dutch background, who was Ontario's first minister of education and helped found the public school system in Ontario as well as Ryerson Polytechnical Institute.

Toronto's Dutch population grew dramatically in the 1920s and 1930s as southwestern Dutch farmers migrated to Toronto in pursuit of jobs in skilled trade and industry. Following the Second World War, another wave made up primarily of Dutch war brides, skilled workers, and professionals came to the then-active industries in Toronto while Holland rebuilt after the devastation of occupation.

There are now approximately 50,000 Dutch Canadians living in the Metro Toronto area, most having arrived within the last forty years. Dutch-owned companies, including Voortman Bakeries and Holtzheuser Brothers Importers, are prominent among Toronto industries. Another area of accomplishment is the Dutch Credit Union, one of the largest and most successful in Ontario. This fraternal organization also offers a variety of social and cultural facilities for the community.

Toronto has also been the metropolis of the many productive farmers in the nearby Holland Marsh area. Their work over the years has provided some of the richest and most fertile farmland in Canada and has helped Toronto develop an extensive food processing and exporting business.

Toronto is a twinned community with Amsterdam and to commemorate this fraternal relationship a small park was built in 1974 at Saint Clair Avenue West and Avenue Road. The park has a replica of the 1928 Van Karnabeek fountain that stands in the Hague. The Dutch community also donated an artistic horticultural maze to the city in 1967. This can be found in the Toronto Islands Park on Centre Island. A large collection of tulip bulbs is housed on the grounds of the Harbourfront Park outside the York Quay Centre; close by is the Amsterdam Bridge which leads to the Pier Four complex.

Among the prominent Torontonians of Dutch descent is Albert Franck, a Dutch painter prominent in Toronto's old Gerrard Street artist's colony, who is well known here for his sleepy almost naive paintings of city streets and neighborhoods. Other Dutch artists from the city include Jake Mol, Hubert Sabelis, photographer John de Visser, and museum designer Jan Hiller.

The Belgian community in Toronto is relatively small but, like its Dutch counterpart, it acts as the focus for a much larger community of fellow nationals who live throughout Ontario. Belgian farmers are particularly prominent in the southwestern Ontario areas around Lake Saint Clair, where they developed and reclaimed an enormous amount of lake-bottom lands after World War II and maintain very prosperous and productive properties there to this day.

Many Toronto Belgians arrived in the years immediately following World War II, coming over as war brides or relatives of war brides. Although the community numbers only a little over 1,000, it is divided linguistically in the same way as its home country with an equal number of French, Dutch, and Flemish, as well as some German, speakers.

A Belgian presence in Toronto actually goes back to the very earliest days when the area was known as Temetegon and was a stop on the portage route up the Humber River to the Georgian Bay. Father Louis Hennepin, a Recollet missionary, accompanied the French explorer Cavalier de La Salle on his journeys through this region, and Belgian settlers and soldiers accompanied the first French settlers in the area.

Immigration on a wider scale began in the 1880s, with Belgian immigrants migrating primarily to rich farming areas around Delhi, Chatham, and Leamington in southwestern Ontario. A few others settled in Toronto, working as teachers and small merchants and eventually becoming active in the early paper and mining industries.

The opening of many armaments factories in the Toronto area during the Second World War attracted many second-generation Belgian immigrants to the city, and many Belgian youths joined the Canadian armed forces after the invasion of their homeland by the Nazis.

Immigration continued after the war and, while the Belgian community remains small, its members have been prominent in their contributions to the city in fields like fashion design, chocolatiers, diamond cutting, and the arts. The community remains active in developing and sustaining its cultural and linguistic heritage.

Swiss

A small but active community, the Swiss have had a role in Canadian life going back to the first settlements in Acadia; Swiss soldiers served there in 1604. Pioneer Sebastian Fryfogel was credited with opening the western area of Ontario known as the Huron Tract in the mid-1800s. Swiss Mennonite communities have been living in Ontario since the late 1700s with early settlements including a town called Zurich.

A Swiss-Canadian governor of Quebec, Sir Frederick Haldimand, was responsible for helping to settle the Loyalist refugees from the American Revolution in Ontario. Most of the settlers who came to Toronto were agriculturists and dairy farmers. Toronto became the focal point for both rural and urban Swiss in the area and a Swiss Club of Toronto was formed in 1918.

Many Swiss immigrants in the 1900s also migrated from Quebec. They were skilled craftsmen, watchmakers, chocolatiers, and chefs whose skills helped provide Toronto with a wide array of locally manufactured specialty products. A final wave of immigration in the 1960s and 1970s brought a number of skilled professionals and academics trying to escape the high prices and tight real estate market in Switzerland.

Many Swiss natives are present in Toronto's hospitality industries as hoteliers and restaurateurs. The Swiss in the area still celebrate the midwinter holiday known as the **Basel Carnivale,** which brings singing and dancing to the wintry early morning streets of Toronto at the end of February.

Czechs and Slovaks

The history of Czech settlement in Canada goes back to the earliest days of the colonization of Upper Canada. In 1791 a group of settlers arrived in Ontario's rural Moraviatown settlement. They were primarily religious nonconformists who were part of the Moravian brotherhood. Some later moved into the Toronto area as opportunities opened up in the 1830s and were joined in the 1880s by a new wave of skilled immigrants from the Czech areas of the Austrian-Hungarian empire.

Many newcomers were miners attracted by the opening of the rich Canadian shield areas. Others were farmers, skilled laborers, and artists who came searching for opportunity in the growing Canadian economy. In Toronto the Czech community settled into the growing Pan-Slavic neighborhood of Parkdale around Queen Street West. A few Czech delis, bakeries, and butcher shops can still be found in this area, though the community as a whole has dispersed throughout Toronto.

Renowned Canadian entrepreneur Thomas Bata was himself responsible for the immigration of many skilled Czech shoemakers to work in his growing firm in the 1930s and 1940s. Another wave of Czech settlers arrived after the Soviet takeover of Czechoslovakia in 1948 and again after the crushing of the Prague Spring in 1968.

One of the first community organizations formed was the Czechoslovakian National Association of Canada, originally created in the wake of the Nazi takeover of the Sudetenland in 1938. In the 1950s Masaryk Hall in Parkdale became the focus for community cultural and social events. Sokol units, organizations designed to promote physical fitness, also became more popular with the Czech community and began to have an important influence on Canadian interest in physical fitness during this period.

In the 1960s Masaryk Hall was sold to the City of Toronto, and a new cultural and recreational complex, called Masaryktown, was built in Scarborough. Czechoslovak Day celebrations have been held here to honor the founders of the Republic of Czechoslovakia as well as to pay tribute to Canada. Toronto's 15,000-member Czech community is by far the largest in the country and has made a number of important contributions to the city's artistic and cultural life. Opera singer Jan Rubes, pianists Oskar Morawetz

and Antonin Kubalek, and author Josef Skvorecky are all internationally acclaimed artists who came out of this community.

Czech-born artist Lea Vivot's sculpture can also be found throughout the
city, including *The Endless Beach* outside the Hospital for Sick Children,
Mother and Child outside Saint Joseph's Health Centre, *The Lover's Bench*
in the new CBC Building, and *The Secret Bench* near Yonge Street and
Summerhill Avenue. Other prominent Torontonians of Czech descent include Hanna Gartner, a news commentator and documentarian with the
CBC, and Chaviva Hosek, former MPP and provincial minister of housing.

Toronto's Slovak community has been very active and visible due to the
success some of its members have had in Canada over the years. The most
visible community landmark is the golden domes of the Cathedral of the
Transfiguration at Woodbine Avenue and Major Mackenzie Road in
Markham. Built in 1984, it is the only cathedral in North America to be
blessed by a pope. Inside, a massive mosaic made from over 5 million pieces
of glass and ceramic tiles towers above the altar. It is a striking symbol of the
success the community has enjoyed in Canada.

Slovak emigration to the Toronto area first began, like that of many other
Slavic peoples, in 1870. Joseph Bellon, a flower shop owner, is the first
recorded immigrant. He later was to fight in the Canadian brigade sent to
quell the Riel Rebellion and later founded a wireworks factory. Many Slovaks originally came to Ontario to work in the mining industries of the north
only to wind up settling in the Toronto area.

The community first formed around the Queen Street West and Bathurst
area, later moving west to Parkdale and eventually to the suburbs. Slovak
churches in these areas trace the evolution and movement of the community,
and Slovak shops, delis, and restaurants mark the former neighborhood's
boundaries.

As more Slovaks arrived in the 1930s and 1940s, community groups and
Protestant churches were founded as well. The community received a large
increase in population following the 1948 takeover of Czechoslovakia by
the Communists and the intervention in 1968 to eliminate the Prague
Spring. These migrations brought many skilled tradesmen, professionals,
and academics to Toronto.

Slovak entrepreneurs have been very successful in the Canadian climate.
The patron of the Cathedral of the Transfiguration, the late Stephen Roman,
is probably the best known. Founder of Denison Mines, Roman also played
a key role in the creation of a World Nationalist Slovakian movement that
eventually led to the setting up of an independent Slovak republic. Athletes
such as the hockey-playing Ihnacek brothers, tennis champion Helen Ke-
lesi, and rhythm gymnast Jana Lazor, are also examples of successful Slovak Canadians.

Hungarians

Toronto's Hungarian community has long been focused around the Bloor Street West area, known generally as The Annex or as Little Budapest. Over 50,000 Hungarians have immigrated to Toronto over the years, mainly following the abortive 1956 uprising against the Communists, when almost half of all Metro's Hungarians arrived.

The earliest Hungarian immigrants arrived in the 1880s, drawn to Canada by promises of cheap farmland and job opportunities. In addition to the population in Toronto, there are large Hungarian communities in many of the nearby cities in the Niagara Region. Many immigrants went on to become successful tobacco farmers in southwestern Ontario, and as a result the community has had a strong presence in Canada's tobacco industry.

Many Hungarians also arrived in Canada at the beginning of the twentieth century due to quotas imposed by the United States at this time against Slavic immigration. By the 1920s, Toronto's Hungarian population was large enough to form its own community organizations. The neighborhood at the time was centered around Queen Street West and McCaul Street and vestiges of it remain in some of the shops and services still found in the area.

In the 1940s, the current center of the Hungarian community at Bloor Street West and Spadina Avenue took shape, and the first overall community organization—the **Canadian Hungarian Society**—was formed. Many émigrés joined this emerging community in the years immediately following World War II, as numerous political refugees arrived in the wake of the communist political victories in Hungary.

Many of these refugees and those who followed in the fifties were from artistic, cultural, and intellectual groups that created an active and thriving Hungarian-language theater and literary scene in Toronto. A number of language schools were started, in addition to cultural, music, and folk dance groups. Toronto, as a result, is one of the world's biggest Hungarian-language publishing centers.

A number of prominent Hungarians have gone on to further fame in Toronto, including author George Jonas; television producer Andras Hamori; and doctors Janos and Paul Rekai, who founded Toronto's Central Hospital for patients who speak little or no English. **Budapest Park,** at Wells Hill Park in Sunnyside, is a site with sculpture by Victor Tolgesy commemorating the struggle for freedom in Hungary.

Scandinavians

Scandinavians were among the first European people to come to Canada. Small, isolated settlements were established in Newfoundland near the end of the first millennium AD, and Icelandic peoples have fished the seas off the eastern coasts of Canada since their early days in Iceland as well. Since the active period of European settlement; immigrants from Norway, Sweden, Finland, Denmark, and Iceland have all settled in the Toronto area.

Early Danish sailors were among the first Canadian traders and explorers. Jens Munk was one of a number of Danish explorers to search for a Northwest Passage, and he sailed in the Hudson Bay area. The mouth of the Churchill River is called Munk's Bay in his honor. The first Danish settlement in Canada was New Denmark, established in New Brunswick in 1872. A second was established near London, Ontario, in 1893 by John Ginge, who built a large pork-packing plant that attracted many Danish butchers and sausage makers to the province.

The Danes continued to live in the rural areas of Ontario until general migration to the cities began in the 1950s. In Toronto, churches and community groups began to establish themselves as well, although the earliest groups date back to 1925 when Toronto acted as the metropolis for many nearby Danish households. Danish skilled workers and professionals were actively recruited by the Canadian and Toronto-area governments for the many skilled job opportunities that opened up at the time. Today over 20,000 Danes live in the Metropolitan area, constituting the largest of the Scandinavian communities.

One of the best-known Toronto Danes was Erik Bruhn, a former principal dancer, choreographer, and artistic director of the National Ballet of Canada. A park in Mississauga is named for Richard F. C. Mortsensen, a Danish community worker and member of the Committee of Adjustment, honoring his long years of service to the people of the area.

The smallest of Toronto's Scandinavian communities are those of Icelandic Canadians. Most of these immigrants have come from other parts of Canada and most are second-, third-, and even fourth-generation families. Icelanders were among the settlers who joined Eric the Red's colonies in Newfoundland and Greenland. The first Icelander to settle in modern Canada was Sigtryggur Jonasson, who arrived in 1872.

Settlement in Toronto began when Icelandic settlers who were taking the trains to the Western prairies had to stop and stay temporarily in Toronto's immigration sheds. During the process, many families decided to stay in the city rather than proceed farther westward. Other settlers began arriving in the Muskoka Lakes district, just north of Toronto around Lake Rousseau. Their settlement was called Hekkla, after a volcano in Iceland. Immigrants from this area also began to trickle into Toronto.

There are now around 2,000 Icelanders living in the Toronto area. Among the best known were patron of the arts and wife of John Eaton, Signy Stephenson Eaton; Magnus Peterson, a real estate developer who started the development of the Brampton/Bramalea area; and well-known rock singer Tom Cochrane.

The Norwegian community is also a relatively small, but important, Scandinavian community, with over 3,500 members in the city. Norwegians settled western Canada in the 1880s along with many other Scandinavian people. Most who settled in Toronto were originally from this area. They were later joined by some of the over-3,000 men of the Norwegian Air Force, who trained with the Royal Canadian Air Force in World War II. Training took place at Little Norway, an air force base on the mainland just opposite Toronto Island Airport, and the first foreign air training camp set up on Canadian soil. Little Norway Park, at the foot of Bathurst Street and the lakefront, is a memorial to these fliers. David Peterson, former premier of the province of Ontario and chairman of Chapters Books and the Toronto Raptors Basketball club, is probably the best-known member of this community.

Toronto's thriving 8,000-strong Swedish community is only one reflection of the city's strong ties with Sweden. It is also home to more Swedish and Swedish-affiliated companies than other city in North America. Swedes first settled in the area in the 1870s, attracted by the opportunities for purchasing land and farming. Sweden at the time was just beginning to come out of a long decline and was far from being the modern, prosperous country of today.

After World War II many Swedish businessmen and engineers were attracted to the Toronto area, sensing the economic opportunities awaiting the post-war era in North America. They were joined by Swedish Canadians who were emigrating from other parts of Canada as well as Swedish immigrants from the United States. A memorial road dedicated to the memory of Swedish war hero Raoul Wallenberg, who helped thousands of Jews escape Nazi Germany in World War II, can be found in Earl Bales Park.

Toronto's 10,000 Finns have an active array of social and cultural institutions working to keep the Finnish language and traditions alive. Finns have been emigrating to Toronto for over 100 years, since Finnish tailor Jaako Lintala first arrived here in 1887 and encouraged other tailors from his homeland to join him. His shop was at one time the largest employer of Finns in Toronto and included a public sauna.

Many Finns came in the early 1900s searching for new opportunities in North America. In Canada many worked in the northern mines and on large engineering projects like the Welland Canal. They were joined by many professionals and scholars who arrived in the 1950s and 1960s and by internal second- and third-generation Finnish immigrants from major Canadian centers like Thunder Bay. Among the best-known Torontonians of Finnish background are designer Peter Nygaard and Andrea Hansen, second violinist with the Toronto Symphony.

Religion

The majority of Dutch people in Canada are Protestants, belonging to a variety of different congregations, including:

Canadian Reformed Church, *148 Thornridge Drive (416-889-5143).*

Christian Reformed Church, *1088 Bathurst Street (416-535-6262).*

First Christian Reform Church of Toronto, *67 Taunton Road (416-481-4912).*

Free Christian Reform Church—Elijah Church, *1130 Finch Avenue West (416-661-0216).*

Grace Christian Reform Church of Scarborough, *25 Channel Nine Court (416-293-0373).*

Reformed Church in America, *174 Maple Leaf Drive (416-244-1598).*

Rehoboth Fellowship Christian Reform Church, *800 Burnamthorpe Road (416-622-9647).*

Second Christian Reform Church of Toronto, *265 Albion Road (416-747-0110).*

Willowdale Christian Reform Church, *70 Hilda Street (416-221-7829).*

Most Belgians are Catholics and belong to one of many of the Roman Catholic churches in the city. Several bishops in the Canadian Catholic church are of Belgian descent.

The Swiss do not have any particular parishes or churches representing a national affiliation but belong to a variety of Catholic and Protestant churches in the Toronto area.

Canadian Czechs belong primarily to two churches:

The **Roman Catholic Church of Saint Wenceslaus,**
496 Gladstone Avenue (416-532-5272).

The main church of Czech Catholics and the oldest Czech church in the city. It also supports a variety of community and cultural groups.

The **Czechoslovak Baptist Church,** *200 Annette Street (416-767-2027).*

The main Protestant church in the Czech community. Czechs on an individual level belong to a variety of other churches.

Slovaks belong to a number of parishes:

The **Cathedral of the Transfiguration,** *Woodbine Avenue at Major MacKenzie Road (905-887-5706).*

Now the main church of the Slovak community. This beautiful new cathedral is a Slovak church of the Byzantine Rite.

Saints Cyril and Methodius Church, *115 Robinson Avenue (416-363-2532).*

The main Catholic church for Slovaks in Toronto. Built in 1941, it also houses a number of Slovak cultural and community groups.

Nativity of the Blessed Virgin Mary Cathedral, *257 Shaw Street (416-531-4836).*

Home to another large Catholic congregation.

Saint Paul Slovak Evangelical Lutheran Church,
1424 Davenport Road (416-656-5259).

The main Lutheran church for the Slovak community.

The majority of Hungarians are Catholic, but there is a broad range of other Protestant churches that provides services for the community as well:

Saint Elizabeth of Hungary Roman Catholic Church, *432 Sheppard Avenue East (416-225-3300).*

The oldest church in the area. Established in 1928, it moved to its present location in 1985 and played an important role as a community center and as a home for many Hungarian social and cultural groups. In 1978 it established a Hungarian Jesuit Noviciate, the only one of its kind outside of Hungary in the world.

First Hungarian Baptist Church, *157 Falkirk Avenue (416-783-2941).*

First Hungarian Presbyterian Church, *439 Vaughan Road (416-656-1342).*

Hungarian Full Gospel Church, *51 Scarlett Road (416-766-0079).*

Hungarian Lutheran Church, *116 Bond Street (416-977-4786).*

Hungarian Reform Evangelical Christian Church, *8 Robert Street (416-923-9416).*

Hungarian United Church, *73 Mackay Street (416-652-3809).*

The Lutheran church has the largest influence among Scandinavians, and a number of national Lutheran churches support different Scandinavian congregations:

Danish Lutheran Church, *72 Finch Avenue (416-222-2494).*

This lovely unassuming church includes a beautiful Danish pipe organ, a library, and a Danish-language school.

Finnish Lutheran Agricola Church, *25 Old York Mills Road (416-489-7600).*

Other than a similar church in Stockholm, this is the second largest Finnish church in the world outside of Finland. Near it is a granite monument to the Finnish soldiers who perished in the two world wars defending Finland's borders.

Toronto Laestadian Congregation, *1330 Bathurst Street (416-883-9445).*

Saint Ansgar Lutheran Church, *Lawrence Avenue West and Avenue Road (416-783-3570).*

Swedish Lutheran Church of Toronto, *72 Finch Avenue (416-222-2494).*

Finnish Pentecostal Church, *2570 Bayview Avenue (416-222-2291)* and **Finnish United Church,** *65 Sheldrake Avenue (416-488-8425).*

Two Scandinavian Protestant congregations separate from the Lutheran church.

══════ Organizations ══════

The main social and cultural organization for the Belgian community is the **Belgian-Canadian Association,** 121 Chillery Avenue (416-261-4603). Activities include an annual carnival dance, an archery club which has won several national competitions, a folk dance group, and other Belgian cultural events which often take place at the Harbourfront complex.

Belgian businesspeople meet at the **Belgian Canadian Business Association,** 1 Eva Street (416-621-9601). There is also a **Consulate General of Belgium,** 8 King Street East (416-364-5283), in Toronto.

Classes in the Dutch language are available at:

Dutch Classes, *265 Scarborough Crescent (416-266-6420).*

Canadian Association for the Advancement for Netherlands Studies, *50 Quebec Avenue (416-922-2475).*

The main community group for Dutch Canadians in Toronto is the

Dutch Canadian Association of Greater Toronto, *207 Newton Drive (416-229-1753).*

This is the umbrella organization for many other cultural and social groups, which include:

Dutch International Social Club, *10 Campbell Crescent (416-489-4487).*

Dutch-Canadian Senior Citizens Organization, *23 Stuart Crescent (416-221-8523).*

DUCA Community Credit Union, *PO Box 1100, 5290 Yonge Street (416-223-8502).*

This credit union, one of Canada's oldest, sponsors a variety of community and social programs.

DUCA Choir, *74 Sabrina Drive (416-244-9867).*

DUCA Social Dance Club, *113 Elnathan Crescent (416-749-2457).*

Gezelligheid Kent Green TIJD, *28 Mayo Drive (416-247-4784).*

Klaverjasclub "Zonder Naam," *83 Bob O'Link Avenue (416-669-4625).*

Ladies Contact Club Welkom, *110 Galley Avenue (416-535-9450).*

Netherlands Luncheon Club, *3 Danville Drive (416-223-0827).*

A businessmen's luncheon club.

Netherlands Bazaar, *15 Pavilion Street (905-477-4321).*

Puts on charitable events.

Netherlands Folklore Group, *8 Jocelyn Avenue (416-444-0821).*

Supports Dutch dance, music, and performing arts groups.

Toronto-Amsterdam Twin Cities Association, *Toronto City Hall (416-489-2897).*

An active cultural exchange program is enjoyed by the two cities.

Canadian Netherland Business and Professional Association, *90 Eglinton Avenue East, Suite 603 (416-482-5818).*

Netherlands Centre Charitable Foundation,
1 Dundas Street West, Suite 2106 (416-598-2590).

The **Swiss Club of Toronto,** PO Box 823, Station Q (416-979-3216), is an umbrella organization for most Swiss groups in Toronto. It has over 1,000 members and includes clubs such as the **Swiss Men's Group** (416-451-4353); the **Swiss Women's Section** (416-449-6818); the **Gymnastics Club** (416-425-5647); the **Yodel Choir** (416-249-2076), and the **Swiss Rifle Club** (416-480-1483).

The Czech community supports a number of excellent social and cultural organizations designed to promote the Czech language and culture. The main organization, sometimes known as **Masaryktown,** is maintained and run by the **Masaryk Memorial Institute,** 450 Scarborough Golf Club Road (416-439-4354). A wide range of cultural activities including dance and music groups, lectures, and language classes are available here.

Other community groups include:

Moravanka Czechoslovak Dancers, *2532 Evelyn Court (416-279-0209).*

A folk dance troupe.

Royal Canadian Legion Branch 601
(Czechoslovak), *41 Lakeshore Drive, #706 (416-259-2643).*

A veterans' association for Czechs who fought with the Canadian military forces in World War II.

Sokol Gymnastics Association of Toronto, *PO Box 1187, Station A (416-762-6846).*

Credited with developing Canadian consciousness regarding gymnastics sports. The association sponsors a major festival and contest in Masaryktown each year.

Women's Council of the Czechoslovak Association
of Canada, *22 Reid Manor (416-239-2456).*

Czech Association of Canada (CAC), *740 Spadina Avenue (416-925-4221).*

A political and cultural organization fighting for Czech concerns in Canada.

Czech Society of Arts and Sciences, *740 Spadina Avenue (416-925-4221).*

A subgroup of the CAC, focusing on support for Czech Canadians working in the arts and sciences.

Slovak community groups include:

Slovak Canadian Professional and Business Association, *PO Box 40, Royal Bak Plaza (416-865-1991).*

Slovak Lutheran League, *1424 Davenport Road (416-656-5259).*

Canadian Slovaks have been heavily involved in current affairs such as the setting up of the Slovak Republic. Among the organizations offering support have been the **Slovak Canadian National Council,** 50 McIntosh Drive (905-513-1215); the **Canadian Slovak League,** 1736 Dundas Street West (416-533-6924); and the **Slovak World Congress,** PO Box 40, Royal Bank Plaza (416-865-1991), which used to be headquartered in Toronto. Most of these organizations were heavily endowed by entrepreneur Stephan Roman when he was alive.

Classes in the Hungarian language can be taken at:

Arany Janos Hungarian Weekend School, *840 Saint Clair Avenue West (416-654-4926).*

Hungarian Credit School, *Central High School of Commerce, 570 Shaw Street (416-393-0030).*

The **Canadian-Hungarian Cultural Centre,** 840 Saint Clair Avenue West (416-654-4926), is the main focus for community activities. It houses a Hungarian military history museum, shows weekly movies in Hungarian, and holds the Dr. Halasz Janos library of over 25,000 Hungarian-language books. There is an auditorium, a dance hall, a restaurant, and an art gallery as well. Some of the community groups under its auspices include the **Kodaly Choir and Dance Group,** the **Hungarian Helicon Society,** and the **Korosi Csoma Sandor Historical Society.**

The **Magyar Hungarian Theatre,** 392 Saint Germain Avenue, has long been one of the most active non-English theater companies in the city. It produces plays in Hungarian on a variety of classic and contemporary themes.

The **Hungarian Freedom Fighters,** 840 Saint Clair Avenue West (416-654-4926), is an active group fighting for the extension and continuation of democratic reform in Hungary.

Many organizations and societies have been created to support the cultural and social needs of the various Scandinavian communities. The best known include:

Danish Women's Association, *4 Glenfern Avenue (416-699-1470).*

Royal Danish Guards Association, *11 Redland Crescent (416-266-6979).*

Dansk Samvirke/Association for Danes Abroad, *54 Lesgay Crescent (416-493-1594).*

The main political and community association for advancing the interests of Danish Canadians.

Toronto Finnish Language School, *York Mills Collegiate (416-881-1429).*

Active in preserving and teaching the Finnish language.

Finnish Canadian Cultural Federation, *191 Eglinton Avenue East (416-425-4134).*

The main umbrella group for a number of Finnish cultural and community groups. It also acts as the main lobbying group for the Finnish community in Canada.

The **Finnish Cultural Centre,** *276 A Main Street (416-421-9614).*

Another active location for Finnish community activities. Also operating out of this location are the **Sisu Athletic Club** (416-286-2228), the **Toronto Finnish Male Choir** (416-284-4844), and the **Toronto Karelian Club** (416-497-9652).

Finnish Canadian Arts Society, *118 Lord Simcoe Drive (905-451-4891).*

Finnish Social Club, *126 Manville Avenue (416-752-4177).*

Toronto Suomi Finlandia Club, *11 Babcock Road (416-755-5995).*

Icelandic Canadian Club, *North York Memorial Hall (416-978-6212).*
The main community organization for Icelandic Torontonians.

Downsview-Norway Royal Canadian Air Force Association, *91 Stormount Avenue (416-782-4604).*
A social club made up of many Norwegian veterans who fought in the Royal Canadian Air Force in World War II.

Scandinavian Business Association, *54 Lesgay Crescent (416-495-8591).*

Scandinavian-Canadian Club of Toronto, *91 Stormount Avenue (416-782-4604).*

Scandinavian Canadian Business Association, *1075 Bay Street (416-324-8597).*

SWEA Toronto, *1075 Bay Street (416-324-8597).*

═══ Holidays and Celebrations ═══

February 28	*Kalevala Day,* marking the reading of epic Finnish poems from Finn mythology.
March	*Thorrablot,* an Icelandic celebration of spring's coming with a smorgasbord meal, including a variety of traditional foods.
March 7	Celebration of the birthday of Thomas Masaryk, founding president of the Czechoslovak Republic in 1918.
March 15	Commemorates the anniversary of the 1848 revolution led by Louis Kossuth. For a short time an

independent Hungary broke away from the rule of the Austrian Hapsburgs and ended feudalism in the country. Ironically, given Hungary's future under communist Russia, czarist Russia was called in by Austria to reconquer Hungary and end this brief revolution.

April	*Arpad Day,* honoring the Hungarian national hero.
	Queen Beatrix's Birthday Ball (Dutch holiday).
	Czech Memorial Day, on the third weekend of the month
April 9	*Memorial Day,* marking the day of the German invasion into Norway in World War II.
April 16	The Queen of Denmark's birthday.
April 18	Memorial for Monsignor Joseph Tiso, first president of the Slovak Republic.
April 30	*Walpurgish,* a Swedish festival marking the arrival of spring.
May	*Heroes Day,* honoring the martyrs of the 1848 and 1956 revolutions, on the last Sunday of the month.
May 1	*Vappu-Carnival Day,* the Finnish version of Walpurgish.
May 4	Commemoration of General Milan Stefanik, one of the founders of the Independent Czech Republic.
May 5	*Liberation Day,* commemorating the end of the Second World War.
May 17	*Norwegian Constitution Day.*
June	*Icelandic Day* celebrations.
June 5	*Danish Constitutional Day,* commemorating the establishment of a democratic constitution in 1849.
June 6	*Official National Day of Sweden.*

June 21	*Slovak Awareness Day.*
June 24	*Saint Hans (Johannes) Day,* honoring John the Baptist and the summer solstice. Celebrated by all Scandinavians.
July	*Slovak Day,* on the second Sunday of the month.
July 21	*Belgian Independence Day,* marking the day King Leopold I took the oath of allegiance for a new constitution.
August 1	*Swiss National Day,* celebrating Switzerland's independence as a confederation back to 1291.
August 20	*Saint Stephan's Day,* held in recognition of the medieval king of Hungary who brought Christianity to the country.
August 20/21	Remembrance of the 1968 Russian invasion of Czechoslovakia.
September 15	*Our Lady of Sorrows Day,* for Slovaks following the Byzantine Rite.
October 6	Honors thirteen Hungarian generals who took part in the revolution of 1848 and were subsequently executed by the Austrians after their rebellion was put down by the Russians in 1849.
October 23	Anniversary of the Hungarian Revolution of 1956.
October 28	*Czech Independence Day.*
November 11	*Mortensaften,* honoring the Bishop Saint Martin of Tours (Scandinavian holiday).
November 15	*Dynasty Day,* paying tribute to the Belgian monarchy. An annual dinner and dance is held for members of the Belgian Canadian Association.
December 5	*Saint Nicholas or Sinterklaas Day.* An annual Saint Nicholas Day children's party is organized by the Dutch Canadian Association in Toronto, and there is a black-tie dinner on the Saturday closest to December 5th where Sinterklaas and Black Peter are the guests of honor.

December 6	*Finnish Independence Day.*
December 13	Winter solstice celebrations, also the celebration of Saint Lucia. Celebrated by Norwegians and Swedes.
December 24	*Christmas Eve.* A traditional twelve-course meatless dinner is served.

═══ Restaurants, Cafés, and Nightclubs ═══

Dutch cuisine has been heavily influenced by Holland's role as a crossroads of trade as well as the colonial ruler of Indonesia. Indonesian specialties are served at most Dutch restaurants, as are more specifically Dutch specialties, like marinated herring or a mixed lunch of meat, eggs, and cheese. Amstel, Heineken, and Orangeboom beers are available in Toronto restaurants, and the excellent Dutch brewing traditions are captured in a couple of brew pubs in the city.

Belgian cuisine includes some of the best French cooking traditions, as well as specialties such as a wide array of mussels dishes.

Swiss chefs are among Europe's best, and Swiss cooking has long been renowned for its subtlety and delectability. Swiss cuisine is an amalgam of the cultures that make up Switzerland, drawing heavily from French, German, and Italian cuisines. Fondue is probably the best-known uniquely Swiss meal, although I think they should be better known for their rosti potatoes (shredded potatoes fried and crisped in a pan and served like a crunchy potato pancake).

Czech and Slovak food is an interesting crossroads cuisine of flavors from Eastern Europe and Germany. Main German favorites like schnitzel and spaetzel are subtly altered into spicy, paprika-flavored variations often served with rich, creamy sauces. Other Polish and Hungarian dishes such as palacinka and paprikash make their way onto Czech menus, as do excellent Pilsener beer (originally named for the town in Czechoslovakia that first brewed it) and fiery Czech liqueurs.

Hungarian food is hearty, borrowing from German, Polish, and other Eastern European cuisines as well as having some unique attributes of its own. The country's position on the edge of the Balkans has caused it to blend certain Balkan spices with Central European flavors to produce stews like the goulash for which it is most noted. Other specialties include *tokany* (a paprika-seasoned pork and beef dish), *nokedi* (noodle dumplings), and *kobasa lecos* (a stew with garlic sausages, onions, green peppers, tomato, and paprika). Toronto has a number of good Hungarian restaurants, particularly in the "Schnitzel Strip" of Bloor Street West between Spadina Avenue and Bathurst Street.

A number of restaurants in Toronto serve Scandinavian specialties, from the Swedish smorgasbord to the small open-faced sandwiches of Denmark.

Amber European Restaurant, *2372 Bloor Street West (416-763-6164).*

This pleasantly decorated, country-style restaurant serves a variety of Polish and Baltic foods, including specialties like *nalesniki* (Polish crepes) and *kotlety* (meatballs). Service is friendly; prices are modest.

Bali Restaurant, *1554 Avenue Road (416-782-5928).*

Specializing in Indonesian dishes such as *rijsttafel* (rice table) and *bahmi goreng* (spicy Indonesian noodles). Long established in the Toronto area.

Bistro 422, *422 College Street (416-963-9416).*

Features Finnish specialties like Reindeer Lapland served in beer sauce with vegetables, thick Finnish pea soup with pork, and meatballs with lingonberries. The Finnish liqueur lakka, made from cloudberries, is also available in this pleasant, moderately priced restaurant.

Bistro Bernard, *6 Saint Joseph Street (416-926-1900).*

An excellent Swiss restaurant with a French flair. Specialties of the house include Swiss barley soup, grilled veal steak, and rack of lamb served with rosti potatoes. *Buenderfleish* (Alpine air-dried beef) is a popular Swiss appetizer, and beautiful Swiss-influenced desserts top off the meal.

Black Peter Buffet, *221 Dufferin Street (416-534-5846).*

An inexpensive buffet restaurant serving Czech specialties.

Budapest Diner, *778 Saint Clair Avenue West (416-653-0207).*

Housed in a quaint cottage of a building complete with cedar paneling, frilly lace curtains, wall plates, and handicrafts from Hungary. The restaurant features schnitzels, goulash, and the enormous Hungarian Wooden Plate, which is a mixed grill designed to feed an army. Entertainment is provided by a musical duo from Budapest.

Café Brussel, *786 Broadview Avenue (416-465-7363).*

A pleasant, unpretentious café near Toronto's Danforth area that serves a variety of Belgian café foods, light snacks, and superb Belgian pastries, including *frangipan* (almond tarts), mousse soufflés, eclairs, truffles, waffles, streusel, and apple almond cake. A variety of excellent Belgian beers are also available.

Chris' Diner, *709 The Queensway (416-251-1466).*

Coffee Mill, *99 Yorkville Avenue (416-920-2108); 110 Bloor Street West (416-944 1771).*

Two cafés with a distinctly Hungarian flavor, offering a variety of daily specials from Hungarian cuisine.

Copenhagen Room Restaurant, *101 Bloor Street West (416-920-3287).*

Serves a full array of Danish specialties, including blue cheese soup, over sixty different open-faced sandwiches, and entrées such as crisp duck with sweet red cabbage, *hakkebof* (spiced chopped beef steak), and *frikadeller* (Danish meatballs). Very classy setting with great service.

Copper Pot Restaurant, *1648 ½ Queen Street West (416-532-2602).*

A well-known restaurant for Czech and Slovak dishes. Roast pork, sauerbraten, pot roast, and palaczinkas are the highlights here.

Country Style, *450 Bloor Street West (416-537-1745).*

One of the best bargains in town, this restaurant still produces the best and least expensive schnitzels in the city, as well as the best strudels. Portions are generous, prices inexpensive, and service fast. Particularly recommended is the Parisian schnitzel, apple strudel, and fresh-made palaczinkas, though the full gamut of Hungarian cuisine is available.

Csarda, *43 Elm Street (416-971-8843).*

A charming Hungarian cottage-style restaurant with a sumptuous Wooden Plate for two, as well as excellent *chicken paprikash* (chicken slowly simmered in a paprika and sour cream-based stew) and stuffed cabbage. A gypsy trio entertains throughout the week.

DANWICH Shop, *4204 Dundas Street West (416-231-5951).*

Specializes in a wide array of Scandinavian open-faced sandwiches with dozens to choose from, such as beef tartare and gravlax sandwiches.

Dutch Freites Good Food, *111 Cherry Post Road (416-979-5739).*

A new restaurant serving Dutch and Canadian specialties at reasonable prices.

Dutch Kitchen, *71 Lakeshore Road East (416-278-2296);* also **Klogs Pub** at the same location.

Serves a variety of Dutch beers, coffees, and liqueurs. Probably the best-known Dutch restaurant in the area, it serves Indonesian specialties as well as Dutch specialties such as Hollandia Schnitzel with gouda cheese, *croquets* (a deep-fried cheese specialty), Dutch sausages, and a variety of Dutch liqueurs and beers.

First Step Restaurant, *2977F Lakeshore Boulevard West (416-252-2771).*

Garuda Restaurant, *373 Eglinton Avenue West (416-487-6426).*

An Indonesian restaurant with some additional Dutch specialties.

Gypsy Hungarian Restaurant, *105 McCaul Street (416-598-1650).*

Good food, fast service, and a comfortable modern environment. Excellent Wooden Plate, cabbage rolls, and paprikashes.

Hungaria Bar and Diner, *4923 Dundas Street West (416-239-9468).*

A West Toronto location complete with musical entertainment, a bar stocking a full array of fiery Hungarian liqueurs, and a restaurant serving specialties such as kobassa lecos and chicken soup with liver dumplings.

Hungarian Dining Room, *2448 ½ Kingston Road (416-261-2415).*

Hungarian Goulash Party Restaurant and Tavern,
498 Queen Street West (416-863-6124).

Hungarian Hut, *127 Yonge Street (416-864-9275).*

Hungarian Pot, *2729 Weston Road (416-749-4209).*

Hungarian Rhapsody Restaurant, *1252 Bay Street (416-960-3900).*

IKEA, *15 Provost Drive (416-226-1900).*

This big Swedish chain has a café along with the many other Scandinavian gifts, interior design accessories, carpets, and textiles stocked here. The café includes a wide variety of Scandinavian foods.

Jantar Restaurant, *403 Roncesvalles Avenue (416-537-5733).*

Krak Restaurant, *153 Roncesvalles Avenue (416-536-6119).*

Movenpick Restaurants of Toronto, *129 Yorkville Avenue (416-926-9545); 165 York Street (416-366-5234); 270 Front Street West (416-979-0060).*

Locally well known for its clean restaurants, excellent cuisine, and diverse menus, the Movenpick chain constantly ranks in the top ten of Toronto's favorite restaurants. Particularly recommended is the new **Palavrion** on Front Street West, which takes the old-fashioned cafeteria/buffet restaurant and stands it on its ear in a modern lively display of Swiss ingenuity. It requires a little getting used to at first but is a thoroughly enjoyable experience in the end.

Pepo's Bistro, *676 Queen Street West (416-860-0514).*

One of the best-known Czech restaurants in the city, it is celebrated for its Czech-flavored schnitzel dishes, as well as specialties such as tripe and stuffed peppers.

Prague Restaurant, *450 Scarborough Golf Club Road (416-439-2053).*

Part of the Masaryktown complex, this restaurant's cooking has to be good to appeal to the demanding tastes of its Czech clientele. Open Wednesday through Sunday with some entertainment on weekends, the menu covers the gamut of Czech specialties from sausages to schnitzels.

Raclette Restaurant, *361 Queen Street West (416-593-0934).*

Toronto's best-known fondue restaurant, the Raclette serves a full array of Swiss fondues, including wonderful chocolate fondue for dessert.

Rotterdam Brewing Company, *600 King Street West (416-868-6882).*

An excellent brew pub with a continental menu but superb locally brewed beers in the Dutch tradition. A popular place with outdoor tables for summertime dining or socializing.

Sveik's Dining Lounge, *40 Orchard View Boulevard (416-489-3215).*

Another popular spot with the Czech community, Sveik's is named after the Good Soldier Sveik, Jaroslav Hasek's antihero in the novel of the same name. Good schnitzel, sausage, and palaczinkas.

Swisse Marmite Restaurant, *136 Lakeshore Road East (905-274-8860).*

A heavily German-influenced Swiss restaurant serving jaeger schnitzel and wiener schnitzel as well as sausages, smoked pork chops, and rosti potatoes.

Valhalla Inn, *Highway 427 and Burnamthorpe Road (416-239-2391).*

This hotel restaurant serves a wide range of Nordic and Germanic foods, including extensive smorgasbords and other specialties.

Food Sources

The Dutch and the Belgians make some of the best pastries in the world, including lovely meringue cookies and tarts, puff pastry, Yule logs, and other chocolate, almond, and nut-cream specialties. The best of these bakers in Toronto are:

Dutch Treats, *500 Rexdale Boulevard (416-674-5543).*

Petit Paris Cake and Coffee Shop, *2384 Bloor Street West (416-769-9881); 2390 Haines (905-566-4401).*

Rood's Pastry Shop, *10 Headdon Gate (905-883-5813).*

Belgian Chocolate Shop, *2455 Queen Street East (416-691-1424); 2487 Yonge Street (416-322-6213).*
Specializes in fine Belgian chocolates.

Two of the butchers who specialize in Dutch food products are:

De Wit Quality Meats, *1224 Dundas Street West (905-896-4222).*
An excellent butcher for sausages and specialty meats, as well as Dutch specialties like salt herring.

Simon De Groot Meat Products, *481 Church Street (416-967-7429).*
When first built this landmark butcher shop was surrounded by Toronto's Dutch community. The community has left, but the market still contains a variety of exotic Dutch mustards and condiments as well as Indonesian spices and excellent cuts of meat.

The Swiss are world renowned for their superb-quality chocolates and pastries. Two Toronto stores that carry on this fine tradition include:

Swiss-Master Chocolatier, *2538 Bayview Avenue (416-444-8802).*
Locally made chocolates in the Swiss tradition.

Teuschers, *55 Avenue Road, Hazelton Lanes (416-961-1303).*
Brings in fresh chocolates from Switzerland daily.

Czech sausages and deli products are among some of the best in Central and Eastern Europe. The main center in Toronto for these products is **Prague Meat Products,** 638 Queen Street West (416-504-5787), which has an excellent array of specialty foods made on the premises or imported to Canada.

A couple of good spots to go for Hungarian meats, sausages, and imported specialties are **Elizabeth's Delicatessen and Meat Market,** 410 Bloor Street West (416-921-8644), and **Hungarian Honey Bear Delicatessen,** 249 Sheppard Avenue West (416-733-0022).

The people who gave us the Danish pastry have a number of good bakery cafés located throughout the city, many serving sandwiches and other food in addition to the ubiquitous fruit- and cheese-filled pastries. Among the stores selling Scandinavian foods and baked goods are:

Danish Food Centre, *101 Bloor Street West (416-920-3287).*

Features an extensive café menu, as well as baked goods and take-out gourmet products.

Danish Style Bakeshop and Cafe, *1027 Kingston Road (416-694-5333).*

Carries a wide array of Danish baked goods, café sandwiches, and imported foods.

Danish Pastry Shop, *1017 Pape Avenue (416-425-8877).*

Finnish Bakery, *133 Manville (416-751-0066).*

Finnish baked goods and breads.

Hillside Bakery and Delicatessen, *2851 Lawrence Avenue East (416-261-2238).*

Pasquale Brothers, *217 King Street East (416-364-7397).*

Brings in hard-to-find Norwegian cheeses.

Rooneem's Bakery, *484 Queen Street West (416-504-5205).*

Includes a number of Swedish baked goods among its extensive offerings.

Scandinavian Select Meat Products, *5229 Yonge Street (416-222-3181).*

Scandinavian Shop, *364 Danforth Avenue (416-469-3886).*

Shops

A few shops carry Dutch specialties, including the **Holland Store,** 2524 Weston Road (416-247-8659), which carries a number of Dutch imports and specialties such as fine china and glassware. **Speelman Book House,** 5010 Steeles Avenue West (416-741-6563), is a long-established bookseller specializing in Dutch-language books.

Dutch porcelain dolls are available for collectors from **Carriage Trade Dolls,** 584 Mount Pleasant Road (416-481-1639), and the **Little Dollhouse,** 617 Mount Pleasant Road (416-489-7180), which are near each other. Other stores selling these dolls include **Sandy's Dolls and Gifts,** 172 Bullock Drive (905-294-3655), and **Dolly Madison Doll Co.,** 220 Highway 7 (905-294-1247).

A number of shops carry Swiss health and beauty products, as well as watches, clocks, and other Swiss-made products:

Swissmar Industries, *35 East Beaver Creek Road (905-764-1121).*

Imports a variety of Swiss precision instruments, fashions, and health and beauty aids.

Swiss Herbal Remedies, *181 Don Park (905-475-6345).*

Sells a number of Swiss herbal teas and herbal remedies.

Swiss Health and Beauty Aids, *1975 Yonge Street (416-489-9626).*

Sells a variety of specialty Swiss skin creams, perfumes, and other beauty products.

Swiss Time, *40 Dundas Street West (416-595-9709),*
and **Swiss Watchmakers,** *512 Yonge Street (416-922-2622).*

Sell a wide array of Swiss watches and other precision instruments.

Lincraft, 506 Yonge Street (416-925-5895), specializes in hand-cut lead crystal from the Czech Republic, a highly prized specialty of that area.

The **Hungarian Book Store,** 344 Bloor Street West (416-966-5156), houses an extensive Hungarian-language bookstore, as well as the largest Hungarian-language publishing house outside of Hungary.

Scandinavian products are known for their craftsmanship and beautiful design. A number of stores carry a variety of Scandinavian products in the Toronto area, including:

Finnish Place, *5463 Yonge Street (416-222-7575).*

Finnish art objects, designer furnishings, and interior accessories.

Georg Jensen, *153 Brookdale (416-486-4070).*

Beautiful Danish silverware and collectible porcelains.

Icelandia, *162 Cumberland Avenue (416-927-9317).*

Icelandic sculptures, art objects, and gifts.

IKEA, *15 Provost Drive (416-226-1900).*

A big Swedish chain with a huge furniture store, a café, and many other Scandinavian gifts, interior design accessories, carpets, and textiles.

Jose Plaza Imports, *271 Park Home (416-223-1456).*

Imports an extensive array of Scandinavian gifts and crafts.

Klas Olsson Optical, *1407 Yonge Street (416-924-0900).*

A Swedish brand of eyewear.

Magnafaxi Farm, *RR1, Palgrave, Ontario (905-936-2228).*

Breeds and raises Iceland horses, noted for their ease of handling and stamina.

Scandia Interiors, *1911 Kennedy (416-291-7990).*

Scandinavian furniture.

This and That Baby Shop, *1089 Victoria Park Avenue (416-755-1873).*

Imports Swedish-built Emmaljunga baby prams and strollers.

Viking Foods and Imports, *19 Industrial (416-696-7011).*

═══════════════ **Media** ═══════════════

Publications

De Nederander Courant (Dutch Canadian Weekly),
Box 2236, Station B, Scarborough (416-264-2672).

A biweekly newspaper published for the Dutch-Canadian community for over forty years.

K-231, *PO Box 2323, Station B (416-261-2365).*

A bimonthly magazine produced by former Czech political prisoners.

Kanadai Magyarsag/Canadian Hungarians, *412 Bloor Street West (416-924-2502).*

Kanaden Suomalaine, *6303 Yonge Street (416-229-4469).*

A Finnish weekly.

Kanadsky Slovak/Canadian Slovak, *1736 Dundas Street West (416-531-2055).*

The main weekly newspaper of the Slovak community in Canada. *The Bulletin,* also at the same address, is published monthly by the Slovak World Congress.

Kronika/Chronicle, *840 Saint Clair Avenue West (416-654-4926).*

Hungarian.

Magyar Elet/Hungarian Life, *6 Alcina Avenue (416-654-2551).*

Magyar Naplo/Hungarian Newspaper, *PO Box 771, Station A (416-921-6161).*

Modersmaalet, *Box 306 (905-825-2229).*

A biweekly tabloid in Danish.

Novy Domov (New Homeland), *450 Scarborough Golf Club Road (416-530-4222).*

A biweekly newspaper covering events in Canada and in the Czech homeland.

Our Voices, *2098 Dundas Street West (416-533-4242).*

A biweekly publication covering issues of concern to the Czech community.

Scandinavian Forum, *54 Lesgay Crescent (416-493-1594).*

A quarterly publication in English.

SWEA Bladet, *1075 Bay Street (416-324-8597).*

A Swedish weekly.

Swedish Canadian Chamber of Commerce Newsletter, *150 Bloor Street West (416-967-3770).*

Tell Tale, *PO Box 823, Station Q (416-842-2073).*

A monthly newsletter produced by the Swiss Club of Toronto on events of interest to the Swiss community.

Vapaa Sana/Finnish Weekly News*, 50 Weybright Court (416-321-0808).*

A Finnish weekly.

Vapaus, *215 Danforth Avenue (416-465-8981).*

A monthly Finnish publication.

Windmill Herald, *Box 1064, Station B, Rexdale (416-621-6139).*

A twice-monthly news magazine covering issues of interest to the Dutch-Canadian community.

Radio and Television

The **Canadian-Finnish Television and Radio Association,** *2 College Street (416-488-4754; 928-5994).*

Produces television programs in Finnish for cable television.

"Dutch Program," *CHIN-FM 100.7, 622 College Street (416-531-9991).*

A half-hour religious show followed by an hour-long Dutch-language radio magazine on Saturday morning from 8:30 to 10:00.

"Hungarian Cultural Centre Program," CHIN-AM 1540, *622 College Street (416-531-9991).*

The main Hungarian language music and current events show.

"Swiss Radio," CHIN-AM 1540/FM 100.7, *622 College Street (416-531-9991).*

A weekly news and variety program covering issues of interest to Toronto's Swiss community.

—Nearby Excursion: The Holland Marsh—

Approximately fifty miles (or eighty kilometers) north of Toronto is one of the richest farming areas in all the world. The Holland Marsh is reclaimed black-soil bottomland from the delta marshes where the Holland River estuary meets Lake Simcoe. Using techniques perfected in Holland, Dutch farmers reclaimed over 10,000 acres of this soil to support one of the most intensively farmed areas in all Canada. These 10,000 acres furnish nearly all of the local farm produce for the huge Toronto area market.

An interesting summer or early fall excursion, the area includes a number of excellent farm and garden markets as well as numerous greenhouses,

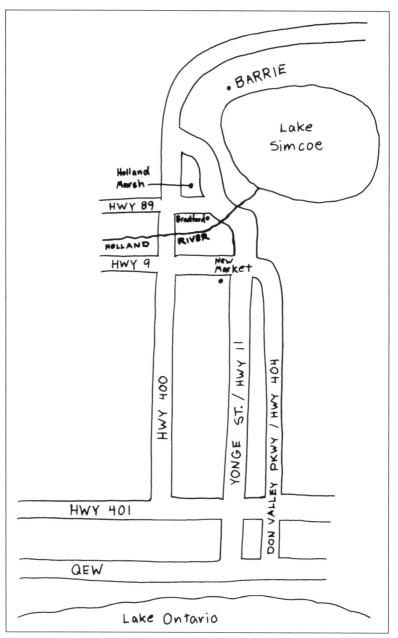

Holland Marsh

some of which sell a variety of exotic plants and produce. One farm sells over 300 different varieties of leafy green vegetables. Most of this area is near or surrounds the town of Bradford, Ontario.

How to Get There: *Take Highway 404/Don Valley Parkway north to its termination and then turn left. Follow the road to Highway 11 (Yonge Street); turn right and drive north to Bradford. You can also take Highway 400 to the Holland Marsh exit or exit east on Highway 89.*

—Little Poland: West Parkdale/Roncesvalles Village—

This lovely neighborhood on Toronto's West Side is a wonderful destination for those who wish to enjoy one of the city's many ethnic neighborhoods. Home to Toronto's Polish community, as well as many other eastern European and Germanic immigrants, the Roncesvalles area is filled with little grocers, produce sellers, bakeries, delis, restaurants, and cafés. Movie theaters showing foreign-language films abound here, with the sounds of passing streetcars going by twenty-four hours a day. The other thing that's great about this area is that it's a living neighborhood, not a tourist destination.

The houses are solid brick dwellings going back to the 1920s, and they get larger and more interesting as one walks west from Roncesvalles toward nearby High Park. Well-known cafés and restaurants, including Cafe Polonez, Cafe May, Granowskas Bakery and Cafe, and the Sir Nicholas Restaurant, are everywhere. The best way to experience the area is to take a walk on a beautiful, sunny summer day and undertake a moveable feast between the various shops on the street, starting at the top of the village where Howard Park Avenue intersects Roncesvalles and walking south to the lakeshore and the Katyn memorial. You will enjoy the feeling of urban central Europe in the sights, sounds, and tastes that abound.

How to Get There: *Take the Bloor/Danforth subway to the Dundas Street West station, then catch the King streetcar south to Howard Park Road. Walk south along Roncesvalles Avenue to the lakeshore.*

—Schnitzel Strip: Bloor Street West Annex—

The Schnitzel Strip, or Annex neighborhood, has long been a popular shopping and eating area. Close to the University of Toronto, the neighborhood abounds in student and faculty housing and was one of the areas of early Hungarian settlement in the city. While many of the original Hungarian residents have moved on, it remains, along with the Hungarian Cultural Centre on Saint Clair Avenue West, the main commercial focal point for the community.

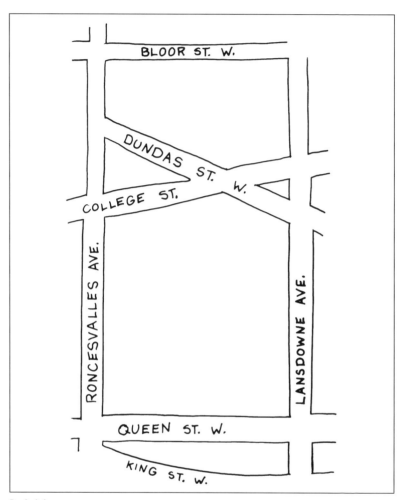

Parkdale

A host of restaurants, schnitzel houses, delicatessens, and other shops abound, catering not only to the Hungarian community but to many other Germanic and Eastern European cultures and a growing Hispanic presence. The area has long been supported by university students looking for bargains, so prices by and large have remained inexpensive for the casual visitor, and the high volume of traffic from area residents has ensured the continuity of most of the restaurants and shops. Particularly noteworthy for those interested in Hungarian culture is the Hungarian Bookstore/Pannoia Books outlet, which houses both the largest Hungarian-language bookstore

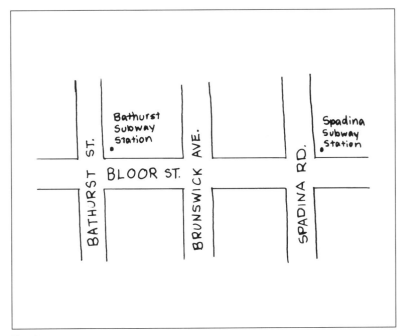

The Annex

and the largest publishing program outside of Hungary. In fact the publisher, Pannoia Books, is one of the biggest Hungarian-language book publishers in the world.

How to Get There: *Take the Bloor/Danforth subway to either the Bathurst or the Spadina station. The Bloor Street West Annex area runs from Spadina west to Bathurst, where it then meets up with the Koreatown area, taking you to Christie Street.*

Other Nationalities

Although not large, there are several other ethnic groups that have their place in Toronto's multicultural mix. This chapter discusses the Australian, Maltese, and Native Canadian contingents.

══ Australians and New Zealanders ══

Immigrants from Australia and New Zealand came to Canada after World War II to take advantage of the employment opportunities offered by Canada's newly developed industries. There are now over 30,000 people from these two countries residing in Canada, many of whom socialize at the **TRANZAC Club,** the gathering place for this community's clubs and social organizations.

Many Australians and New Zealanders originally arrived in Canada as a stop toward working their way around the world. The TRANZAC Club derived from a gathering of these travelers on April 25, 1948, to celebrate the landing of the Australian and New Zealand forces at the Battle of Gallipoli.

Cultural activities include organizing the community's presence at the annual Caravan celebrations, which include everything from sheep shearing to Maori dancing as well as a celebration of Australia's and New Zealand's fine beers and wines.

Many members of this community are part of Toronto's professional and academic communities, in particular the locally well-known author Eric Ross Arthur, an architectural historian who helped revive the interest of Torontonians in their own history and architectural heritage. Among his better-known restoration projects in the city was the restoration of Saint Lawrence Hall near the Saint Lawrence Market.

Other prominent members from this community include Jack Cahill, a local columnist for the *Toronto Star,* and Colin Vaughan, a former city councilor and now a broadcaster.

Religion and Organizations

There is no specific religious affiliation that attracts this community. Like most Canadian groups, it is an admixture of Anglicans, Catholics, United Church members, and other believers and nonbelievers. The most important cultural organization, however, is the aforementioned **TRANZAC Club,** 292 Brunswick Avenue (416-923-8137). The club is open every evening from 4:30 PM to 1:00 AM and has two licensed lounges. Set up to foster friendly relations between Canadians, Australians, and New Zealanders, the club also offers Australian/New Zealand foods like roast lamb and meat pies, and on Sunday afternoons features folk music from the region. Every Saturday an Australian- or New Zealand–produced film is also shown.

Other groups that help develop awareness of Australian and New Zealand culture are:

Maori dancers.

A group of thirty dancers of a variety of nationalities that perform native Maori dances and performances throughout the year, as well as at the annual Caravan celebrations.

NAGS.

A theater troupe and improvisational comedy company who have performed throughout the Toronto area for over fifteen years.

NOMAD Rugby Club.

Maintains an Australian team that plays in Toronto's rugby leagues.

ANZAC Club (Mississauga) *(905-567-3600).*

A suburban branch of the TRANZAC Club.

Holidays and Celebrations

January 26	*Australia Day,* marking the arrival of the first European settlers to Australia.
February 6	*Waitangi* or *New Zealand Day,* marking the signing of the Treaty of Waitangi guaranteeing peaceful cooperation between the native Maoris and the immigrating Europeans, as well as protection of Maori lands. The TRANZAC Club sponsors an annual celebration.
April 25	*Anzac Day,* in memory of those who and died at the Battle of Gallipoli.

Shops

Australian and New Zealand imports can be purchased from the following stores:

Australian and New Zealand Imports, *374 Brookdale (416-783-5780).*

Imports gifts, clothing, oilskin coats, food favorites like vegemite, records, and tapes, as well as wool clothing and outback hats, Maori and aboriginal shell necklaces, koala bear and kangaroo toys, and eucalyptus oil products.

Australian Boot Company, *791 Queen Street West (416-504-2411).*

Australian-produced work boots and shoes.

Outback, *Sherway Gardens (416-622-5256).*

Carries coats, jackets, and hats from New Zealand and Australia.

Media

Australian Monitor, *184 Swanwick (416-693-0300).*

A monthly publication covering events in Australia.

Tranzaction, *104–255 Glen Lake Avenue (416-766-3939).*

A monthly newspaper covering events of interest to the community.

Maltese

The small Mediterranean island of Malta has provided a small but steady stream of immigrants to the Toronto area over the years. The community now numbers over 9,000 and is one of the largest in North America. A small park in the West Toronto neighborhood called "the Junction" is named Malta Park in honor of these immigrants and the area they inhabit. Shops, clubs, and a community center remain in the area.

The community traces its history back to 1840 when settlers first arrived. Some were among the early shipbuilders and workers who were involved in the construction of the Welland Canal. At the turn of the century, Toronto had substantial Maltese communities in both the Junction and Dundas/McCaul areas. As citizens of a British territory, Maltese people found it relatively easy to emigrate to Canada and the influx continued throughout the early 1900s.

Many Maltese found work in the leather-tanning and meatpacking businesses near the Junction area and on the railroads. In 1922 the first North American Maltese organization, **The Maltese-Canadian Society of Toronto,** was organized to build the first Maltese Catholic church, which was erected in 1930. **Saint Paul the Apostle Church** in Toronto's West End remains the focus of the community to this day.

During the Second World War the Maltese community was active in providing relief efforts to fellow Maltese, and a spurt of immigration occurred in the immediate post-war years. The community refocused its settlement around its present location in the Junction area, and Saint Paul's was expanded to encompass its larger congregation. Second- and third-generation Maltese have become active entrepreneurs and professionals. **Our Lady's Chapel** in **Saint Michael's Cathedral** was designed by the Maltese-Canadian architect John Farrugia. Other prominent Maltese citizens include Larry Attard, one of Canada's top jockeys; Sid, Joe, and Tino Attard, top horse trainers; and fashion designer Emily Zarb.

Religion

Saint Paul the Apostle Church, *3224 Dundas Street West (416-767-7054).*

The main church in the Maltese community. Dedicated to one of Malta's two patron saints (Paul preached there during his travels throughout the Roman Empire), it also houses an auditorium and a choir.

Organizations

Maltese-language classes are available from the **Maltese Heritage Class Parents and Teachers Association,** 154 Prescott Avenue (416-658-6370).

The **Maltese-Canadian Federation,** PO Box 206, Station M (416-762-6613), is the umbrella group for most Maltese organizations in Toronto and Ontario. Among those that are a part of the federation are the **Maltese Veterans Association of Canada** and the **Maltese Actors Group.**

The **Maltese Canadian Society of Toronto,** 3278 Dundas Street West (416-767-3645), sponsors a variety of sports and social activities in the community, as well as charitable works.

Other clubs and associations include:

Melita Soccer Club, *3336 Dundas Street West (416-763-5317).*

Malta Band Club, *235 Medlund Street (416-767-9821).*

Gozo Club, *3265 Dundas Street West (416-767-7135).*

Holidays and Celebrations

February 10	*Feast of Saint Paul the Apostle,* who first converted the Maltese to Christianity in 60 AD.
April	*Feast of Our Lady of Sorrows.*
June 29	*Feast of Saints Peter and Paul.*
September 8	Commemorates the victory of the Maltese in two great sieges in 1565 and 1942.
December 13	Recognizes the day in 1974 that Malta officially became an independent republic in the British Commonwealth.

Food Sources

Maltese food has a Levantine Mediterranean flavor. Specialties include *fenkatta* (rabbit stew), *bragioli* (beef roulades), octopus stew, and *tumpani* (puff pastry, macaroni, meat, and eggs). These specialties and other baked goods and imported delicacies can be found at the **Malta Bake Shop,** 3256

Dundas Street West (416-769-2174). A great dessert here is the *strizzi* (pastry filled with chocolate, fruit, and almonds).

Other bakeries and delis serving Maltese specialties are located in the area between Keele and Jane Streets off Dundas Street West. They include:

Buskett Bakery, *3029 Dundas Street West (416-763-2562); 1750 Victoria Park Avenue (416-755-8688).*

Valletta Bakery, *3082 Dundas Street West (416-762-0702).*

Media

L'Abbar, PO Box 272, Station M (416-766-1443), is a monthly tabloid covering events of interest to the Maltese-Canadian community.

"**Bejnietnail-Maltin,**" Graham Cable 10, 35 Scarlett Road (416-762-3622); "**Mill Maltin Ghall Maltin,**" Brampton Cable Maltese Show, 10 Wheatfield Road; and "**Mill Maltin Ghall-Maltin-Servizz Xandir Malti,**" Graham Cable 10, 35 Scarlett Road (416-762-3622), are all weekly television shows on community cable covering news and issues of interest to the Maltese community.

The **Annette Street Public Library,** 145 Annette Street (416-393-7692), has an extensive collection of Maltese-language books and current magazines.

══════ Native Canadians ══════

In the debate over whether Canada is one nation united by a British monarch with two dominant linguistic cultures, or two nations with separate linguistic and cultural heritages, native groups are quick to point out that *they* were the true founders of Canada and that everyone else is essentially a guest. It is an apt point, though slightly moot, now that Native Canadian life has been overwhelmed everywhere with the exception of, perhaps, the far north. Happily, while Native Canadians have suffered tremendous deprivation as a result of these historic changes, their culture has begun to make an important comeback in recent years.

The native presence in Toronto is not quite as great as it is in many western Canadian cities, but still constitutes a population of over 40,000. Toronto itself owes its name and origin to the Ojibwa, Iroquois, and Huron tribes, who first used the area as a short cut for canoe routes between Lake

Ontario and Lake Huron. The Humber River was at that time named Taronto, first by the Huron Indians who once populated this area, and later by the Senecas who dominated it until the mid-seventeenth century only to be replaced by the Ojibwa and the Mississauga. Their most important village, in fact, was in the western Toronto neighborhood known as Baby Point overlooking the Humber River.

By 1805 all of the native lands in this part of Ontario had been appropriated through what was called the Mississauga Purchase. Most native people remained in the area on reserve lands, but some were attracted to the trading and work opportunities afforded by the growing city of Toronto. Unlike western Canada, there was not extensive warfare in this area, and native groups were well integrated into the broader European and North American economies for over 200 years (through the fur trade) before extensive European settlement began in this area.

People from the Ojibwa and Iroquois tribes make up the largest percentage of the native population in the area. While immigration from the reserves to the city was a steady trickle for many years, in recent times it has grown more dramatically as the opportunities in the city have attracted many younger native people. An interesting counterpoint to this has developed in that many Native Canadians are going through a major revival of interest in their heritage and background.

As a result groups like the **Native Canadian Centre of Toronto** have developed both to bridge the gap between the reserves and the city and to help Native Canadians regain and redefine their heritage in the wake of the changes that have occurred to their societies in recent years. A number of prominent members of the theater and arts community in Toronto have emerged in recent years, including Thomson and Rene Highway. Roberta Jamieson was the first native woman lawyer in Canada and the Ontario Ombudsman as well. Bill Montur, chief of the Six Nations tribe, was also chair of the Ontario Economic Board. Native Canadians have been able to succeed in all walks of life, and more and more are taking their places in professions such as medicine and the law as educational opportunities have opened up.

Religious and Cultural Organizations

Native religion has made a very strong comeback in recent years with many Native Canadians trying to practice and/or resurrect the practices of their longhouse cultures. In Toronto itself a religion close to the traditional Algonkian practices is observed. Given the nomadic nature of most native groups, ceremonies are not held in traditional churches or buildings. Feasts and healing rituals that are part of native culture are private affairs and should be respected as such.

First Nation School of Toronto, 935 Dundas Street East (416-393-0555), teaches native ways, traditional beliefs, customs, and languages. While some of its classes are open to the public, the aim is to reinvigorate the traditional ways of Native Canadians rather than act as a museum or archive of native culture.

A permanent display of Native Canadian art is located on the mezzanine level of the **Toronto Dominion Centre Tower.** There is also a permanent display of animals and mythical creatures taken from native mythology at the **Canadian National Exhibition** grounds.

The **Native Canadian Centre of Toronto,** 16 Spadina Road (416-964-9087), hosts plays, literary readings, art exhibits, and conferences. It also houses a library and gift shop for native crafts.

Art-I-Crafts of Ontario, 2 Carlton Street (416-977-4442), is a nonprofit organization aimed at helping native people promote their arts and crafts.

The **Association for Native Development in the Performing and Visual Arts,** 9 Saint Joseph Street (416-961-8744), is a group aimed at helping Native Canadians develop skills in the visual and performing arts, while **Native Earth Performing Arts,** 506 Jarvis Street (416-922-7616), is a successful theater company developing and performing productions from the native perspective and experience.

The **Ontario Federation of Indian Friendship Centres,** 234 Eglinton Avenue East (416-484-1411), is an umbrella organization for native friendship centers in the province.

The **Union of Ontario Indians,** 27 Queen Street East (416-366-3527), is a political advocacy group of fifty-four Ontario reserves.

Other Native Canadian community, cultural, and political groups include:

Canadian Council for Native Business, *777 Bay Street (416-977-0008).*

Canadian Native Arts Foundation, *77 Mowat Avenue (416-588-3328).*

Chiefs of Ontario, *22 College Street (416-972-0212).*

Indian and Northern Affairs Canada, *25 Saint Clair Avenue East (416-973-2281).*

Indian Commission of Ontario, *236 Avenue Road (416-973-6390).*

Native Women's Resource Centre, *245 Gerrard Street East (416-963-9963).*

Southern Ontario Metis and Non-Status Indian Association, *35 Struthers Street (416-588-4825).*

York Metis Association, *4201 Kingston Road (416-798-1488).*

Canadian Alliance in Solidarity with the Native Peoples, *245 Lippincott Street (416-588-2712).*

Nishnawbe-Aski Nation, *14 College Street (416-920-2376).*

Ontario Native Council on Justice, *2 Carlton Street (416-592-1393).*

Holidays and Celebrations

October	*Thanksgiving Day,* which we have come to view as a very North American feast, in fact goes back to native harvest celebrations at which people gave thanks to the earth and nature for providing for them over the course of the previous summer so they could survive the oncoming onslaughts of winter.

Shops

A number of art galleries in the city carry Native Canadian works of art, including paintings, prints, and sculpture.

Algonquin Sweetgrass Gallery, *668 Queen Street West (416-703-1336).*
Offers art and crafts such as moccasins, beadwork, and pottery.

Armen Art Gallery, *16 Wellesley Avenue (416-924-5375).*

Carries contemporary Native Canadian artwork, as does **Gallery Phillip,** Don Mills Centre (416-447-1301), and the **Isaacs Gallery,** 179 John Street (416-595-1677).

Skin and Bones, *180 Queen Street West (416-599-0216).*

Carries Indian furs, crafts, moccasins, jewelry, and sculpture.

The **Longhouse Bookshop,** 497 Bloor Street West (416-921-9995), carries an extensive array of publications by Native Canadian authors and on Native Canadian life.

Media

Boozhoo, 16 Spadina Road (416-964-9087).

A bimonthly publication of current events.

Ontario Native Experience, 234 Eglinton Avenue East (416-484-1411).

A contemporary monthly periodical on Ontario native life.

—Nearby Excursions: Six Nations Reserve—

Near the city of Brantford, Ontario, approximately 1 ½ hours from Toronto by car, is the Six Nations Reserve. This is the largest and most heavily populated reserve in Canada and features the **Woodlands Culture Centre, Her Majesty's Royal Chapel of the Mohawks** (built in 1785), and the historic home of **Emily Pauline Johnson,** is best known for her poetry celebrating native life and culture. The reserve also has retail outlets selling native crafts and artifacts. Other reserves near Toronto include those of the Chippewas of Rama, north of Toronto, who have constructed a heritage Indian Village for visitors to see, and the Tyendenega Reserve, east of Toronto and north of the Cobourg on Highway 45.

How to Get There: *The Six Nations Reserve is just south of Brantford on Highway 54. Take the Gardiner Expressway/QEW to the Highway 403 exit to Hamilton; take that to its end at Highway 2 and proceed west to the junction of Highway 54. Go left (south) at this junction approximately 6 miles (10 kilometers).*

Index